The Roosevelts
and Their
Descendants

The Roosevelts and Their Descendants
Portrait of an American Family

F. MARTIN HARMON

McFarland & Company, Inc., Publishers
Jefferson, North Carolina

LIBRARY OF CONGRESS CATALOGUING-IN-PUBLICATION DATA

Names: Harmon, F. Martin, 1951– author.
Title: The Roosevelts and their descendants : portrait of an American family / F. Martin Harmon.
Description: Jefferson, North Carolina : McFarland & Company, Inc., Publishers, 2017. | Includes bibliographical references and index.
Identifiers: LCCN 2017027991 | ISBN 9781476668437 (softcover : acid free paper) ∞
Subjects: LCSH: Roosevelt, Theodore, 1858–1919—Influence. | Roosevelt, Franklin D. (Franklin Delano), 1882–1945—Influence. | Roosevelt, Eleanor, 1884–1962—Influence. | Presidents—United States—Biography. | Presidents' spouses—United States—Biography. | Roosevelt family.
Classification: LCC E757 .H324 2017 | DDC 973.91/1092—dc23
LC record available at https://lccn.loc.gov/2017027991

BRITISH LIBRARY CATALOGUING DATA ARE AVAILABLE

ISBN (print) 978-1-4766-6843-7
ISBN (ebook) 978-1-4766-2805-9

© 2017 F. Martin Harmon. All rights reserved

No part of this book may be reproduced or transmitted in any form or by any means, electronic or mechanical, including photocopying or recording, or by any information storage and retrieval system, without permission in writing from the publisher.

Front cover image of Teddy Roosevelt holding his infant grandson, Kermit Roosevelt, Jr., in 1916 (Library of Congress, Prints & Photographs)

Printed in the United States of America

McFarland & Company, Inc., Publishers
  Box 611, Jefferson, North Carolina 28640
    www.mcfarlandpub.com

For Sharon, TR, ER, and FDR,
the one who gives purpose to my life
and the three who gave purpose
to America's 20th century

Table of Contents

Acknowledgments   ix
Preface   1
Introduction   3
Prologue: Setting the Stage—America's Dynamic Duo and Their Remote Outposts of Destiny   5

Part One—Reunion Recap

1. Roots, Rivalry, Renewal   11
2. The Reunion Roster   21

Part Two—Eleanor's Place

3. The Common Denominator   27
4. The Val-Kill Cousins   35
5. Life Lessons   47

Part Three—Reunion Realizations

6. Must Be the Genes   51
7. Family Preservationists   57
8. Generational Genetics   65
9. Generational Go-Between   70

Part Four—Descendant Dictates

10. In the Line of Fire   75
11. Too Close   81

Table of Contents

12. Like Father, Like Son?	87
13. External Family	92
14. Unfulfilled Offspring	109
15. Stretching Limits	114

Part Five—Extended Family

16. True Heirs	119
17. Embracing Influence	129
18. Secretly Significant	135
19. The Unknown Brother	141
20. Overcoming Class	145
21. French Born	150
22. Intriguing In-Laws	154
23. Northwest Branch	164
24. Writer's Roots	170
25. Inclusive Legacy	176
Epilogue: Roosevelt Reminders	180
Appendix: Eleanor's "My Day" Observations	187
Chapter Notes	193
Selected Bibliography	207
Index	211

Acknowledgments

This addition to the ever-expanding library of Roosevelt books was made possible by one of the family's number who has withstood her share of arrows throughout life and measured up in truest Roosevelt fashion. Indeed, the granddaughter of Franklin and Eleanor Roosevelt, born Anna Sturgis Roosevelt but known by a childhood nickname, "Nina," survived polio at a very young age, lived through the tragic death of a little sister as a teenager, and has even endured a heart transplant, now more than 15 years ago. She is living proof of one of their most recognized Roosevelt maxims: carrying on without complaint in the face of adversity.

While some of this internal fortitude may be due to acquired skills as an esteemed psychologist, there's more to it than just that. Consider the fiber of the family of which she's a part—the same enduring fiber her grandmother gave voice to following the death of her sister. The words Eleanor Roosevelt chose that day, "You must be brave," and her caring conviction are the kind of memories Nina Roosevelt Gibson has treasured most. Now in her seventies, Nina knows well the stories of Theodore Roosevelt's battles with asthma as a child; Franklin Roosevelt's comeback as an adult from crippling polio; and Eleanor Roosevelt's depressing youth following the deaths of her parents. She's also aware of the trials and tribulations faced by other Roosevelts since then, a family burdened by the glare of history but one that remains, justifiably, proud.

To Nina belongs most of the credit for their latest family reunion, the idea for which started with her first visit to Warm Springs, Georgia. That's when she learned one of the best Roosevelt stories of all, one that truly impressed her: how her grandfather provided hope for so many others crippled by polio in the West Georgia hills. It's one most

Acknowledgments

of the family had never thought much about until being enticed to gather there for a weekend in the fall of 2013. Like their previous family reunions, this one was made special by location—not because of any fancy amenities but as a place of living Roosevelt legacy through ongoing rehabilitation nearly 100 years old.

Nina's leadership, along with her first cousin Chris Roosevelt and more distant cousin Stephen Jeffries, provided the motivation to make it happen. Each exhibited qualities shared with their most famous ancestors, including Nina's tireless support for a cause, much like Eleanor; Chris's charisma in getting people on board, much as FDR's famous charisma always came through; and Stephen's out-front leadership skills, charging ahead as Theodore Roosevelt always did to pave the way. For a year, it was a distinct pleasure to work with this trio of Roosevelts in the planning, organization, and coordination that brought this great family together once again at one of the little, out-of-the-way places forever connected to their history.

The reunion lasted for just one weekend, but for everyone involved it was memorable in a very special way, as most of the Roosevelts who remain were there. But make no mistake: the 2013 Roosevelt reunion was due to just one of them, Nina Roosevelt Gibson. As a result, so is this book.

Preface

Truly some of the most written about times in American history, the "Age of Roosevelt"—as some people have termed it—might even be labeled a separate era by college history majors wishing to concentrate on one specific or influential segment of our national story. Perhaps only the great American wars—Civil, Revolutionary, and World War II—have been written about more than the three related individuals from New York State who dominated and largely authored United States history in the early to mid–20th century. With this in mind, any fresh attempt at this massively documented genre had better come with a new twist and special access, essential components for any historical narrative wishing to find a niche among the many volumes already written about this trio and their family. Fortunately, such access and new aspect were both available to an old reporter turned historian at the tiny village of Warm Springs, Georgia, in the fall of 2013, a place of reunion and a place made famous by a Roosevelt.

Unique access was provided this author because of 13 years as public relations director (now retired) at the state-managed Roosevelt Warm Springs, the rehabilitation center Franklin Delano Roosevelt founded in 1927 and made world famous for its integral role in the treatment and work toward eradication of polio. It was the same access that provided impetus for a previous book, *The Warm Springs Story: Legacy and Legend,* in 2014.

Both were made possible in large part through interaction with significant players in the Roosevelt saga. While it is only a fraction of the Roosevelt legacy, Warm Springs, nonetheless, remains a microcosm of the influence these Roosevelts had on any landscape or agenda they came in contact with during the first half of the 1900s. Its past status

Preface

and recognition were possible only because of the presence and commitment of one of the family's primary players, a presence finally (and fittingly) recognized by family members who attended the latest family reunion.

As a member of the reunion planning committee (and the person responsible for securing Ken Burns and Florentine Films for a well-timed screening of the documentary *The Roosevelts: An Intimate History*), I was afforded opportunities for interviews with family members before, during, and after the reunion. This unique insider's perspective was combined with a longtime interest and study of everything Roosevelt, which had only intensified during my years and daily presence on the Warm Springs campus. It was there that previously little-known Roosevelt history was made available through records of the Roosevelt Warm Springs Archives and its well-versed archivist Mike Shadix, as well as veteran tour guide Linda Creekbaum and a multitude of informants as they consistently returned as visitors to the National Historic Landmark halls. These visitors included former patients, staff and descendants of the three most famous Roosevelts. Following more than a decade of that kind of exposure, additional research came on a trip to the Hudson River Valley and the FDR Library and Museum in Hyde Park, New York, during the summer of 2014.

Added to that was an extensive personal library of contemporary works by some of the most renowned Roosevelt biographers, including Doris Kearns Goodwin, Edmund Morris, H.W. Brands, Nathan Miller, Jonathan Alter, and Douglas Brinkley; related historians like Stacey Cordery, Michael Hiltzik, Laura Kalman, Noah Feldman, and David Pietrusza; and books written or edited by family members such as Eleanor Roosevelt II, Curtis Roosevelt, David Roosevelt, John Boettiger, Joseph Alsop, Elizabeth Winthrop, Eleanor Seagraves, and, of course, Eleanor and Theodore Roosevelt. In addition, influential periodicals such as *Life* and *Time* added much to a countless array of Roosevelt resources. As one might imagine, this wealth of information made for a veritable smorgasbord of better-known Roosevelt facts along with little-known Roosevelt minutia, resulting in a far-reaching stew of Roosevelt reflections, the personal kind one might uncover at any other family reunion. As shall be revealed, however, theirs has never been just any other family.

Introduction

There has never been a royal family in America, no ruling lineage that stretches from one generation to the next in authentic or even ceremonial leadership roles. At the same time, there have been families elected to the seats of government so frequently that the mere mention of their last names seems synonymous with various eras in the American saga. Examples would be the Tafts of Ohio, the Kennedys of Massachusetts, and the Bushes of Connecticut, Texas, and Florida.

No other family, however, has achieved the historic significance and lasting influence of the Roosevelts of New York. Perhaps that's why so many books have been written about them, particularly their amazing trio of national leaders: Theodore Roosevelt and Franklin D. Roosevelt, two of our most dynamic presidents born a little less than 25 years apart, and Eleanor Roosevelt, a First Lady who distinguished herself on both the national and international stage more than any other First Lady has done so far. This book is about them, but it is also about their descendants and the many interesting connections shared with these famous forebearers, some of the connections coming to light during a three-day family reunion in Warm Springs, Georgia, in the fall of 2013. It's about Roosevelt lore, Roosevelt relationships, Roosevelt remembrances, both documented and otherwise, and the Roosevelt legacy. You might say it's about all things Roosevelt, not just Theodore, Franklin, and Eleanor.

Obviously still proud of their famous heritage, modern-day Roosevelts are located coast to coast and even overseas. Being subject to life's pitfalls like any other family, their heritage includes highs and lows, good times and bad, and more than their share of public scrutiny. Although occasionally obscure, many of them have lived under the

Introduction

microscope. Even if their last name was not Roosevelt (in other words, related from the maternal side) their place in this family genealogy is nevertheless sure to resonate during each of their lifetimes.

Like their "Big Three"—Theodore, Franklin, and Eleanor—many Roosevelts have been in the business of making a difference at one level or another. It's a family trait that has been fairly typical and one with seemingly genetic implications. Occasionally, they are still singled out, but their profiles, for the most part, are much lower key than before, and based on the realization there could never be a more famous Roosevelt.

Prologue
Setting the Stage—America's Dynamic Duo and Their Remote Outposts of Destiny

Is there any doubt that Theodore Roosevelt (TR) and Franklin D. Roosevelt (FDR) set the stage for the 20th century? They were, in essence, America's dynamic duo when the United States assumed world prominence. It's ironic they were also cousins. Although TR was born almost 25 years before FDR, their fathers were contemporaries, with only three years' difference in their ages. In fact, both fathers avoided service in the Union army during the Civil War, a fairly common practice among Northern elite but a perceived family flaw that Theodore struggled mightily to accept, while Franklin, apparently, did not just a generation later.

Direct descendants of the earliest New York European settlers, the Dutch, the two men represent two branches of the van Rosenvelt clan—brothers who went their separate ways in the 1700s. One side, that of Johannes, the merchant branch, eventually moved east of the city onto Long Island and the other, that of Jacobus, migrated north into the beautiful Hudson River Valley, thanks to real estate earnings before the American Revolution and the British occupation of New York City. We now refer to this separation as the Oyster Bay branch (TR's home community) and the Hyde Park branch (FDR's home). Regardless of the location, their legacies both center around the city and state of New York.

This fact would be reinforced once TR established his political legacy by becoming a New York assemblyman (state representative), assistant

Prologue

secretary of the navy, and governor of New York before being elected vice president and president. FDR provided the reinforcement with an avowed desire to follow in his distant cousin's footsteps by also becoming a New York state senator, assistant secretary of the navy, a candidate for vice president, and governor of New York, all before being elected president four times. The biggest difference in their progressive sagas is FDR's decision to remain a Democrat (like his father) despite most of his neighbors and family associates being Republican, including TR's four sons and the very distinct possibility one or more of those sons would follow in their illustrious   father's Republican footsteps.

Earlier, both TR and FDR had been Harvard graduates and the obvious beneficiaries of aristocratic upbringings, including trips to Europe and other rare opportunities not available to most American youths. The old saying about being born with "silver spoons" would have certainly applied to both men, and yet their adoption of the common man and what's-good-for-all approach would shape their political beliefs and programs. Where did

Above and opposite: **Theodore Roosevelt (TR) as a buckskin-clad ranch owner headed to the Badlands and later, as the youngest U.S. president, age 42.** COURTESY SAGAMORE HILL NATIONAL HISTORIC SITE, NATIONAL PARK SERVICE, OYSTER BAY, NY; LIBRARY OF CONGRESS, PRINTS AND PHOTOGRAPHS DIVISION, PACH BROTHERS—REPRODUCTION NUMBER LC-DIG-PPMSCA-35950 OR LC-USZ62–13026.

this sense of fairness come from? FDR has been termed a "traitor to his class" by one of his many biographers. TR was categorized by an early acquaintance as someone whose likely reelection would "come from the common people and not from the moneyed class." In her 2013 Pulitzer Prize-winning book, *The Bully Pulpit*, historian Doris Kearns Goodwin traces TR's concern for the masses and ultimate turn to government intervention on their behalf to his two years as a New York City police commissioner, when he first experienced the urban slums. And we know of FDR's initial experience with such squalor while accompanying his cousin and future wife, Eleanor, on some of her earliest benevolent sojourns for the city's Junior League prior to their marriage.

Although their individual and personal histories are not nearly as identical as their shared family and career backgrounds, there is at least one other obvious comparison to be drawn from them that deserves to be considered when reviewing the lives and connections of the Roosevelts. In fact, destiny might be the simplest word available to describe and compare the impact of two remote, different, and yet very similar

places in the massive legacies of these two American giants. What better way is there to connect the similar roles played by the Badlands and Warm Springs in the lives of TR and FDR, respectively, than to consider them remote outposts of American destiny? After all, both represented retreats from tragedy at the lowest moments in their respective lives. One does not have to be a trained psychologist to see the similarity in the reasons why both happened and the influences they had, not only on TR and FDR but on history.

Prologue

For TR, February 14, 1884, was his date that would live in infamy—the day both his wife (Bright's disease following childbirth) and his mother (typhoid fever) died only hours apart and less than six years after the death of his father (gastrointestinal tumor), all three shockingly gone before their time. His wife of only three years was 23 and his mother 48; his father had died suddenly at 47. In his diary, TR wrote, "The light has gone out of my life." Fortunately for TR (and the world) it came back on again in that most barren of places—the Badlands of what was then Dakota Territory, where he spent approximately one-half of his inheritance to become a cattle rancher.

For FDR, his personal tragedy would be just as shocking and linger the rest of his lifetime. Polio, that most dreaded and crippling of diseases in the early 20th century, struck him at age 39 in the midst of political promise. For three years he struggled with its impact until new hope and purpose surfaced in another of the most unlikely of places: a run-down resort in rural West Georgia, a place eventually called Warm Springs, which he purchased with two-thirds of his personal worth over the strenuous objections of his wife, mother, and law partner.

It's odd how greatness can manifest itself when and where it's least expected. In the Badlands TR found solitude, a new kind of respect, and the strength to resume and achieve great public service. He also found causes that would transform the still-infant western United States and benefit all Americans. In much the same way, Warm Springs taught FDR patience and empathy for his fellow man, and gave him a confident, never-say-die spirit and style that exuded hope. Years later, he credited his experience in Georgia with also providing insight into politics, economics, and the American dream; his New Deal policies and management of World War II would exhibit these acquired attributes and abilities.

In the American Experience documentary entitled *TR*, Theodore Roosevelt's granddaughter Edith Derby Williams made the statement, "If it hadn't been for the time he was in the Badlands, I don't think he would have been president." And TR himself called his time there "the romance" of his life and a period that "enabled him to interpret the spirit of the West," according to Goodwin. In much the same way, FDR's fellow polio survivor and historian Hugh Gallagher wrote in his book *FDR's Splendid Deception*, "Roosevelt was at home in Georgia; only at

Setting the Stage

Franklin Delano Roosevelt (FDR) poolside in Warm Springs and later, as the longest-serving U.S. president. COURTESY ROOSEVELT WARM SPRINGS ARCHIVES; LIBRARY OF CONGRESS, PRINTS AND PHOTOGRAPHS DIVISION, GOLDENSKY AND ELIAS—REPRODUCTION NUMBER LC-USZ62-117121 OR LC-US762-26759.

Warm Springs could he relax his guard." FDR's wife, Eleanor Roosevelt (ER), even stated, "Although I don't think it changed him completely, he certainly learned to understand suffering and people in ways he never had before." As with TR, a case can be made that without Warm Springs FDR might have never been president; and even if he had, he would certainly not have been as effective or as enduring.

Prologue

It was Warm Springs that taught him what most of the rural South was in need of: cheaper and more accessible electricity, which was accomplished through his Rural Electrification Administration as part of his "New Deal." Before FDR's tenure in office was finished, he was also known for working with Senator George Norris (of Nebraska) to bring even more extensive electrification to the people of the South via the dams and power plants of the Tennessee Valley Authority. In the same way as FDR had at Warm Springs, TR gloried in the majestic surroundings of the West, the type of majesty he first experienced in the Badlands. Along with his trust-busting and development of the Panama Canal, he is perhaps best remembered as the president who nurtured the conservation movement, including efforts to protect the great western landmarks, working along with Senator John Lacey (of Iowa) through the Antiquities Act of 1906, which led to the establishment of the National Park Service in 1916. And just as FDR's 41 visits to Georgia made him an adopted son of the South and helped ensure what was then the Democrats' "Solid South" at election time, TR's three years in the Dakotas earned him the respect and lasting admiration of westerners, as evidenced by his carrying every state west of the Mississippi in the election of 1904 except the three southern trans-Mississippi states—Louisiana, Arkansas, and Texas.

Such facts provide a mere sampling of the influence these two remote places had on the lives and leadership characteristics of TR and FDR, and the unique parallels that can be seen as a result. Episodes during their time in the Badlands and Warm Springs illustrate how these influences became fixtures in their individual personas and interesting additions to better-known Roosevelt stories throughout their political careers. To better understand such parallels, what better place is there to infiltrate than a Roosevelt reunion involving both branches of this historic family? That was the opportunity afforded the author when Roosevelts from all over the country came to Warm Springs. Not always harmonious, theirs had been an intense family rivalry before such reunions were possible. However, that kind of internal intrigue seemed long forgotten as they gathered amidst the Georgia pines for the latest in a series of such renewals, a series that had once included TR's Badlands just as it ultimately did FDR's Warm Springs.[1]

PART ONE—REUNION RECAP

1

Roots, Rivalry, Renewal

There they stood ... 160 Roosevelts by blood or marriage ranging in age from six months to several well into their 70s or 80s and all posing for a group picture in front of Warm Springs' Columbus Colonnade on November 2, 2013. For most of them, it was the first time they had ever been there—the place their forebearer, Franklin Delano Roosevelt, had made famous during the polio era of the early to mid–1900s. There for a family reunion, they had just witnessed an exclusive screening of Ken Burns' documentary *The Roosevelts: An Intimate History*, scheduled for release in 2014, and as they emerged outside on the lawn of the historic Quadrangle at Roosevelt Warm Springs, the rehabilitation center FDR started so many years before, a classic family photo was in the offing with a long-ago gift from the nearby city of Columbus, Georgia, as their backdrop. With the early evening light rapidly disappearing, time was of the essence as they readied themselves for this keepsake photo op. Taking charge of the moment, the photographer ascended a 14-foot ladder in front of them and gave them instructions for the impending visual record of their visit, a moment in time Franklin D. Roosevelt would have been proud of, as would have his cousin Teddy, whose branch of the family, surprisingly, was almost equally represented at this out-of-the-way, FDR-inspired location.[1]

They had come from all over the country—Arizona and California, New England and New York City, and lots of places in between. Admittedly, the Ken Burns event was a big draw, but their participation was no less enthusiastic than it had been for seven previous family reunions in decades past, reunions at places like Hyde Park and Oyster Bay in New York; Campobello Island off the coast of Maine; the Netherlands, honoring their Dutch ancestry; and even the TR-inspired Badlands of

Part One—Reunion Recap

North Dakota. As with Warm Springs, all those previous locations offered much in terms of family history, identifiable stops or connections for arguably the nation's most influential brood.² The youngest was named Elliott Roosevelt IV and went by the nickname "Thatcher," which was embroidered on the front of his toddler attire. Although Thatcher was unable to stand on his own yet, his adoring father was nevertheless only too happy to playfully identify him as the next Roosevelt president. Among the oldest was Elizabeth Roosevelt, the last Roosevelt still residing at Oyster Bay and a lifelong history teacher. She gladly confirmed that many of her lessons through the years had indeed involved her own famous ancestors.³

Also in their midst were many identifiable namesakes—the Eleanors, Annas, Elliotts, Kermits, Halls, and Corinnes of the family with their uniquely handed-down Roosevelt given names, as well as perhaps the most challenged of all—Theodore Roosevelt IV and Franklin Delano Roosevelt III. Imagine living with the burden of being named specifically for one of the most famous Americans ever, with the former namesake once described as "a steam engine in trousers" and a "force of nature" the equal of "Niagara Falls," and the latter generally acknowledged as chief architect of America's 20th century. Remarkably, both of these attendees measured up. One is a well-known investment banker and conservationist and the other a leading economist and author.

Like extended families everywhere, this Roosevelt reunion was one of renewal, remembrance, and getting reacquainted, but it was also a reunion of their collective Roosevelt roots. Of necessity, their family legacy must constantly be addressed. Although they had nothing to do with the extensive American history their deceased relatives made, altered, or shaped, they must, nonetheless, have been mindful of at least some of it from an early age. Some were obviously more mindful than others, but all are ingrained with being a Roosevelt in much the same way it must have been for an Adams in our nation's earliest days or for a Kennedy or Bush in more recent times.

Theirs is a large family made even larger by the fact that so many of them during and after the last Roosevelt White House married multiple times (in a few cases as many as five). FDR and Eleanor had 28 grandchildren, natural or adopted, and 56 great-grandchildren (and

1. Roots, Rivalry, Renewal

Gathered on the lawn of Georgia's historic Warm Springs Quadrangle, Roosevelts from throughout the country and both sides of the famous family posed for this photograph during their most recent Roosevelt family reunion, November 2013. Their shared legacy remains that of the most influential family in American History. COURTESY ROOSEVELT WARM SPRINGS ARCHIVES, PHOTOGRAPH BY LEE CATHEY.

that does not count those from one union where they were not Roosevelts at all until their surname was legally changed). At the same time, TR had 17 grandchildren and 26 great-grandchildren.[4] Many, on both sides, have long been used to the ritual of constantly making selections among themselves as to whom should represent the family on any given day. So as to limit inconvenience and possible controversy, this seemingly hierarchical requirement of famous families has repeatedly forced them to pose this question: "Do you want to be a Roosevelt today or shall I?"[5]

In a 1994 book entitled *The Roosevelts: An American Saga*, Peter Collier with the help of David Horowitz touched in the epilogue on another unique feature of the family legacy—the reportedly intense rivalry that existed between the two branches for many years over the

Part One—Reunion Recap

political divide that blighted family relationships following FDR's (and ER's) ascension to the throne of national leadership. Collier's book points to the mellowing of this rivalry by the 1980s, which was about the time the family reunions were born. In fact, highlighting a 1989 reunion at Hyde Park, the book emphasized that the "bitterness that had driven the two branches of the Roosevelt family apart and created a state of civil war between them" was by that time finally on the mend. "For those who had witnessed this conflict, that event was extraordinary," the book goes on to state. "It was a peace meeting between the descendants of Theodore and those of Franklin and Eleanor."[6]

Much of what has always been credited with fueling this earlier animosity was the lifelong bitterness that existed between first cousins Eleanor Roosevelt, TR's favorite niece, and Alice Roosevelt Longworth, his eldest daughter by his first marriage and apparently the focal point of much ill-will when it came to the FDR-ER ascendency. A national celebrity in her own right and international debutante during her adolescent years in Teddy's White House, Longworth grew into a Washington insider and was a D.C. lightning rod her entire life. *Alice* (Stacy Cordery, 2007), a provocative and long-overdue biography of TR's eldest child, confirmed as much, stating at one point, "Alice's vituperation toward Franklin and Eleanor during the years they inhabited the White House, and even after, was relentless."[7]

Earlier in the book, Cordery also revealed that such malice was not just a one-way street when she quoted ER as saying to a mutual acquaintance, "Of course Alice isn't a bit changed and it is always entertaining to be with her, but now that I am older and have my own values fixed a little, I can only say what little I saw of her life gave me a feeling of dreariness and waste. Her house is charming, her entertainments delightful. She's a born hostess and has an extraordinary mind, but as for real friendships and what (they) mean, she hasn't a conception of any depth, or so, at least, it seems. (Her) life seems to be one long pursuit of pleasure and excitement, and rather little real happiness either given or taken on the way."[8]

These first cousins of almost identical age had seen much of each other growing up. Despite the fact that the early, untimely deaths of both Eleanor's "beautiful" mother and "beloved" father had destined ER to a sequestered and unhappy childhood in the care of her mother's

1. Roots, Rivalry, Renewal

Alice Roosevelt Longworth, TR's only child by his first marriage, was a Washington, D.C., insider her whole life and lived to 96. She was also a constant critic of her cousins Franklin and Eleanor Roosevelt during their 12-plus years in the White House. LIBRARY OF CONGRESS, PRINTS AND PHOTOGRAPHS DIVISION, HARRIS AND EWING—REPRODUCTION NUMBER LC-DIG-HEC-24400.

aging mother, she and younger brother Hall were always welcome guests of TR's large and boisterous household. It's just that they never fit in—not in the games and competitions constantly being waged or in the riding, swimming, and other outdoor activities that one would deem natural for the family of a born adventurer like their Uncle TR.[9] At the same time, Alice was a schemer, even at a young age, as she competed for her famous father's attentions amidst her younger and more accepted half brothers and half sister. The Burns documentary even referenced her feelings of not belonging—an ironically similar emotion to Eleanor's familial insecurities. In *Theodore Rex*, Edmund Morris acknowledged as much when he quoted this from Alice's diary: "Father doesn't care for me. That is to say one eighth as much as he does the other children. Why should he pay attention to me or things

Part One—Reunion Recap

that I live for, except to look upon them with disapproval?" Later Morris wrote, "She was the only one who resented him [TR] though loving him with equal violence. Her attitude toward herself was equally confused."[10]

Never one to take no for an answer even when it put her at odds with her parents, Alice was the extrovert that Eleanor never could have been or wanted to be until thrust into the suddenly satisfying role as the most outgoing and admired First Lady in American history, an obviously bitter pill for her attention-seeking first cousin to swallow. Only when family honor was threatened by outsiders or in moments of loss is it documented how these two Roosevelt women would rally to each other.[11]

Perhaps it was inevitable, their permanent split, especially when Eleanor moved from wallflower to political player during the Teapot Dome scandal of 1921, which involved the illegal leasing of navy oil reserves, a sordid tale that sullied the reputations of many in the Republican Party. It sucked everyone in, even naive (though innocent) bystanders like Alice's oldest brother, Ted, by then assistant secretary of the navy and a logical candidate to follow in the footsteps of his father for governor of New York. That's when Eleanor, picking party (and her husband's future) over blood relatives and the ideology of Oyster Bay she had grown up with, became a promoter of Ted's perceived involvement in the scandal by personally working for Al Smith on the Democratic side and determinedly trailing her first cousin's campaign around the state in an automobile with a papier-mâché–shaped teapot on top. Such representations of guilt by association apparently left only one Roosevelt a viable candidate in the state of New York and left many on the Oyster Bay side feeling Ted's political birthright had been stolen by "the upstart FDR."[12]

When asked about this supposed, long-ago family disparagement at their most recent reunion, members of the TR side confirmed its rather sinister existence. In fact, the previously mentioned Elizabeth Roosevelt, surviving matriarch of Oyster Bay, whose great-grandfather,

Opposite: **Among the oldest attendees at the 2013 family reunion in Warm Springs was Elizabeth Roosevelt, from the TR side, the last of the Oyster Bay Roosevelts; the youngest was Elliott Roosevelt IV from the FDR-ER side, a member of today's Dallas branch of the family. Photographs property of the author.**

1. Roots, Rivalry, Renewal

Part One—Reunion Recap

James Alfred Roosevelt, had been the first to transfer his residence from New York City to Long Island, said, "Until everyone in my father's generation died, you couldn't have had a joint reunion like this. Until then, my family didn't care for them [FDR-ER side]. They [her family elders] were private bankers, you see, and they didn't consider FDR a friend of private investment. My father [John Kean Roosevelt] offered his congratulations when FDR won [the presidency] the first time, but that was the end of that and I will never forget my father's first statement on the day FDR died: 'Well, he can't do any more harm.'"[13] Tweed Roosevelt, another great-grandson of Teddy and often the TR side's family historian or spokesperson, added, "Of course there was a rivalry—around the time Uncle Ted was running as a Republican and FDR was running as a Democrat. Then there was Teapot Dome, which involved Standard Oil and even though TR's kids were among the whistle-blowers, like all whistle-blowers they absorbed some of the fallout. In fact, it's true, Eleanor really did take to following Ted's campaign around in a vehicle that looked like a teapot and that only widened the rift. It wasn't until the great aunts died off that we could move forward with a joint reunion like this."[14]

Meanwhile, speaking for the other branch, Christopher du Pont Roosevelt, the FDR grandson and descendant most responsible for organizing family reunions to date, doesn't buy into the rivalry in such definite terms. He does admit, however, that the media may have created one simply by referencing the political differences of the two sides over and over again. At Warm Springs he surmised as follows:

> It was largely a myth. In fact, there wasn't a rift until the media reported it so many times that they developed one. Actually, there was a letter produced at our first joint reunion that clearly showed TR supported FDR when he was running for office in New York despite their different parties. Uncle James [FDR's eldest son] chaired a panel that included representatives from both sides of the family and their findings revealed there was no definitive rift. I actually think TR steered FDR away from the Republican Party when he first entered politics because the Republicans were in such disarray at the time with the advent of the Bull Moose Party and all the internal warfare that went with it.

The Burns documentary also highlights a note of congratulations that Teddy sent his "nephew-in-law" upon FDR's being named assistant secretary of the navy, which acknowledged the irony of his following TR's own path to that office.[15]

1. Roots, Rivalry, Renewal

FDR's father, James, had been a Democrat, but much of his family was not and certainly not the local community from which he came. It would have been easy for him to switch just starting out, and Chris Roosevelt does not believe "the old fairy tale" that he stayed Democratic just because the presence of TR's sons made it too crowded for any other Roosevelt on the Republican side. No, in at least one of his grandsons' eyes, FDR had an obvious, behind-the-scenes TR influence in making his initial political choice, something Republicans would have trouble believing unless documentation could be found.[16] In their eyes, as H.W. Brands so aptly titled his 2008 biography, FDR will forever remain a *Traitor to His Class*, an aristocrat who practiced class warfare, casting himself as a modern-day Andrew Jackson, one of his historical favorites and the first American president to come from "the common people" (to drive home this point in the midst of the Great Depression, FDR's first inaugural parade included a replica of the front of Jackson's home, the Hermitage, as his temporary reviewing stand).[17]

At the same time, Collier's book indicates that any mellowing that may have been necessary between the family's two branches had actually begun almost 40 years before the reunion in Warm Springs. Again, according to his *The Roosevelts: An American Saga*, it began developing as early as 1976 when representatives of the family's' two sides established a "mutual interest in cooperating in the hiring of a pair of researchers to produce a comprehensive and accurate genealogy of the (entire) family." This project was eventually published by the Theodore Roosevelt Association, and the cooperation it inspired was deepened further through a Roosevelt Study Center established in the Netherlands and a coming together of the two branches for a grand opening of that place, an event "humorously" referred to at the time as "the peace of Utrecht."[18] (Ironically continuing such rivalry humor at the most recent reunion, grandchildren of ER and by extension FDR drew mischievous pleasure from the idea that they were actually generationally closer to Uncle Teddy as great-grand-nephews and -nieces than were his own great-great-grandchildren of the same age bracket.)

Whether the rivalry was ever as intense as TR old-timers still depict, most of the dramatics have long since been in the rearview mirror, especially by the time the family was together again in Warm Springs. By that time the 40 or so attendees at the milestone Hyde Park

Part One—Reunion Recap

reunion of 1989 had, indeed, quadrupled, with few, if any, of the younger Roosevelts aware that any such family intrigue ever had reasonable cause to exist. Just one big happy family, these descendants of Johannes and Jacobus van Rosenvelt were simply renewing the connection originally confirmed on St. Patrick's Day 1905, the day Franklin Roosevelt married his distant cousin Eleanor.[19] That was the day the clan from Oyster Bay, the so-called "Rew-sevelts," and their relatives from Hyde Park, the "Rose-velts," were actually ("for better or worse") again made one.[20]

2

The Reunion Roster

Based on the list of addresses provided by the family's planning committee prior to the gathering of Roosevelts in Warm Springs, the 2013 reunion roster proved about as diverse as any coast-to-coast configuration of an American clan could possibly be—at least among those of European descent. And that would undoubtedly include those equally recognizable from the annals of American History such as the Vanderbilts, Rockefellers, Kennedys, or Fords.

Representing a total of 38 states and five foreign countries,[1] they were all contacted and informed of the upcoming weekend proceedings months in advance. Those who made the effort to be there were rewarded with FDR's so-called "spirit of Warm Springs," a classically southern setting he originally intended to mimic Thomas Jefferson's renowned University of Virginia. In other words, he wanted the central campus of his Georgia Warm Springs Foundation (GWSF) to resemble a college rather than a hospital. To accomplish this, he instructed his Georgia-born architect, Henry Toombs, to design it in the image of the Jeffersonian model in Charlottesville, Virginia (and to anyone who has seen both, the resemblance has always been striking).[2]

As a result, the column-lined Roosevelt Warm Springs Quadrangle that greeted reunion attendees—most of whom were first-timers, especially from the TR side—for the main events that Saturday evening in November proved an elegant if aging backdrop of buildings and covered walkways constructed between 1930 and 1954.[3] In fact, the Quad's final addition was the GWSF's appropriately named 300-seat Roosevelt Auditorium, the nation's first fully accessible theater when it opened in 1954 (nine years after FDR's death), in which the family and special guests were treated to their exclusive screening of the Burns documentary.[4]

Part One—Reunion Recap

Master documentary filmmaker Ken Burns was in Warm Springs for the 2013 family reunion to personally introduce the exclusive screening of his 2014 film *The Roosevelts: An Intimate History.* **Afterwards (as shown here second from left), he met with members of the family at a reception in historic Georgia Hall.** PHOTOGRAPH PROPERTY OF THE AUTHOR.

As to the breakdown of that roster, as might be expected more hailed from the family's state of origin, New York, than any other state but, surprisingly, not by much. Whereas 36 of the individuals or couples listed were from the Empire State in 2013, thirty were from California and twenty-eight from Massachusetts. In order, the remaining states of residence broke down this way: Pennsylvania 16, Texas 13, Connecticut 11, Florida 11, Maryland 9, Virginia 9, Washington 8, Colorado 7, the District of Columbia 7, Oregon 6, Arizona 5, Illinois 5, Maine 5, Delaware 4, Vermont 4, Iowa 3, South Carolina 3, Arkansas, Georgia, Louisiana, Minnesota, New Mexico, Ohio, and Rhode Island, all with 2 each, and Idaho, Kansas, Michigan, New Hampshire, North Carolina, North Dakota, Tennessee, Utah, Wisconsin and Wyoming each with

2. The Reunion Roster

one. In addition, Great Britain and France both had three Roosevelt entries listed within their borders, while Canada, Germany, and Switzerland each had one.[5]

Among the diverse resumes represented was an expert in digital marketing; an early pioneer of American video games; an orthopedic surgeon; married veterinarians; a Canadian-based guitarist/vocalist with her own record label; both a current and former writer for the *Los Angeles Times*; a disease intervention specialist; one who worked for the Smithsonian Institution for three decades; a Texas oilman; an environmental consultant; a California winery CEO; an ordained minister; a concert violinist; two former ballet dancers; a stained-glass artist; an Oregon trucker; a massage therapist; and even an Iron Mountain, Tennessee, bed-and-breakfast innkeeper.[6] Robert T. Gannett, Jr., of Chicago, Illinois, a great-grandson of TR, authored one of the most important books ever published on the French Revolution, *Tocqueville Unveiled*[7]; Samuel Roosevelt Hornblower of Brooklyn, New York, another of TR's great-grandsons, was a reporter, writer, researcher, and producer of CBS's long-running *60 Minutes* and won Peabody (2006), Edward R. Murrow (2007), and Emmy awards (2008) during his time with the TV network[8]; and Dr. Anna C. Roosevelt of Evanston, Illinois, a great-granddaughter of the great TR and yet another member of an obviously impressive generation of Teddy descendants, has been one of America's leading archeologists through her work on the prehistory of the Amazon River and as curator of archeology for Chicago's Field Museum.[9]

Other examples of noteworthy descendants included a granddaughter of Eleanor Roosevelt, another Anna Eleanor Roosevelt of Portland, Maine, who is an ER namesake and look-alike, and is now CEO of Goodwill Industries of Northern New England.[10] Yet another TR great-grandson, Mark Roosevelt, now serves as president at St. John's College of Santa Fe, New Mexico, after serving in the same capacity at Antioch College in Ohio and making an unsuccessful run for governor of Massachusetts two decades ago.[11] Also attending was Corinne Zimmerman of Washington, D.C., TR's great-grandniece whose husband, Warren Zimmerman, once served as America's ambassador to Yugoslavia before it was forcibly torn apart and turned into seven individual nation-states.[12] Another attendee was Kermit Roosevelt III, TR's great-grandson and an already-esteemed representative of the "next generation," as

PART ONE—REUNION RECAP

well as a distinguished law professor at the University of Pennsylvania, who like his great-grandpa has authored a number of books. In typical Roosevelt fashion, his standard bio also lists his connection to FDR—"fifth cousin, four times removed."[13]

The Roosevelt roster contained some less obvious connections as well, with historic name recognition all their own, such as William Sheffield Cowles. Formerly an architect and commercial apple grower in Vermont, William S. Cowles has resided on a ranch near Rowe, New Mexico, since 1984 after previously developing Sugarbush Valley, one of New England's largest ski resorts, and Pine Cay, a privately owned island turned exclusive resort in the British West Indies. The grandson of a well-known navy rear admiral of the same name who married TR's oldest sister and confidant, Anna (better known as "Bamie" or "Bye"), his father was also William S. Cowles and a frequent playmate of his first cousin of the same age, Quentin Roosevelt, in the years when their families were Washington, D.C., neighbors. As a result, both were constantly underfoot in the Roosevelt White House of the early 1900s.[14]

In addition, if looking on the roster for names to drop, one could consider Susan Weld of Washington, D.C., another great-granddaughter of TR whose ex-husband was governor of Massachusetts at a time when both were close friends of Bill and Hillary Clinton,[15] and Nancy Roosevelt Jackson, of New York City, TR's very articulate granddaughter and the wife of William E. Jackson, a prominent attorney (and son of a Supreme Court justice) who counted Jackie Kennedy Onassis and the Shah of Iran among his many clients.[16] Equally impressive, as you might expect, are some of the places many call home, including Martha's Vineyard, Massachusetts; Berne, Switzerland; Pembridge Gardens, London; Park City, Utah; Manchester by the Sea, Massachusetts; San Francisco's Presidio Boulevard; Greenwich, Connecticut; St. Bonnet du Gard, France; the seaside Corona del Mar community of Newport Beach, California; and the Clintons' famously adopted home, historic Chappaqua, New York (for residency purposes), prior to the former First Lady's successful run to the U.S. Senate in 2000.[17]

Counted among the professionals listed were at least a dozen college professors and a like number of lawyers, physicians, schoolteachers, journalists, and architects. Other persons of noteworthy interest included a six-foot, eight-inch grandson of FDR, perhaps the tallest

2. *The Reunion Roster*

Roosevelt ever; an American rowing participant in the 1976 Summer Olympics; a recovering alcoholic who has helped many others with the same addiction; and two heart transplant recipients, truly a mixed bag of individual success stories, varied career paths, and unique story lines that TR and FDR, for the most part, would have been proud to claim as their progeny—Roosevelts all, regardless of station or background, party or creed.[18]

Part Two—Eleanor's Place

3

The Common Denominator

Along with ancestral origin and the remarkable consistencies of their early lives and careers, there was one other rather obvious link in the famous lives of Theodore and Franklin Roosevelt, as well as the conduit for the family's two branches: Anna Eleanor Roosevelt. As the third icon of the famous Roosevelt triumvirate in American history, ER was the connection that ultimately welded the two branches back together when she married Franklin on St. Patrick's Day 1905.[1] Long before her marriage to FDR, Eleanor grew up adoring TR, "her uncle and surrogate father," according to at least one of her grandsons.[2]

The eldest child of TR's younger brother, the first Elliott Roosevelt, Eleanor—"Little Nell" or "Granny," as she was dubbed by her parents (on obviously opposite ends of the nurturing spectrum)—suffered an equally devastating personal tragedy as TR and FDR at a far younger age when her much-loved but misguided father essentially ended his own life at 34 from injuries received in a suicide attempt, the tragic fulfillment of an alcoholic past. That was after her mother and one of two younger brothers had died even earlier of diphtheria (when she was only eight), and after she and her other brother, Hall, had been carted off to live with their maternal grandmother in 1892 in the austere Hall family residence, Oak Terrace, at tiny Tivoli, New York.[3] As a result, ER never enjoyed the kind of childhood that ensures sense of place. As previously noted, with both parents deceased, she and her brother were orphans and wards of extended families, including the up-and-coming Roosevelt clan of soon-to-be New York Governor Theodore Roosevelt, their magnetic uncle.[4] In her autobiography, the

Part Two—Eleanor's Place

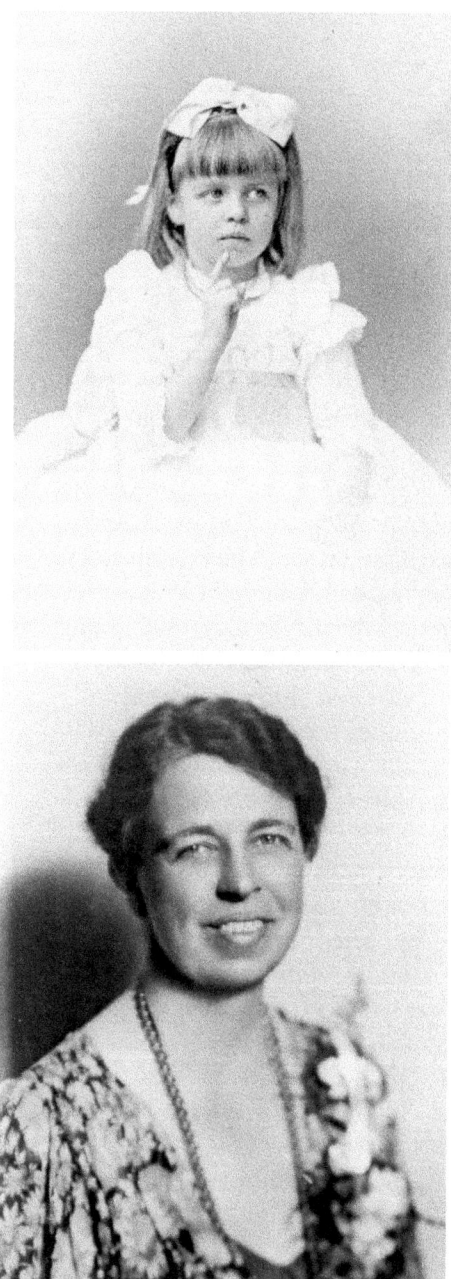

first Anna Eleanor Roosevelt even admits to having been somewhat afraid and "in awe" of her uncle's oldest daughter of the same age, Alice, while they were growing up.[5]

Although admittedly shy, awkward, and withdrawn during the formative years spent with her grandmother, Eleanor was fortunate when her life changed at age 15 with the opportunity to visit family on her mother's side in England, followed by placement in a private girls' school near London. That opportunity was arranged through the uncompromising efforts of her "Auntie Bye," the eldest of TR's two sisters.[6] And because she was a good and willing student, that's where Eleanor's life started over. Whether mastering French, devouring history and Shakespeare, learning to dance, or overcoming her lack of physical prowess to become a starter on the school's field hockey team, ER began to come out of her

Eleanor Roosevelt (ER) as a (soon-to-be orphaned) child and later, after becoming First Lady. Courtesy FDR Library and Library of Congress, Prints and Photographs Division—reproduction number LC-US762–54474.

3. *The Common Denominator*

shell. Eventually she would see Europe with teachers, friends, and the family of friends, and despite having to return stateside during summers, the school became her refuge.[7]

Unfortunately, with time she also had to become more and more responsible for her younger brother, almost his surrogate parent as her aging grandmother was involved less and less. While he was away at private school, she moved in with an unmarried aunt on her mother's side in New York City.[8] From there she acquired more friends, survived an uncomfortable debutante's coming out party, and began to see and date her fifth cousin, Franklin, whom the Burns documentary revealed was on a romantic rebound. In the autumn of 1902 FDR asked Eleanor to marry him. She was only 19 and he (at 21) would not graduate from Harvard University until the following spring.[9]

A year later, in the autumn of 1904, their engagement was finally announced and Eleanor spent time with the entire Delano side of FDR's family, his mother's side. In her autobiography, she stated, "It was an ordeal, but I knew so many of them already and they were so kind and warm in their welcome that I began to feel I was part of the clan—and a clan it was." A wealthy, former seafaring family, the Delanos apparently always stood together "and the whole family profited." Their big family gatherings were to Eleanor something of a "revelation," with a sense of security that she had never known before. She wrote, "The Delanos were the first people I met who were able to do what they wanted to do without wondering where to obtain the money. They watched their pennies, which I had always seen squandered. They were generous and could afford to be in big things because so little was ever wasted or spent in inconsequential ways. If misfortune befell one of them, the others rallied at once."[10]

Among the last things Franklin and Eleanor did together prior to their wedding was attend her Uncle Teddy's presidential inauguration in Washington on March 4, 1905, at the start of his second term. "I was interested and excited, but politics still meant little to me, for though I remember the forceful manner in which Uncle Ted delivered his speech, I have no recollection of what he said," she later admitted.[11] She also never expected to be at another presidential inauguration. Just two weeks later, TR was again the unintended main attraction at their wedding in New York City. While taking the place of his deceased brother by giving away the bride, the President also took well-wishers

Part Two—Eleanor's Place

away from the newlyweds and their receiving line when he went into an adjoining room where refreshments were being served, enticing the majority of the guests to follow.[12]

Their first home was a small apartment in a New York City hotel. Later that summer, after FDR finished his first year at Columbia Law School, they "went abroad," a belated honeymoon to England, Scotland, France, Italy, Germany, and the Swiss Alps. On the way back they spent even more time with family and friends in Paris, England, and Scotland and did not arrive back in New York City for the start of FDR's second term at Columbia until September 1905.[13] Not long after their return, Eleanor realized she was pregnant and eight months later, after a difficult and illness-filled pregnancy, she gave birth to the first of their six children on May 3, 1906. Their only daughter, the baby was christened another Anna Eleanor Roosevelt, but unlike her mother she would always go by her first name. A year and a half later, their first son, James, was born and that trend would continue through March of 1916, with the birth of their youngest, John.[14] Five of the six would survive to adulthood and all together be married a total of 19 times.[15] Their third son, Elliott, suffered through the most ill health as a child and his mother's grief over the preceding death of their second son, the first Franklin Jr., at only eight months due to complications from the flu. Fatefully, Elliott would become the most contentious and controversial of the children.[16]

Shortly after Elliott was born in 1910, FDR left his New York City law firm and entered politics, running and winning the first of two elections for the state senate from a county that had not elected a Democrat in 32 years. Remarkably, he won the first with a hands-on, very personal style that had rarely been seen before, and the second while mostly flat on his back with a severe illness (typhoid), thanks to the astute campaign strategy of his political manager and confidant Louis Howe.[17] In her autobiography Eleanor stated, "My husband's branch and many of the Roosevelt family had been Democrats until the Civil War, when they became Abraham Lincoln Republicans. Later many of these returned to their Democratic allegiance [including, obviously, FDR's father], but some remained Republicans."[18]

This divergence of family political paths was further accentuated when incoming Democratic President Woodrow Wilson, the electoral beneficiary of a split Republican Party in 1912 between incumbent

3. The Common Denominator

William Howard Taft and TR, running again as a third-party, progressive candidate, invited FDR to join his administration as assistant secretary of the navy. It was the same office Teddy had used to catapult his own career to national prominence.[19] Although FDR had been a staunch Wilson supporter during the campaign, FDR's acceptance of this plum Washington assignment was further deviation from the politics of TR, an equally staunch critic throughout Wilson's years in the White House. Although both progressives, TR and Wilson viewed America's future proceeding along differing paths, as exemplified during the campaign by Wilson's "New Freedom" and TR's "New Nationalism." In fact, many considered Wilson's inclusion of a young Roosevelt in his new administration as an astute way to reduce the impact of verbal criticisms sure to continue from the defeated former chief executive of the same last name.[20] In essence, however, TR's once mighty influence had already been reduced and would continue to be diminished in the years ahead, as the split vote made for a Republican loss that would be accentuated by a more and more conservative doctrine within that party in the decades to follow.[21]

On the other hand, Wilson's progressive mantra would become a significant part of Democratic politics and further defined by FDR over the next two decades, a "New Deal" passed on to Truman, Kennedy, Johnson, Carter, Clinton, and Obama in subsequent presidential politics. As James Chace indicates in his book *1912: The Election That Changed the Country*, the rift between Taft and TR and the resulting split vote "inflicted wounds on the Republican Party that have never healed. For the rest of the century and even into the next, the Republican Party was riven by the struggle between reform and reaction."[22] The book *Woodrow Wilson: A Biography*, by John Milton Cooper, Jr., takes this political crossroads a step further. In it, Cooper stated, "For conservatives and Republicans, it was Taft, not Roosevelt (TR), who pointed out the ideological path of the future. (Teddy) Roosevelt's brand of statist-oriented, commercially skeptical conservatism would grow less and less welcome in his former party. Instead, by a quirk of fate, his big-government views and concern for the welfare of workers and consumers would find a home among Democrats. This ideological crossover would happen in part because the next Democratic president after Wilson would be TR's distant cousin and the husband of his niece."

Part Two—Eleanor's Place

Still, this next Roosevelt (FDR) had made TR his role model early on and absorbed much of his approach to politics. The Burns documentary even quotes Eleanor as "wishing Franklin" could have been "fighting" for "Uncle Ted" at the time because "his was the party of the future." Such would not be the case, however, as Franklin Roosevelt gradually became a political heir to Woodrow Wilson. Nevertheless, by his assuming the strong-government legacy of both Theodore Roosevelt and Woodrow Wilson during the 1920s, that legacy would eventually become the sole property of the Democrats a decade later.[23]

In this new, big-government idealism adopted by her husband, Eleanor would flourish and guide, and even surpass, his efforts. Although she would remain constantly connected to those "other Roosevelts" through such things as taking over "Auntie Bye's" former house in D.C. during their early days there and seeing her brother Hall enlist for World War I duty in the same Army Air Corps squadron as her Uncle Teddy's youngest son, Quentin, her political leanings were assured and her own self-assurance would grow immeasurably in the years of turmoil and triumph just ahead.[24] Despite discovering her husband's affair with Lucy Mercer, a personal tragedy that nearly ended their marriage, his tragic affliction with polio in 1921, and her amazing adjustment to being (and remaining) the devoted and valued wife of a sitting president for over 12 years, she obviously grew in individual ways that no one would have ever suspected during her disjointed youth.[25]

Upon his overwhelming victory and elevation to the presidency for the first of four terms in 1932, her autobiography famously noted, "I was happy for my husband, because I knew in many ways it would make up for the blow that fate had dealt him when he was stricken with infantile paralysis; and I had implicit confidence in his ability to help the country. But for myself I was deeply troubled. As I saw it, this meant the end of any personal life of my own. I had watched Mrs. Theodore Roosevelt [her aunt] and had seen what it meant to be the wife of a president, and I cannot say I was pleased at the prospect."[26] Regardless of these feelings, into her life came new direction, interests, people, knowledge, vision, assertiveness, and power. Unlike other First Ladies, those of the past and most of them since, she was consistently visible, involving herself in the issues of the day, serving as her husband's eyes and ears in places he could not (or dared not) go, and

3. *The Common Denominator*

generally garnering double the exposure of most White House couples during their time in office together. Although not always appreciated, her views on great issues of the day became important, almost as important as those of the President, and her influence on him and upon events throughout his administration is undeniable.[27]

Equally undeniable is the fact she emerged from her years in Washington and following FDR's death a very different and much more complete person—someone entirely secure in her own skin, so to speak, and a political luminary. In the remaining years of her life, many considered her "First Lady of the World" (a phrase first coined by President Harry Truman) for her efforts on behalf of such things as human rights, civil rights, and one of FDR's final visions, the United Nations. In fact, it was her stewardship and ultimate leadership in development of the UN Charter that may have been the crowning achievement of her later years. Certainly the recognition she earned as head of a U.S. delegation that had to stand up to the Soviets while also bonding the entire world captured international attention and gained her enormous respect, especially as a woman exhibiting tremendous resolve and ability in what was basically, at that time, the men's-only world of international diplomacy.[28] Like any senior citizen suddenly alone on the home front, she made necessary adjustments, but she never let those adjustments stand in the way of moving forward and continuing to be productive for the remainder of her life.

In her autobiography, she confirmed, "I had to face the future as countless other women have faced it without their husbands. I had few definite plans but there were certain things I did not want to do. I did not want to run an elaborate household again. I did not want to cease trying to be useful in some way. I did not want to feel old—and seldom have. In the years since 1945 [FDR's death], I have known the various phases of loneliness that are bound to occur when people no longer have a busy family life. But without planning it, I made the necessary adjustments to a different way of living and enjoyed almost every minute of it."[29] Indeed, this go-between in the Roosevelt legacy, this common denominator, if you will, enjoyed perhaps her most rewarding years during the final 17 of her earthly existence, a segment brought out and discussed during the Warm Springs reunion by a group of people who lived through some of that time directly with her. Theirs was

Part Two—Eleanor's Place

Seen here at Top Cottage following FDR's death, Eleanor Roosevelt outlived her husband by 17 years and continued to have lasting influence in such things as the creation of the United Nations. COURTESY FDR LIBRARY.

an up-close and personal relationship with ER that only a few others experienced. Both individually and as a group, theirs were the Hyde Park summers of 1950 through 1961, when her brother's daughter and the group we will designate "the Val-Kill cousins" were in residence and interacting with her on a daily basis.[30] Return now to those idyllic days through the words of her niece and namesake, Eleanor Roosevelt II (or "Ellie," as she was called)—who authored an elaborate scrapbook about those times entitled *With Love, Aunt Eleanor*—as well as through the eyes of Ellie's children: Eleanor Calkin and her brothers, Stewart, Lauren, and Ted Elliott. Most of all there are the remembrances of two of her own grandchildren, Haven Roosevelt and Nina Roosevelt Gibson, who spent most of their formative years growing up next door to their famous grandmother at Hyde Park.

4

The Val-Kill Cousins

A "constant presence in my life for 42 years" is the way Eleanor Roosevelt II, the daughter of ER's younger brother Hall, prefaced her published scrapbook, *With Love, Aunt Eleanor*, in 2004. Obviously named for her aunt, Ellie, as she became known, also had to endure a father with the same alcoholic tendency as Eleanor's, an unfortunate, recurring family trait that led directly to Hall's death at the relatively young age of 50.[1] Divided into sections entitled "The Early Years," "The White House Years," "Life After Franklin," "Too Busy to Be Famous," and "The Later Years at Val-Kill," the last section of her book, the one following ER's extraordinary success working for the United Nations and most of her overseas travel, became the object of attention at the reunion in Warm Springs. It was during those later years that Eleanor stayed mostly near home, her beloved Val-Kill Cottage, the place Ellie would bring her children each summer for at least a month to see, and stay with, her famous namesake. Also there during those wonderful summers were the four children of John Roosevelt, Eleanor and Franklin's youngest son, who by that time resided with his family in the neighboring Stone Cottage, which had been constructed even earlier using FDR's designs at the same property. Together these young people—grandchildren, grandniece, and grandnephews—would be transformed into the "Val-Kill cousins," future emissaries of ER's unforgettable life in its final stages.[2]

Val-Kill had not always been used as a home. Originally it was a unique factory (Val-Kill Industries) built along a stream on the Roosevelt estate at Hyde Park with the blessing of both FDR and his mother. It was financed by ER and two female friends for the purpose of manufacturing furniture, pewter, and homespun cloth using traditional, early-American methods and as a means of providing supplemental income for families of the Hudson River Valley affected by the Great Depression. As a factory it lasted from 1927 until 1938.³ After that, it became a home, a nearby retreat for Eleanor away from the Roosevelts' big house—Springwood—and the overseeing visage of FDR's mother, Sara, a well-documented constant in their lives until her death in 1941.⁴ At that point, Val-Kill changed character without changing format. In other words, while the main floor plan remained the same the usage shifted from factory to home—ER's quirky home off the beaten path. It was converted to reflect her personal tastes in ways she had never been able to do before: framed pictures hung illogically over and around doors and windows; a piano featured prominently in the living room, even though she didn't play, so that guests who did would have the opportunity; elegant, heirloom candelabras sharing the same dining room table as inexpensive flatware, an indication of her simple yet sentimental preferences; overstuffed but unmatched chairs filling her entertaining spaces, an obvious nod to comfort over appearance; and an inviting screened "sleeping porch" off her bedroom on the second floor, offering outdoor access at all hours of the day, weather permitting.⁵

Lush Fall Kill Creek forms the most idyllic of settings as it traverses this section of the Roosevelt property, now the Eleanor Roosevelt National Historic Site. Still in evidence is the combination stable-garage; a children's playhouse; two well-tended flower gardens; a tennis court and stone barbecue pit; a large, in-ground swimming pool; a combination bridge and dam over the creek, connecting everything (and everyone) via a long driveway to the outside world; and the large, flat-topped rock outcropping that served as a creek-side picnic spot and identifying location before the property's development.⁶

Within sight of ER's Val-Kill home, the previously mentioned Stone Cottage is much more picturesque and was originally built for Eleanor and her two business partners, who resided there until 1947. Also not far away, at least as the crow flies, FDR's Top Cottage was designed to be his own wheelchair-accessible retreat at a loftier, more remote location. Due to his sudden death in 1945, however, others would ultimately stay at Top Cottage much more than FDR ever did. The Stone Cottage was built in 1925, but Top Cottage didn't take shape

4. The Val-Kill Cousins

until 1939.[7] Somewhat similar in exterior look, their longest-period family residents would prove to be Roosevelt sons John (with his family) and Elliott (with his third and fourth wives), respectively. Exemplifying the colonial Dutch influence of the Hudson River Valley, the cottages were constructed using fieldstone common to the area, the building material FDR expressly preferred.[8] The name Val-Kill came from the combination of the English word valley and the Dutch name of the creek along its perimeter, Fall-Kill, which translated means "valley stream."[9]

Along with her staff, ER always welcomed a constant stream of special guests, visitors, and family to her Hyde Park home. Among the array of international dignitaries to pay their respects at her humble abode were the Soviet Union's Nikita and Nina Khrushchev, Queen Frederica of Greece, Queen Mother Elizabeth of Great Britain, Queen Juliana of the Netherlands, and Ethiopian emperor Haile Selassie, as well as national notables like Harry Belafonte, Gore Vidal, Adlai Stevenson, and John F. Kennedy.[10] Her longest serving personal secretary, Malvina "Tommy" Thompson, enjoyed her own separate apartment. When the factory closed, FDR was the one who suggested Eleanor convert Val-Kill into a home for herself as the private abode she had always longed for during all the rentals, townhouses, mansions, and main Hyde Park manor she had been relegated to as the wife of a Hudson River patrician, Manhattan attorney, Washington bureaucrat, New York governor, and, finally, U.S. president.[11] Later, when both FDR and her mother-in-law (1941) were gone, she was perfectly willing for Springwood to become the Franklin Delano Roosevelt Home National Historic Site (1946), which it has been ever since.[12]

Val-Kill, meanwhile, became a hodge-podge of interior redesign, a place "with many" guest rooms, "adequate bathrooms," and a suite for ER with its previously mentioned sleeping porch in addition to the requisite living room, dining room, and kitchen. According to her niece:

> Aunt Eleanor lacked a clear idea of what the dimensions of the rooms might be, or could not imagine from looking at the blueprints how the actual spaces would work out; in any case, it is not a designer's dream of a house. In fact, it's surprising that the spaces worked at all. You came upon the stairway quite by accident. Narrow and poorly lit, it begrudged the fact that you might be carrying

Part Two—Eleanor's Place

a suitcase. You had to traverse the dining room and the living room in order to get to the porch. The dining room was too narrow for its table; the kitchen too small for the cook; the nine bedrooms were indeed small and often hot; and the five bathrooms were hidden in odd corners. Convenience was never high on Aunt Eleanor's list of priorities.[13]

With John's children in residence "right next door" whenever Ellie's brood was visiting for the summer, Val-Kill would become a childhood adventure land for the eight cousins, chock full of daily activities like swimming, horseback riding, motor scooter racing, and board games. Many times the latter were played at the same time and in the same room as Eleanor dictating her syndicated columns ("My Day"), columns that would be read by thousands throughout the country. In addition, the cousins were required to read books suggested by ER, the titles of which she would post at the beginning of each summer visit and book reviews of which would be given by each child when finished in order to earn $1. "That was my favorite thing whenever we were there," Eleanor Elliott Calkin remembered at the reunion. "She loved to read and she passed that love on to us. There was even a recording made of her reading *Peter and the Wolf* with the Boston Symphony Orchestra."[14] Calkin's middle brother, Ted Elliott, added, "You've got to understand she was a great reader. She was not real socially oriented, but she loved spending time reading." Their eldest brother, Stewart, seemed to take that a level further when he emphasized, "She didn't care which book you picked, but at Val-Kill you were required to read something."[15]

As for their other activities and chores, Nina Gibson, John Roosevelt's eldest daughter, reported, "We were all good riders. We rode bareback at least once a day and sometimes three or four times. The stables were within the compound and there were always three or four

Opposite top: Second cousins who were together at Val-Kill each summer for years were together again at the Warm Springs reunion. From left to right are siblings Stewart Elliott and Eleanor Elliott Calkin and siblings Nina Roosevelt Gibson and Haven Roosevelt. The Elliotts are grandchildren of ER's brother Hall, while Nina and Haven are offspring of FDR-ER's fourth and youngest son, John. Photograph property of the author. *Bottom:* Horseback riding was a favorite activity of the FDR-ER grandchildren and others at Val-Kill, according to Nina Roosevelt Gibson, shown here on horseback during her teenage years in Hyde Park. Courtesy FDR Library.

4. The Val-Kill Cousins

Opposite: The Stone Cottage at Val-Kill was the first and more picturesque building on the property, but it was in the converted furniture factory next door that ER would make her home and where world leaders like Soviet premier Nikita Khrushchev and Ethiopian emperor Haile Selassie came to pay their respects. PHOTOGRAPHS PROPERTY OF THE AUTHOR. *Above:* As someone who loved to be outdoors, Eleanor Roosevelt had a "sleeping porch" at Val-Kill, preserved today as part of the Eleanor Roosevelt National Historic Site. PHOTOGRAPH PROPERTY OF THE AUTHOR.

horses available. We also attended a lot of Hyde Park picnics. At hay baling time, we could pick up as many as 300 bales a day and we often spent time gathering wood for winter."[16] The youngest Elliott brother, Lauren, elaborated further: "You had two families of children roughly the same ages and actually we were assigned lots of chores, including loading hay, gathering wood, and cleaning the stables. Once while doing that, the older cousins played a joke on Sally [one of Nina's two younger sisters] and me by locking us in one of the stalls. It took a long time for the adults to rescue us and when they did, the older ones just acted like we must have accidentally done it to ourselves."[17]

Part Two—Eleanor's Place

4. The Val-Kill Cousins

Meanwhile, Haven, Nina's brother and the oldest cousin in the group, got to drive the tractor whenever they picked up hay. "Because he was the oldest, he always got to drive and I never thought that was fair. It allowed him to avoid the heavy lifting," his sister complained.[18] Haven, who like Nina had the experience of traveling with his grandmother, also offered an example of her well-conceived hectic pace when he remarked, "I know when she took John Boettinger [another grandson] and me to Europe, she had things organized to the last second so that when someone in our party left a purse in the Loire Valley and we had to send the limousine back to retrieve it, she was very upset with how that would affect our schedule. Surprisingly, she also took us to Le Lido, a topless Parisian nightclub. She later wrote my mother that she felt it was good for young men to be exposed to such things and that she stayed with us 'until the bitter end,' but my mother was never happy about it."[19] Prompted by that admission, his sister quipped, "I was in Paris with her [ER] on another trip, but she didn't take me to anything like that. That must have been her big boy's training."[20]

Some of their other ER remembrances were also surprising (if not equally so). As to the less-than-common knowledge of her actually being quite shy, Haven responded, "I know she loved to go swimming, but by herself. She always made sure no one else was around when she went to the pool. She liked company, but really preferred just friends and family."[21] Stewart added, "I remember it was hard for her to offer a toast at dinner. She always wanted someone else to offer the toast."[22] Haven confirmed that while Eleanor attended church every Sunday and always made sure to take the cousins along she was notorious in later years for falling asleep during the service. On that note, Nina said, "I will never forget attending an Easter Sunday service where we all had candles in a small, dimly lit chapel. She kept falling asleep with hers and it would start to tilt in her hand. I was afraid she would catch

Opposite top: **Eleanor Roosevelt's preserved dining room at Val-Kill illustrates her no-frills approach. Notice the elaborate candelabras that were a gift combined with simple everyday dishes and her hodge-podge of pictures on the side wall.** *Bottom:* **As for the living room, even though she couldn't play, she always had a piano handy for any guests who could. PHOTOGRAPHS PROPERTY OF THE AUTHOR.**

4. The Val-Kill Cousins

her clothes on fire, so I kept nudging her to keep her from nodding off and I had to keep that up through the whole service."[23]

ER was also a notoriously bad driver, and Haven remembered her "exiting Val-Kill and almost always forgetting to look both ways, which produced some pretty harrowing highway departures." And Stewart recalled she once surprised everyone by purchasing a bright red Fiat Spider (through her son Franklin, the northeastern Fiat franchise dealer), a convertible sports car that, according to Ellie's book, she felt comfortable driving since it was not like the much bigger, more socially pretentious Cadillacs of her well-to-do Hyde Park neighbors.[24]

Other memories of the great lady included having tea every afternoon. "I can remember it being a pretty regimented process and seeming extremely formal, especially for someone 12 years old, but we were expected to take part and display the proper manners throughout," Stewart recalled. Haven recollected her lack of patience when it came to illness. "I can remember she had no patience when her own body didn't cooperate," he stated. "She was a very private person with little or no patience for personal failings. Any misgivings about health were inappropriate in her eyes. It was a very stoic era and she was among the most stoic."[25]

Because she was a very guarded person, Haven maintained, "She had nervous energy, but she was also very guarded with her private time. It was another regular part of her routine. Even if she had not been First Lady, I think she would have stayed involved in the issues of the day and would have created a niche for herself, especially with her interest in human rights. She had the knowledge, energy, and wherewithal to accomplish great things—even without FDR."[26] At the same time, there was no doubt her lofty position in the world gave her more opportunities to make a difference and she continued to thrive

Opposite top: Now permanently covered, beside the Stone Cottage at Val-Kill was the swimming pool, which was a center of summertime activity even for ER, who preferred to swim alone. *Bottom:* Also near Val-Kill at a higher location on the Roosevelts' Hyde Park property is Top Cottage, the on-site getaway FDR had built for himself in 1938. Notice the earthen slope of the yard to the porch that gave the disabled president unaided wheelchair access. PHOTOGRAPHS PROPERTY OF THE AUTHOR.

in those situations. "Personally, I think it allowed her to become independent," Nina confirmed. "I've always maintained that when Sara [FDR's mother] took over the home front when our father and his brothers and sister were growing up, it freed her [ER] to become more involved in things she enjoyed, especially interaction with other people."[27]

As for her very best memories of being with her famous grandmother at that time, Nina fondly remembered early mornings before anyone else was up. Of those times, she stated, "I often couldn't sleep as late as the others and I would hear her calling the dogs to take them for a walk. Almost always, I would get up and sneak out to join her. In addition to the walks, she would pick flowers every day so we had fresh flowers in every bedroom. She believed they were fresher if you picked them before the sun came up. She had a big flower garden and loved gardens everywhere. One of the things she enjoyed most was being outside in a garden."[28]

Obviously, Nina will also never forget the day Sally died at age 13, the result of a horseback riding accident, and the fact her grandmother was the one who had to break the tragic news about her little sister. In that awful moment, ER offered this admonition: "You must be very brave." Such was the behavior expected … of a Roosevelt.[29]

5

Life Lessons

Along with life-teaching moments for which she will never forget her famous grandmother, Nina Gibson will also not forget one special trip she was a part of at the age of 16, a trip already cleared with her parents and boarding school when ER extended the invitation in 1959 and one that speaks to Eleanor Roosevelt's belief in life-building exposures for herself and those around her. Perhaps such attitudes resulted from her own schoolgirl memories while away in England or on connected trips to the European mainland, when the protective shell she had developed during childhood finally began to crack amidst new experiences and extensive cultural intake. It had been good for her—obviously an awakening that allowed her to transition from the lonely, closeted environment of her early years with the Halls—so why would it not be just as good for a granddaughter of practically the same age growing up right next door under her added guidance at Val-Kill. Needless to say, Nina was ecstatic upon learning that she would be accompanying ER to Iran, Israel, and Turkey before finishing up in France, Italy, and England. At the time, "Excitement turned my face into a perpetual smile!," she has admitted.[1]

Although not the constant powder keg it is today, the Middle East at that time was still not widely traveled by Americans. Twelve years after Israel had been declared a Jewish state (1947) at the conclusion of World War II, its existence was in the early stages of becoming the proverbial problem it has been for the modern world surrounded (and even inhabited) as it is by Muslim Arabs who never intend to recognize its right to exist. Having worked with the United Nations on behalf of the U.S. during attempts to resettle Arabs dispossessed by the massive Jewish influx to their "promised land," ER sought to prepare Nina for

Part Two—Eleanor's Place

some of the tensions she might witness firsthand by giving her a copy of Leon Uris's novel *Exodus*, published just the year before and eventually made into an award-winning movie of lasting significance.

Admittedly, she "devoured" the book, learning how deeply the tensions ran in that part of the world and how difficult it was to travel between Muslim countries and Israel. In fact, when the trip took place, their passports were not stamped as was traditional in those days upon entering Israel so as not to indicate they had previously been to Turkey and Iran. Nina's statement confirmed as much: "Even then it would have been embarrassing for Israeli political leaders to permit one of the staunchest supporters of their right to statehood [ER] admission into their country if her passport indicated she was coming from Iran. However, the precaution of not stamping our passports was not enough to prevent my grandmother from receiving threatening letters from people warning her not to come to Israel by way of Iran."[2]

One of the truly unique experiences derived from that trip actually involved a little camel. Apparently, while visiting a camel market with longtime family friend Abba Schwartz, an American-born attorney living in Israel, the group encountered a determined vendor ready for a sale. In fact, while Eleanor was briefly occupied elsewhere, the vendor's haggling with Abba became so intense that he suddenly turned to Nina and exclaimed, "Since we're here at a camel market, don't you think we should buy a camel to live at Val-Kill?" Surely he was kidding, she initially surmised. But before she realized anything to the contrary, Schwartz was back with more questions: "Do you like this little white camel? Don't you think she would be fun to have in Hyde Park? She is only two years old and the large brown one is her mother."

Although Nina remembered expressing that her father would have "a conniption" if she returned stateside as the owner of a camel, the lively discussion between their Israeli host and the vendor remained intense until both exhibited satisfaction. It was then she realized that, ready or not, the camel had indeed been purchased for her. By that time a crowd had gathered to see what all the commotion was about and her grandmother had returned with a "quizzical expression." Rather than being aghast at her granddaughter's unexpected commitment, however, ER simply smiled and asked, "What will you name your camel, Nina?" "Dutchess" was Nina's unhesitating reply, the name of the New

5. *Life Lessons*

York county in which they resided at Hyde Park. "And what do you think your father will say?" was ER's next well-aimed question. Nina's answer to that one, which included the selling of rides in Hyde Park to help cover the cost of hay and feed, elicited a smile from her grandmother. That's when the teenager knew she had struck the right cord to win acceptance of her newfound dromedary.

What she didn't know, however, and would have never imagined

During a 1959 trip to the Middle East with her grandmother (ER) as a teenager, Nina Roosevelt Gibson was the surprise recipient of a young female camel. Unfortunately, U. S. State Department guidelines at the time prohibited bringing livestock into the country from that part of the world, prompting her to bequeath the little camel to a very appreciative young Bedouin. The American Embassy in Israel provided her this photograph of the proud new owner, a cherished keepsake ever since. PHOTOGRAPH COURTESY NINA ROOSEVELT GIBSON.

Part Two—Eleanor's Place

was the red tape that would eventually prohibit her little camel from ever setting foot in the United States. Upon learning of the impending shipment of a camel from the Israeli desert, the U.S. Department of State and U.S. Department of Agriculture cabled both Schwartz and Eleanor to inform them that such an animal's arrival from Israel would be impossible due to the threat of hoof and mouth disease in that corner of the world. Despite the fact officials in Israel insisted such a malady did not exist among their country's livestock, plans to ship Dutchess were put on hold pending some sort of governmental resolution. In the meantime, news of the former First Lady's trip and her granddaughter's camel leaked to the media, prompting a sympathetic gentleman in Canada to suggest sending Dutchess to his country first and from there to the neighboring U.S. Unfortunately, even that idea would have involved a six-month quarantine or layover in Canada, the time necessary for U.S. officials to make sure Nina's little camel was indeed disease free.

As a result of all this red tape, even for the granddaughter of Eleanor Roosevelt, Nina decided it would probably be best if a good home were found for Dutchess in the animal's native land. With the help of the American embassy in Israel that's ultimately what happened. In fact, Nina still has the photograph they sent her of a young, recently married Bedouin who needed transportation to get his goods to market proudly beaming with his new camel.[3] Although it was not the result Nina would have preferred, it was one of those life lessons ER hoped for when she invited Nina to go along, a Middle Eastern experience to last a lifetime.

PART THREE—
REUNION REALIZATIONS

6

Must Be the Genes

Witnessing firsthand one of the three family icons the way Nina Roosevelt Gibson was privileged to do with her grandmother was not something Theodore Roosevelt IV ever had the opportunity to enjoy, at least not the company of his famous great-grandfather. However, that never stopped the influential Harvard grad, former navy SEAL, Brooklyn investment banker, and environmental trustee from doing his best to live up to his namesake (who died even younger than FDR at age 60). In fact, given his many commitments and constantly hectic schedule, his presence at the family reunion was anything but a given until just a few days before. Even so, from Warm Springs he was slated to head immediately to China for efforts pertaining to at least one of his many international commitments at the time, including chairmanship of the Pew Center on Global Climate Change and counselor for the China-United States Center for Sustainable Development.[1] In addition to those important global initiatives, he's also been part of the governing council for the Wilderness Society, a trustee for the American Museum of Natural History, and has served in the State Department. He once even addressed the Republican Party at its national convention, which, by the way, encouraged him to run for political office in his native New York more than once. His public service and conservation-conscious great-grandfather would have undoubtedly been proud.[2]

Christened Theodore Roosevelt V because Teddy Roosevelt's father, an equally staunch advocate of public service, was really the first (officially listed as Sr.) Theodore Roosevelt, TR IV, as he is known throughout the family, has also entertained thoughts of one other

Part Three—Reunion Realizations

similarity he acquired later in life that he believes mirrors Teddy—one that most people would not suspect. At the reunion he briefly talked about it: "While [I was] growing up, my family lived mostly in Philadelphia. When I began attending boarding school, I can remember developing a sense that I would join the military, probably the Navy. Later, while still in college, I became an ensign and eventually a Navy SEAL when the war in Vietnam began. I felt I would be better at that than being caged up on a destroyer. At the time, I was a raging hawk [pro-war], but I learned a great lesson from that war and my views changed considerably and much more objectively. I came to believe that war was totally unnecessary and I felt the same way about the war in Iraq."[3] As interesting as this statement seemed, given the aggressive Republican dogma at the time of those two wars (the administrations of Nixon and Bush No. 2), it got exceedingly more so when he took it several steps further.

> I think my great-grandfather [Teddy] probably experienced some of the same feelings after his youngest son, Quentin, was killed in World War I. Before that, he was obviously very militaristic as everyone knows; a firm believer in might helping to make things right. I think Quentin's death probably changed him in that respect, but I also think World War I might have been averted if he had been returned to the presidency in 1912 instead of Wilson.[4] I say that because I know how well he knew Europe and Kaiser Wilhelm, the German ruler, as well as all the other European heads of state, especially after his world tour at the end of his presidency and after his work (which garnered the Nobel Peace Prize) ending the Russo-Japanese War in 1905. I believe he might have had the status and capacity to convince them all to cease mobilization, which, of course, led to an endless progression towards war and ultimately to one of history's most horrible and avoidable mistakes. Unlike my great-grandfather, Wilson had no international experience and that made a critical difference.[5]

To be sure, Wilson blamed Germany and its militaristic leadership for "The Great War." As Jack Beaty affirmed in his 2012 book, *The Lost History of 1914*, "What Allied statesmen and publics agreed was the cause of World War I: Prussian militarism. Its first victims, Woodrow Wilson argued, were the German people. The war was ultimately about their 'liberation' from the 'military clique' in Berlin."[6] And equally sure is the fact the German emperor, Kaiser Wilhelm, had a huge personal regard for Theodore Roosevelt, upon whom he had heaped praise for ending the Russo-Japanese War as president in 1905. Kaiser Wilhelm went out of his way to host TR at his royal palace during TR's tour of

6. *Must Be the Genes*

Europe over a year removed from the presidency in 1910.[7] H.W. Brands confirmed as much by paying special attention to their meeting in his 1997 biography, *T.R.: The Last Romantic*. In it he stated, "Roosevelt had what he called 'a most interesting time with the Kaiser,' who he had never met. The highlight of the visit was a mock battle the Prussian forces staged just for Roosevelt's benefit."[8]

Meanwhile, sensing the thought-provoking attention such historic insight exhibited for inquiring minds at the reunion, TR IV continued to talk about family, including his grandfather, TR's oldest son, Theodore Jr., one of the better known members of the U.S. military when America entered World War II.[9] At the time, one veteran war correspondent even labeled him, "the only man I ever met who was born to combat." Proudly reminiscing about such tributes, TR IV commented, "At age 56, my grandfather, despite being a brigadier general [who had been recently named to that rank by none other than FDR, the perceived family rival], was among the first wave on Utah Beach during the D–Day landings. That's when he realized that he and his men had actually landed in the wrong place and made the famous statement, 'the war begins here,' because it was not defended, at least not as well as some of the other areas where the landings were taking place. Carrying a swagger stick, for which he was known in the army, he was not wounded, but later died from a heart attack."[10]

That episode in Roosevelt family lore was prominently played out by Rick Atkinson in his 2013 *The Guns at Last Light*, the third and final book in his award-winning Liberation Trilogy on World War II. In doing so, Atkinson began with this: "Brigadier General Roosevelt intended to see with his own congenitally weak vaguely crossed eyes just how stout the enemy defenses remained." He then set the stage for the entire D–Day Allied landings amidst the personal bravery of TR's eldest son with such soliloquies as the old soldier bantering with "pale, wide-eyed men around him" in the landing craft "because, as he had written [his wife], 'they see shadows when they stop to think,'" as well as his assumption that it helped to see him there with them. Next, Atkinson cites the deeds and awards General Roosevelt earned during the First World War and through the North African campaign of the Second World War, along with wartime correspondent A.J. Liebling's comment that he was "as nearly fearless as it is given to man to be." All

PART THREE—REUNION REALIZATIONS

The eldest son of Theodore Roosevelt—Ted, as he was called—was a decorated soldier in World War I and a Medal of Honor-winning general in World War II whose leadership in North Africa and on D-Day is remembered in books and family lore. He died of a heart attack shortly after the Normandy Invasion. ROOSEVELT, 570.R67T-032/TRC-PH-2, HOUGHTON LIBRARY, HARVARD UNIVERSITY.

6. Must Be the Genes

this is recounted before he acknowledges, "To no one had he disclosed the chest pains gnawing beneath his service ribbons."[11]

Later, after establishing they were on the wrong beach, a determination based on a windmill and other structures he had seen in aerial reconnaissance photos, Atkinson recorded how General Roosevelt "worked the waterline" with cane in one hand and map in the other, "walking around as if he was looking over real estate. 'How do you boys like the beach?' he roared to arriving troops. 'It's a great day for hunting. Glad you made it,'" he reportedly called out as they swarmed ashore.[12] Also, "soon enough" he was racing ahead "in his newly landed jeep," a striking vision of leadership on the type of battlefield his own father had once termed "my crowded hour" after leading the famous charges up Cuba's San Juan and Kettle hills in the Spanish American War. All the while, General Ted Roosevelt apparently ignored the personal pain of a severe coronary thrombosis that must have been building in his chest throughout the D–Day excitement.[13] He would die just over a month later in France, the most decorated soldier of the war. Other generals served as his pallbearers and his remains were interred at the massive Colleville-sur-Mer Cemetery, just one of the many American servicemen who died in Normandy. In a nice touch of historical significance their father would have appreciated, he is buried alongside his younger brother Quentin despite their dying two wars and 26 years apart.[14]

"He was a banker by trade, like many of our family," TR IV continued about his brave grandfather. "He had been governor of the Philippines, a New York assemblyman, and a candidate for governor of New York, but that was the extent of his political efforts."[15] As for any of his own political aspirations, TR IV admitted, "I, too, have been asked to enter the political arena, the last time as a candidate for the Senate, but I have always felt the financial investment it takes and the tenure necessary to actually be in a position to make a difference made it too formidable to consider." At the same time, he has met with the powerful Politburo in Communist China and surprised this writer when he indicated the Chinese are actually well versed in the science of climate change. "In fact, they know a lot more about it than we do," he added, "but their whole political system is dependent on continued economic development and the jobs they need for their millions. By

Part Three—Reunion Realizations

overly addressing climate issues, they know they would be putting their power and security at risk, the same power that constant construction and development provides. [The official Chinese approach to climate change has since been altered, becoming more proactive and focused on global leadership.]"[16]

Such reunion revelations were not uncommon. In fact, a sense that there was a lot more to the genetics of this remarkable family and a lot less to the weight carried by their name seemed to gradually permeate the proceedings. "There's absolutely nothing special or different about us when compared to any other American family," Chris Roosevelt offered on more than one occasion during their Warm Springs visit. "We're ordinary people with our goods and our bads, just like everybody else." But as with TR IV, the impressive persona of Christopher du Pont Roosevelt, one of FDR's grandsons and a family mainstay, seemed to belie such rationalizations even as he spoke.[17]

7

Family Preservationists

As noteworthy as the name Roosevelt will always be in American political annals, the name DuPont ranks just as prominently near the top of U.S. business. In fact, the actual last-name spelling for the French Huguenot family that settled along the Brandywine River near Wilmington, Delaware—and became synonymous with the production of gunpowder long before branching into many other chemical industries and providing employment for over 60,000 people worldwide—is du Pont.[1]

Any marriage between such prominent families (and political opposites), portrayed by newspapers of the time as "a Capulet and Montague union" for the famous family feud in the story of Romeo and Juliet, has always been society page fodder and thus it was for Franklin Roosevelt, Jr., and Ethel du Pont, a true, 1937 society headliner.[2] It also produced the exclusive lineage for their son that has been a lifelong feature of Christopher du Pont Roosevelt's existence, with both the advantages and disadvantages conferred by such noteworthy breeding.

Fortunately, this lofty familial connection has never kept Chris Roosevelt (CDR) from remaining very involved in Roosevelt comings and goings, to the extent that he's always been a leader in family events, including his previously acknowledged leadership role with their reunions. On being a Roosevelt, he stated in Warm Springs, "Some handle it better than others. It's all in how you set yourself up. You go back enough in the history of this place [Warm Springs] and you find that FDR just wanted to be a patient like everyone else." Taking that desire for simplicity a step further, he added, "FDR actually said once that no memorial for him should be bigger than a desk. He really did not want any edifices built in his memory. Grandiosity was not in his

Part Three—Reunion Realizations

vocabulary and like the Little White House [in Warm Springs], Top Cottage, which he had built for himself on the family property at Hyde Park, was a modest house."[3]

Even monumental Washington, D.C., reflects FDR's understated tastes. Unlike the much older, grandiose structures that celebrate legendary leaders Washington, Lincoln, and Jefferson in the nation's capital, the FDR Memorial that opened along the Potomac River in May 1997 is an outdoor configuration of sculpted walls, gardens, and statuary designed to share significant moments from his presidency, including a second statue of him clearly in a wheelchair that surprisingly proved divisive when it was first considered. The memorial was designed by Lawrence Halprin of San Francisco and originally did not include the wheelchair statue.[4] According to CDR, "A couple of our cousins said you can't do that, when the wheelchair came into discussion, that FDR would have never approved, but the rest of us said you had to do it, that it was a symbol that disability should not be a reason for lack of opportunity."[5]

His statement can be confirmed by a July 1996 Associated Press story in which FDR's oldest grandson, Curtis Roosevelt, who spent considerable time during his formative years in the Roosevelt White House, stated that his grandfather would have been disturbed to be shown as a handicapped person. "He was a very private person and went to great lengths to avoid any comment or discussion of his illness," Curtis said.[6] In April 1997, yet another grandson, David Roosevelt, a member of the FDR Memorial Commission, emphasized to the *New York Times*, "At no time did this commission consider hiding FDR's disability. His disability will be depicted for all to see, but it will not, and in my opinion should not, be a primary focus."[7] Meanwhile, Chris Roosevelt was among 16 other FDR grandchildren, along with then President Bill Clinton, to give active support to inclusion of the additional wheelchair statue at the memorial's entrance. In the *Washington Post* that same April, CDR stated, "Without [illustrating] what polio did to this man, you really can't understand this man. Trying to ignore his polio is like trying to depict Helen Keller without blindness."[8]

Actually, such involvement in preserving the illustrious history of his grandfather and family is right up Chris Roosevelt's alley. A longtime member and more recent chairman of the Roosevelt Campobello

7. Family Preservationists

International Park Commission, having been appointed by President George H.W. Bush to succeed his father (Franklin Roosevelt, Jr.) in 1989, CDR was also instrumental in efforts to include then privately owned Top Cottage, the retirement getaway FDR had planned and built for himself, in the overall Franklin Delano Roosevelt Home National Historic Site at Hyde Park in 2001. Working with and through the Franklin and Eleanor Institute and the Henry Luce Foundation, he led efforts to have FDR's final residence returned, adding it back to the federally owned and maintained historic home place.[9]

CDR also shared the story of his earliest involvement with his grandfather's "beloved island," the traditional family vacation home off the coast of Maine. A joint venture originally proposed by President John F. Kennedy, this truly international historic site became an example of the close relationship that exists between the United States and Canada after the Roosevelt International Bridge (linking Lubec, Maine, with the little Canadian island of Campobello) was dedicated by James Roosevelt in 1962.[10] Five years later, in 1967, the opening of the Roosevelt Campobello International Park Visitor Center took place, the result of this U.S.–Canadian partnership.

Technically located in New Brunswick, the park had been in existence only a couple of years when CDR was informed by his stepmother and one of his aunts that as the eldest Roosevelt male scheduled to be at the opening he would be required to take England's visiting Queen Mother on a tour of the former family compound. "The only problem—" he admitted, "I had never seen the cottage myself before Roddy [his wife] and I got there after driving cross-country from Montreal in a torrential rainstorm. As a result, we sat around a table all night working on my speech, talking about the house, and getting up to speed on royal protocol."[11] He continued: "The next day I gave my address, stepped off the dais in front of the historic cottage, and upon presenting my arm as an escort for the Queen Mother [Elizabeth Angela Marguerite Bowes-Lyon] explained that my guided tour of the building might be somewhat inadequate since it would be my first time inside as well. Her response is one I will never forget. She said, 'Well, Christopher, isn't that wonderful? You and I will be seeing it for the first time together.'" From that day forward the two of them remained good friends and corresponded regularly until her death in 2002.[12]

Part Three—Reunion Realizations

Of equal substance on the other side of the family, especially when it comes to such things as lineage and leading the way at family functions, Stephen Jeffries of Boston learned early on the importance of his famous heritage, despite the absence of the actual name of Roosevelt (thanks to its being from his maternal ancestry), as part of his own. In fact, one of his favorite family legends passed down through the generations, which he shared at the reunion, had to do with a so-called English language professor of the New York State Teachers Association who once conveyed to the family by letter that the name Roosevelt should actually be pronounced Rews-uh-velt and, thus, they had been saying it all wrong. The family's written response at the time follows, as related by Jeffries and later confirmed by the pages of the *Theodore*

7. Family Preservationists

Opposite and above: Two of the most respected leaders at the reunion in Warm Springs, one from each side of the family, were Theodore Roosevelt IV (TR IV) and Christopher du Pont Roosevelt, one of five FDR-ER grandsons in attendance and the organizing mainstay for every Roosevelt reunion in recent memory. PHOTOGRAPHS PROPERTY OF THE AUTHOR.

Roosevelt Association Journal: "It is rather a dangerous proceeding to assume that a man does not know how to pronounce his own name, and the writer who attempts not only to criticize but to dictate may find himself in the unhappy position in which 'angels fear to tread' even if he be a 'chairman of reading and culture.'"[13]

A business management consultant and devoted reunion planner, much like CDR, Jeffries is actually a direct descendant (and look-a-like minus the mustache, beard, and receding hairline) of the man who wrote that response, TR's uncle, an uncle who might have been among the best known Roosevelts ever had it not been for the obvious ascension of the Big Three (TR, FDR, ER). In fact, Robert Barnwell Roosevelt (RBR) was a well-known conservationist before his nephew ever attained that status from his promotion and nurturing of the national park idea in America.[14]

Along with a well-developed reputation as a womanizer and man about town, RBR is also remembered as "the great U.S. conservationist

Part Three—Reunion Realizations

during the years from the Civil War to the Spanish-American War," according to Douglas Brinkley's *The Wilderness Warrior*, a theme-focused biography of Theodore Roosevelt published in 2009. To be sure, Theodore Sr.'s brother, who for a time lived right next door on East 20th Street in Manhattan, was a prime shaper of the young TR's interest and future concern for all things outdoors. Brinkley even termed him "more than any other direct influence" the person responsible for turning Theodore Roosevelt "into a conservationist as a teenager."[15]

An editor for the *New York Citizen* and several times a published novelist in the mid–1800s, RBR was, unlike his brother (TR's father), a Democrat by choice and a lifelong advocate for "fish rights," having often fished the waters of New York Sound as a teenager and grown into someone who fought for protection of North America's fish populations. Indeed, his *Game Fish of the Northern States of America and British Provinces* was a book that garnered extensive praise. Along with the simple concerns it voiced for recreational fishing, it was among the first to analyze the potential loss of a great American "foodstuff" should the rivers and lakes become "fished out," an idea that led directly to the development of fish hatcheries (including, ironically, a national hatchery at Warm Springs in 1899). Brinkley points out that such "wildlife management was embryonic in the mid–19th century" and that TR's uncle RBR actually "pioneered in introducing scientific concepts" related to fish before going on to head the New York State Fish Commission.[16]

It is no wonder such a close and influential family member became a role model for the young and aspiring TR and surprising his influence could be overlooked until Brinkley by historians and biographers alike, especially given the knowledge and pride exhibited by descendants like Jeffries. Even the great Edmund Morris, TR's most recognized biographer, barely mentioned him in his Pulitzer-winning *The Rise of Theodore Roosevelt*; and H.W. Brands offered not much more on Uncle Robert in *T. R.: The Last Romantic*.[17] Among more recent TR biographers other than Brinkley, only David McCullough in his *Mornings on Horseback* delved into this intriguing uncle very much.[18] "He clearly started the conservationist movement in this country and influenced TR heavily," RBR's great-great-grandson emphasized over the phone.[19] Further proof

7. Family Preservationists

of the outspoken exuberance RBR must have imparted to the young TR was Jeffries' retelling of how an extended family, the result of an indiscreet relationship, fostered several additional claimants to the Roosevelt name and a desire to be invited to an upcoming family gathering. RBR is reputed to have addressed the brewing controversy with the brash proclamation, "We should just let the bastards in!"[20]

Among those in between Jeffries and his colorful great-great-grandfather were his grandparents, Philip James Roosevelt, a New York City banker who would form one of the oldest partnerships on Wall Street, and Jean S. Roosevelt. They were cousins (second cousins to be exact), the marriage of which happened fairly frequently within the Roosevelt clan, much like the better known union about the same time between more distant cousins Franklin and Eleanor. Jeffries also mentioned the historic home built by his great-grandfather John Ellis Roosevelt, which is still standing at Sayville, New York: Meadow Croft. It's now the property of Suffolk County and, like TR's National Historic home at Oyster Bay, Sagamore Hill, a relic of the significant roots the TR branch put down on Long Island.[21]

All these Roosevelts and all of their relations were cataloged in that previously mentioned amazing family genealogy near the end of the 20th century. Entitled "The Roosevelt Family in America" and published in 1990 by the Theodore Roosevelt Association in its journal, it included 13 generations of American Roosevelts and basically replaced an earlier family genealogy that spanned 1649 through 1902. Along with the two U.S. presidents, the genealogy also includes six other family members who made the *Dictionary of American Biography*. Well indexed throughout its 161 pages, "The Roosevelt Family in America" breaks down known family members and their children from one generation to the next, regardless of how many marriages and additional family units that entailed (and, as established, rather amazing numbers of those resulted).[22]

Among its later listings on page 92 is one Ann Keating Luskey, a descendent of TR's younger sister Corinne on her mother's side but someone who grew up rather oblivious to her influential lineage until recent adulthood. Now in her forties, she, in fact, never thought much about it until becoming interested in how many of her ancestors on both sides of her family had attended Harvard University (17), and

Part Three—Reunion Realizations

coming face to face with a genetic reality tying her to the famously adventurous TR in a seemingly indisputable way.[23]

Of similarly recent genetic awakenings is the previously mentioned granddaughter of FDR and ER to be found on pages 67 and 82 of the genealogy, Anne Sturgis Roosevelt, now known as Nina Roosevelt Gibson, the result of a nickname given to her while she was still very young (a family derivative of a Russian word apparently meaning little princess). Now in her 70s, she too only recently realized a genetic connection to her famous grandfather that she had never considered before despite spending many of her formative years growing up near (and with) her grandmother at Hyde Park after FDR's death in 1945.[24]

Together these two Roosevelt women, Ann and Nina, would seem to provide proof of the influence of genetics on succeeding generations. Their stories, one from each branch, offer powerful statements about history repeating itself within families—even the better known ones.

8

Generational Genetics

After attending the Roosevelt reunion in Warm Springs, Ann Luskey could admit she had never even thought about such things until the last couple of years. Although in her mid–40s and knowing that Roosevelt blood ran through her veins, having been told on more than one occasion that part of her family's lineage could be traced to President Theodore Roosevelt's younger sister Corinne, she had never previously considered the undeniable similarities.[1]

She's not even sure when the idea first crossed her mind or what prompted its genesis, but it had occurred nonetheless. As a former board member of the African Wildlife Federation and committed ocean conservationist, she suddenly realized for the first time the rather remarkable similarity her life's interest and work had taken to her most famous forebearer, the formidable TR. "I have to admit, I thought the same thing myself," she confirmed when contacted by telephone. "I had never read or known much about him, except, of course, that he was a prominent American president and that I was related. My interest in Africa, wildlife, and conservation had actually started much earlier as a child, when my immediate family went on a safari to Kenya. I was only 12."[2]

Interestingly, the most famous African safari in American history was undoubtedly the one TR undertook with his second son, Kermit, immediately after TR's second and final term as president in 1909. As portrayed, he was always a man of abundant energy and action and he was obviously anxious for a getaway of the most elaborate kind, a chance to continue the kind of exploration and adventure he had always been known for in America. In other words, putting his disappointment at having to leave the White House aside in the most flamboyant way

Part Three—Reunion Realizations

possible while at the same time focusing on the exotic excursion (and hunt) he had always dreamed about, TR moved on with his life in the kind of macho way he was famous for, one sure to test him through new experiences, even dangers. It was—the press, his family, and everyone involved knew—typical Teddy.[3]

Designed to acquire taxidermy specimens for American museums, TR's African safari began in Mombasa in April 1909 and lasted all the way to Khartoum in March 1910. Brinkley described how, "armed to the teeth" and "with a retinue of hundreds," "free from the shackles of the White House," TR disappeared from the American political scene for a full year. Already a Nobel Peace Prize winner, he envisioned his post-presidential role as being "a global spokesperson for big game animals, wildlife protection, and natural resources conservation." He made

As a man and president who loved action and the strenuous, outdoor life, TR was frequently photographed on horseback. ROOSEVELT R500.P69A-064, HOUGHTON LIBRARY, HARVARD UNIVERSITY.

8. Generational Genetics

arrangements with the Smithsonian Institution to sponsor the trip only weeks after his presidency ended and entered into a strenuous training regimen before advancing into the most remote recesses of the Dark Continent, never imagining that the political landscape he had shaped so much during the previous decade would be significantly altered while he was away.[4]

In *Alice and Edith*, a biographical novel about the two wives of Theodore Roosevelt by Dorothy Clarke Wilson, the anticipation of TR's return from his safari is examined through the eyes of Edith Carow Roosevelt, the childhood friend who returned to his life as his second wife after the untimely death of his first. Even in this fictional account are seen the seeds of political dissent that he would embrace once he realized his handpicked presidential successor, William Howard Taft, had not followed TR's progressive approach as completely as expected. While he was away, a more conservative course had been charted by Republican leaders glad to see him gone, and Wilson's concept of his wife's expectations illustrate the personal eruption sure to come once he realized the full extent of what she knew he would consider his successor's back-stabbing departure.[5]

The resulting intra-party squabble, as significant as it would be to the ensuing history of American politics, had nothing to do with the realization of Ann Luskey.[6] Her understanding of such things as TR's conservationist leanings, his love of wildlife and wide-open spaces, and his extended African sojourn were the only part of his story that grabbed her attention.[7] She emphasized:

> My family's trip to Africa was the start of everything for me. I basically fell in love with the place and went on to major in African studies at the University of North Carolina. By the time I finally realized what an avid conservationist and explorer Theodore Roosevelt was, I already knew I came from an explorer gene pool because my mother's father was the son of the famous archeologist Alfred Kidder, who discovered so much in the American Southwest, including his excavations at what is now Pecos National Historical Park. I understand how my life emulates TR, but I also know I came by the explorer gene from both sides of my mother's family.[8]

Indeed, the combination of TR and Kidder genes probably left little to chance in Luskey's makeup. Born in 1885, Kidder has long been regarded as "the foremost American archaeologist of his day." Her maternal great-grandfather even has an anthropological award named in his honor for his work in pottery typology, the use of stratigraphy in archeological assessments, as well as his discoveries in Arizona, Utah, Colorado, and New Mexico, and his leading role in a far-reaching survey of the cultural history of Mayan Mexico and Central America.[9] Combine that resume with TR's exploration of the Amazon; his big game hunts and ranching adventures; and his basic fathering of conservation in this country, including the National Parks movement, and you surely have the makings of an overpowering personality trait in just about any genetic code.[10]

Nothing quite that transparent was passed down from Franklin D. Roosevelt to his last-born granddaughter before he died in 1945. In fact, Anne Sturgis "Nina" Roosevelt Gibson was just two years old when FDR succumbed to a massive cerebral hemorrhage at his Little White House in Georgia and years before her family moved to Hyde Park to live next door to her famous grandmother. Those, in fact, would be school-age years and quality time with Eleanor of a kind she obviously never got to enjoy with her equally famous grandfather.[11] No, she was far too young when he passed away to have any such personal recollections of him. That has not stopped her, however, from realizing a series of traits common to her grandfather throughout a very productive life that now stretches into eight decades. First and probably most troubling was the onset of polio when she was only nine. In fact, both she and her older brother, Haven, contracted the same dreaded disease as their grandfather, but in milder forms that did not inhibit their mobility the way it did his.[12]

Later in her life, as an accomplished psychologist, she would also learn of a heart defect in both herself and her daughter, a family characteristic that some feel may have contributed to FDR's own cardiovascular problems and eventual death at just 63.[13] The result of that discovery for Nina R. Gibson was a heart transplant, an obviously very successful transplant that she had already lived with at this writing for more than 15 years and one she feared her daughter might eventually need.[14]

Ever since her own operation and recovery at the University of Arizona Medical Center, a hospital that specializes in "cardiothoracic and multidisciplinary transplant programs," Nina has used her experience and psychological skills to assist others waiting for and going

8. *Generational Genetics*

through similar ordeals, helping to ease and even stimulate the sense of shared burden for the families of transplant victims by providing a special apartment environ near Tucson.[15] And it is because of her volunteer efforts there as an outstanding example and resource for transplant patients and their families that she has drawn her own genetic conclusions in terms of what she found upon visiting Warm Springs, today home to a state-managed rehabilitation center that began as a historic community of polio survivors founded by her grandfather in 1927.[16] Of this discovery she said, "I see a lot of similarities between what he started in Warm Springs for polio survivors and in what I've been involved with in Arizona for organ transplant patients, but I didn't make that connection until I visited Warm Springs and saw for myself the hospital and cottage community he loved and was so much a part of. That's when it hit me—hey, there really must be something to genetics because I suddenly sensed a kinship with him that I had never felt before. "[17]

Because that "kinship" has helped, and continues to serve, so many people, theirs could even be viewed as a shared legacy, one that lives on through compassionate care in both Georgia and Arizona.

9

Generational Go-Between

Perhaps no living member of the Roosevelt family is as well positioned to write a book someday as Mary Winskill Roosevelt, who resides in the seaside community of Corona del Mar in Southern California. The last of the four wives of James Roosevelt, FDR's and Eleanor's first son, she admits to having extensive family letters and documented remembrances under lock and key, just waiting for the proper moment to go through it all and share it for posterity. It is hoped, as she is in her late 70s, she won't wait too much longer.[1]

The reunion in Warm Springs was her first return to a Roosevelt family gathering in a decade. Prior to that period, years in which she was helping to raise her own grandchildren on the West Coast, she had attended several reunions, including some with James, who was 32 years her senior and died in 1991.[2] A very educated person in her own right, she has been in the unique position of observing Franklin and Eleanor's children, grandchildren (most of whom are her peers age-wise), and great-grandchildren during a sort of bridging, generational lifetime.[3]

Even though of British descent and living somewhat distant from most of them, she has always made an effort to remain connected and on good terms with James's older children from his previous marriages. Every Christmas she still makes an effort to telephone them all and even views herself as a conduit of information among the extended family groups of stepbrothers and stepsisters, most of who don't regularly communicate with each other. Only in the reunion setting (or at their father's funeral) have these divergent groups been brought

9. Generational Go-Between

together, but she has nonetheless done her best to keep tabs on the influential brood she found herself thrust into after repeated courtship attempts by James in the late 1960s. She was able to connect again in person with several at Warm Springs, including her contemporary Kate Whitney, one of two daughters from her husband's first marriage, as well as Michael and James Jr., look-a-like brothers from his second.[4] As to this assumed role within the family, she remarked, "They're wonderful people who have always gone with the flow. I have been careful not to overstep my bounds but just join in and I think they have accepted me for that reason. For the most part, I would say the grandchildren [FDR and ER's] have been more successful in their personal lives than the children, but I also have wonderful memories of being with James and his siblings, especially John and Franklin, when we were all living in New York. By and large they are a family of very bright and caring people with the collective trait of public service and duty. They make extraordinary volunteers."

Mary Roosevelt also remains an excellent resource when it comes to confirming much of what has been written about her late husband, including his many interests and associates.[5] One such account was included in *The Patriarch*, by David Nasaw, a 2012 bestseller. In fact, Nasaw's biography of Joseph P. Kennedy makes clear the friendship between the two, which began with FDR's 1932 presidential campaign and the extremely wealthy Kennedy's financial support and participatory role on a cross-country train tour. Afterwards, James remembered Kennedy as "a rather fabulous figure to a very young fellow on his father's first campaign."[6]

From what Mary Roosevelt was told, however, their friendship really took off about a year later when Kennedy provided James a temporary job. Nasaw described it thusly: "In the fall of 1933, Kennedy sailed to London to negotiate an agreement with the Distillers Company, which had a near monopoly on aged Scotch. To demonstrate the strength of his Washington connections, [Kennedy] brought with him the President's oldest son," who "did help him get the business going" but never expected to become part of the business, according to James's memoirs.[7] When asked if that initial business proposition confirmed Joe Kennedy as the "bootlegger" he had always been rumored to be, Mary Roosevelt responded with an emphatic "yes," but she also assured the author that all James ever got in return were contracts to insure the Distillers' imports from fire for his budding insurance business.[8]

Meanwhile, what Kennedy got in return was a more direct line to the Roosevelt White House, appointments to head two federal commissions (Securities and Exchange and Maritime) and eventually the ambassadorship for himself and his soon-to-be famous family to the Court of St. James in England. Nasaw touches on this by describing how James briefly assumed the duties of the deceased Louis Howe in 1936, serving as his father's presidential secretary despite considerable charges of nepotism and other expressed concerns, even by his own mother. Some members of the media went so far as to report something sinister about Kennedy's friendship with the much younger Roosevelt.[9]

According to Mary Roosevelt, they remained friends for the rest of their lives with "never a rift," even after Kennedy was perceived to be persona non grata by many in the Roosevelt administration for his appeasing beliefs and comments at the start of World War II, and his perceived lack of support for Great Britain once the British were under attack. She confirmed, "I can remember James being very friendly with all the Kennedys. I can even remember when James, Jr., was running for Congress from Massachusetts [in the 1980s] against Joe Kennedy III, Robert's son, with all of the Kennedys and much of the Roosevelt tribe in contention, but in close proximity at one particular juncture during the campaign. I will never forget finding James and Ethel [Robert's wife], parents of the two candidates, sharing a laugh together at that event, away from the cameras."[10]

Another confirmation she was happy to make was James' support for Republican Richard Nixon in the 1970s and even for Ronald Reagan almost a decade later as a key member of "Democrats for Nixon and Reagan" in California, his adopted state and the place he represented for six terms in Congress.[11] She stated the following:

> Hard to believe as it sounds, James always voted Democratic except when it came to president, when he voted the man. I think he had a problem with George McGovern being the Democratic nominee in 1972 and he knew Nixon personally, having been around him when they were both representing California in Congress. Later, he helped kick off Jimmy Carter's first presidential campaign, but Carter never involved or consulted him again and I think that's what led to him supporting Reagan four years later, once again a Californian who he had gotten to know through the Actors' Guild.[12]

9. Generational Go-Between

Not the only Roosevelt son to switch political allegiances from time to time (John openly supported Dwight Eisenhower for president in 1952 after Elliott and Franklin, Jr., tried to recruit "Ike" as a Democrat in 1948), James also had the film industry in common with Joe Kennedy, who became a producer and better known motion picture investor after his initial Wall Street successes of the 1920s.[13] According to Mary Roosevelt, James also established a friendship with Sam Goldwyn of Metro Goldwyn Meier and from that relationship went on to produce the movies *Wuthering Heights* in 1939 and *Pot of Gold* in 1941. It was during this foray into the motion picture industry that Los Angeles became what she termed "his stomping ground," a factor that made their eventual settling in "less crowded, more conservative, and beautiful" Newport Beach an easy decision.

Being located just south of Los Angeles also put them in close proximity to the University of California at Irvine, the relatively young college (founded 1965) that James would eventually endow with funds from the Roosevelt Warm Springs Foundation,[14] and also the place where Mary would eventually transfer her own international background into an academic legacy. A respected educator in Europe and New York City before marrying (or meeting) James, she would serve in a number of leadership and volunteer capacities with the UCI faculty after his death, earning directorships, awards, and even medals from the school.[15]

Along with her own daughter (and her daughter's family), the child of James who now resides the closest to her in Long Beach is, ironically, the one who brought them together in the first place. Adopted by James as a baby, Hall Delano Roosevelt was only a second grader at the International School in Geneva, Switzerland, at the time his teacher Mary Winskill first made the acquaintance of his father, who at that time was in the middle of a messy divorce from his third wife. After pursuing Mary over several continents, as her work took her repeatedly to other countries, and even resorting to calling her mother to find out where she was, James finally got the "yes" he was seeking. They were married in 1969. "I have always been a gambler to some extent," she quipped in regard to marrying a much older, thrice-married man, "and although I knew from the start he was the son of a president, I didn't realize just how important the Roosevelt name was until coming back with him

Part Three—Reunion Realizations

from Europe and seeing how much he was thrown into public life in this country even in Orange County, California, which is normally very Republican."[16]

Theirs was an interesting 22 years together, to say the least, and it is evident Mary Roosevelt remains devotedly proud of her late husband and his family a quarter of a century later. One other part of his life she emphasized was his decorated service in the Army and Marines during World War II, the eldest son of a prominent wartime president who, unlike at least one other (Robert Lincoln), wasn't asked to avoid the battlefront by his family at the height of conflict. In fact, James Roosevelt was definitely in the line of fire in World War II in the Pacific, one of several segments of his very segmented life that has long since been glossed over following repeated exposure in prominent outlets like *Time* magazine.[17]

PART FOUR— DESCENDANT DICTATES

10

In the Line of Fire

Although a Roosevelt and a du Pont, Chris Roosevelt's mother, Ethel du Pont Roosevelt, was like a lot of other women during World War II—ready to do her part for the war effort. For her, what that involved was driving an ambulance that picked up returning wounded warriors from the European Theater at a no longer existent military airport on Long Island, New York, and carrying them to area hospitals throughout New York City for continued rehabilitation and recovery.[1]

Such were the commendable efforts of even the most affluent home front U.S. citizens between 1941 and 1945, truly a time in our nation's history when everyone pulled together regardless of such things as background, status, religion, race, age, sex, or even politics. Into this atmosphere of volunteerism and rolled-up sleeves four Roosevelt sons, offspring of a president who repeatedly promised to keep us out of the war before being forced by the Japanese at Pearl Harbor to take us into it, were immediately faced with doing their part as service-eligible young men.[2] Each, like so many others, did their duty, with James initially joining the Army Reserve (1936), Elliott the Army Air Corps, and both Franklin, Jr., and John the Navy. Each was decorated, with John, the youngest, winning the Bronze Star for service under attack on the USS *Hornet*; Elliott the Distinguished Flying Cross and Air Medal with 11 Clusters for various missions over Europe; and Franklin, Jr., the Purple Heart and Silver Star for his action in North Africa, Europe, and the Pacific. Elliott also drew substantial attention as a military attaché during his father's famous wartime conferences at Newfoundland, Casablanca, Cairo, and Tehran, when he openly (and somewhat controversially) agreed with the tough-minded, postwar

Part Four—Descendant Dictates

attitude of Soviet leader Joseph Stalin towards Germany, much to the chagrin of British Prime Minister Winston Churchill.[3]

Just as Theodore Roosevelt took pride in, and endured stress with, his four equally decorated sons all playing frontline roles in World War I (in *T.R.: The Last Romantic*, H.W. Brands indicated he wrote to them "almost daily"),[4] so James MacGregor Burns acknowledged a similar World War II emotion by FDR in his biography, *Roosevelt: The Soldier of Freedom*, when he used the quote, "I can speak as one who knows something of the feelings of a parent with sons who are in the battle overseas."[5] Perhaps it was FDR's eldest, James, however, whose wartime exploits and brushes with danger attained the most exposure, especially after he moved from the Army to the Marine Corps as a commissioned lieutenant in the Pacific once Japan's surprise attack assured American entry. "Jimmy," as he was often called, was in fact one of 15 decorated participants (Navy Cross) in one of the most daring early U.S. operations of the war, in August of 1942, the Marine Corps raid on Makin Island, about which the wartime movie *Gung Ho* was made.[6] By that time a major and second in command to Lieutenant Colonel Evans F. Carlson (aka "Carlson's Raiders"), James Roosevelt's citation read: "Through his maintenance of communications, he was able to inform his own supporting vessels of the presence of two enemy vessels, as a result of which the two enemy vessels were destroyed. During the evacuation, he personally saved three men from drowning in heavy surf."[7] After the medal was presented to him by Fleet Admiral Chester W. Nimitz at Guadalcanal later that fall, a mention of it appeared in *Time* magazine in January 1943. It followed an earlier battle report by that same national publication in September 1942. Entitled "Battle of the Pacific: Forty Hours on Makin," it was a very descriptive, blow-by-blow account of the rout of 200 Japanese on the island and 150 more who sank in two warships just offshore. Meanwhile, Carlson's battalion lost fewer than 20 men. "Did you kill any Japs?," reporters later asked Major Roosevelt, who was nursing an injured hand at the time. "Shot at a couple of snipers," he replied. "We got 'em."[8]

Previously, in late December 1940, almost 12 months before Pearl Harbor and nearly two years before Makin Island, then U.S. Army captain James Roosevelt was in Iraq as a special observer assigned by the President during the time Great Britain was attempting to get a

10. In the Line of Fire

pro–Axis revolt in the Middle East under control. Remarkably, while crossing 400 miles of desert with a British expedition, FDR's son came under fire, undoubtedly some of the earliest enemy fire experienced by any American serviceman during World War II, when four German Messerschmitt fighter planes suddenly appeared above the car in which he was traveling and proceeded to rake the entire area with gunfire. According to another *Time* account, "Roosevelt was frank to later admit he did not like his first taste of targetry at all. He scrambled out of the car, he said, 'faster than I ever got out of anything in my life.'"[9]

While these were wartime examples when he was literally under fire, James very often found himself under fire in other ways, especially as it pertained to his four marriages. The first of those, to Betsy Maria Cushing, daughter of the great Cleveland neurosurgeon Harvey Cushing and a known favorite of FDR, came under the famous scrutiny of Hedda Hopper, a well-known Hollywood gossip columnist, after the President's eldest son moved to California and became vice president of Samuel Goldwyn, Inc. In that role he was remembered for producing his two movies and distributing the British film *Pastor Hall*—while also becoming good friends with movie mogul Joseph Schenck, reputed to have had mob connections as well as having been prosecuted for income tax evasion.[10]

It was his married life, however, that garnered the most attention and scrutiny when Betsy left him and returned East, prompting Walter Winchell, another gossip columnist of New York City fame, to hint at a possible breakup. Winchell's speculation, in fact, came after James had been seen in the company of his former nurse at the Mayo Clinic (where he had undergone surgery), Romelle Schneider, who eventually became his second wife. Hopper, meanwhile, "ran" with her story in November of 1939. According to yet another *Time* article of the period:

> On a Saturday night at nine o'clock, with three hours to make deadline for the *Los Angeles Times'* early-morning editions, she picked up the phone and tried to get James Roosevelt at his home in Beverly Hills. Two hours later she was still ringing, but had got no answer. So Hedda Hopper sat down and wrote the story. Afterwards, at 11:15 p.m., Miss Hopper stepped up to the Roosevelt door, rang and rang the doorbell, roused a friend who roused James Roosevelt, who appeared in a woolen bathrobe, one foot slippered, the other bare. Said he graciously 'Oh hello Hedda.' Miss Hopper handed him her story, James Roosevelt studied it a moment, shrugged and said, 'Hedda you know how rumors are.

Part Four—Descendant Dictates

Since Betsy returned to the East to live near her parents and friends, people have been trying to attach some importance to our geographic separation. More than that I'm afraid I can't say.' More than that he did not have to say. Hedda Hopper shook his hand understandingly, hopped in her car, drove straight to the *Times* office, and wrote a new lead quoting Mr. Roosevelt. The front page was re-plated, pushing aside news of the war in Europe, and by four in the morning on a quiet Sunday Hedda Hopper's story ranked as the Pacific Coast's newsbeat of the year.[11]

In fact, for several years, such things seemed to be in the news a lot about Franklin and Eleanor's two oldest sons. While James was married four times, Elliott was married five,

The eldest son of Franklin and Eleanor Roosevelt, James Roosevelt was a decorated veteran of both the Army and Marines and, along with his three brothers, always in the limelight. Today Mary Roosevelt, the last of his four wives, remains a loyal conduit for his very extended family. Courtesy FDR Library; also photograph property of the author.

10. In the Line of Fire

including his third, to actress Faye Emerson, soon after a warplane-purchasing controversy involving reclusive millionaire Howard Hughes (who had introduced them), seemed to implicate Emerson and Elliott in some way. Later, James would survive a well-documented stabbing by his third wife while living in Geneva, Switzerland (1969), after informing her of his intention to seek a divorce.[12]

But it was mostly tell-all books authored by Elliott after his parents' deaths and the alleged facts (or secrets) they purported to reveal, some of which James would refute in later published accounts of his own, that fanned the flames of family controversy for this branch of the Roosevelts in years to come. These exposés and the sibling squabbles they fostered even led to suspicion among the extended families of Roosevelt grandchildren, some of who would continue to regard Elliott and his children as inherently opportunistic.[13]

Along with James and Elliott's various forays into matrimony, Franklin, Jr., would be married five times, Anna three times, and John (remarkably, it seems, by comparison) only twice, so internal comments or even jokes among later generations on the FDR-ER side were certainly not without warrant and fairly commonplace as the years passed and their parents were no longer living. If perceived as a family shortcoming, such matrimonial proliferation was, in fact, deemed okay to acknowledge and joke about if done within the confines of the family.[14] Meanwhile, along with the attack on James, two suicides by former in-laws would further cloud lingering impressions of Franklin's and Eleanor's offspring, as the previously mentioned John Boettiger (Anna's second husband) and Ethel du Pont (the first wife of Franklin, Jr.) would both take their own lives—John's demise coming a year after divorce in 1950 at age 50 and Ethel's 15 years later in 1965 when she was 49 and remarried.[15]

Sad to say, such tragedies also afflicted the family's other side. TR's second son, Kermit, the steadfast companion who brought his ailing father out of the Amazon jungle in 1914 following participation in an ill-advised South American expedition and Teddy's equally ill-fated bid to return to the presidency in 1912, also committed suicide, the result of an adulthood with the same depression and alcoholism that had marred so many other family members, including his uncle Elliott and cousin Hall.[16] For obviously protective reasons, the truth about Kermit's death, which came in 1943 in Alaska, where he was

Part Four—Descendant Dictates

serving a final wartime stint in the military, was kept secret and never revealed to his aging mother, who outlived him by five years. While avoiding the public eye, a policy she maintained from the time TR died in 1919 at age 60 until her own death 29 years later at age 87, Edith Roosevelt was spared those details.[17]

In addition, Kermit was also the perpetrator of perhaps the family's longest running extramarital affair, a liaison with a one-time German masseuse, Carla Peters, that stretched throughout the final seven years of his life even with his wife's knowledge and begrudging acceptance.[18] However, it was Alice who would both concoct and conceal what would have surely been the family's most tabloid-worthy relationship had it been revealed.

Alice was a Washington insider her entire adult life and not only married one of the nation's up-and-coming statesmen, Ohio congressman Nicholas Longworth in 1906 (a future Speaker of the House despite his reputation as something of a playboy), she also had a child by another congressional luminary of that era, Senator William Borah of Idaho. Even though rumors persisted for years, the truth about Paulina Longworth's parentage would never surface during her lifetime, and the only child of Alice Roosevelt Longworth would die at just 42 from an alcohol-induced, medication overdose, six mournful, depression-filled years after the untimely hepatitis-related death of her own husband, Alexander Sturm. Despite many opinions to the contrary at the time, her death was deemed accidental. Officially, at least, it has never become another Roosevelt suicide.[19]

11

Too Close

As the daughter of Anna Eleanor Seagraves, the eldest grandchild of Franklin and Eleanor Roosevelt, Anna Fierst was the lone representative of her immediate family at the Roosevelt reunion in Warm Springs. With her aging mother still living in Washington, D.C., but very limited in her ability to travel, the daughter was nevertheless anxious to make her way south from Bethesda, Maryland, even without her husband David Fierst, a prominent D.C. attorney.[1]

The granddaughter of the Anna Eleanor Roosevelt who was FDR's and ER's only daughter and oldest child and who would become Anna Roosevelt Dall before Boettiger and finally Halsted, Anna Fierst is one great-grandchild who has been privy to tales of the Roosevelt White House throughout life, thanks to both her mother and uncle, Curtis Roosevelt. They were the two oldest Roosevelt grandchildren who resided, along with their mother, at 1600 Pennsylvania Avenue during their formative years and in the midst of their parents' marital separation. In fact, they were termed the "First Grandchildren" by White House media when they first moved in before becoming, more commonly, "Sistie" and "Buzzie," family nicknames conferred at the time of their parents' breakup as a means of separating little Curtis from his suddenly persona-non-grata father, Curtis Dall (a stockbroker by trade), and his sister from simply being another Anna or Eleanor, using instead, the Roosevelt derivative for "Sis."[2]

Acceptance of the nicknames apparently dates to FDR's mother, Sara Delano Roosevelt, the family's domineering Hudson River grande dame, who was around her initial great grandchildren much more than the later ones. This was especially true, as they also visited Hyde Park frequently with their mother and their grandparents during the 1930s and through-

Part Four—Descendant Dictates

out FDR's first and second terms as president.[3] Eventually their stepfather (Anna's second husband), John Boettiger, a newspaperman by trade who had covered the Roosevelt White House, would resettle his acquired and rather prominent family on the other side of the country near Seattle, Washington, a move that did not sit well with his attention-loving stepson, who by that point had grown accustomed to being near the limelight.[4]

Never one to shy away from the notoriety cast upon his childhood by those early White House years, Curtis Roosevelt (aka Buzzie) authored a book in 2008 entitled *Too Close to the Sun*, a first-person account of growing up in the gargantuan shadows of his grandparents. In its preface he confessed: "Intoxicated by the exhilarating environments of Washington [D.C.] and Hyde Park, I created a dream world that protected me and became a form of addiction. In fact, as I grew older, I found it easier to inhabit that fantasy world than to develop and nurture my own strengths and talents in the real one." In his 80s and living in France when he finished the book, he also admitted that it had actually taken a lifetime to fully understand his role as "a tiny planet circling the dual suns" of his grandparents and to accept and adjust to "a world devoid of their reflected glory."[5]

As the eldest male grandchild, perhaps Curtis's lifetime of searching for his own individual direction and identity most closely resembled the sons of FDR and Eleanor, who, he states in his epilogue, "prospered, or didn't, variously. They had large appetites, whetted by being, just as [he] was, too close to the sun—and the course of their lives was closely linked to the family identity. Their stories [were] told often in the tabloid press." Like them, he also freely admitted to the "family tradition" of multiple marriages (in his fourth when he died in 2016).[6]

Meanwhile, unlike her younger brother, this early proximity to power never seemed to alter Eleanor "Sistie" Seagraves' development and approach to life. In very "un–Rooseveltian" fashion, she's been married to the same man, Van Seagraves, a speechwriter, for over 60 years and has resided in the Washington, D.C., area, becoming co-president of the Woman's National Democratic Club in the 1980s, a women's political group that her grandmother ER helped found.[7] According to her daughter, interviewed while at Warm Springs, "She had an obviously fascinating childhood, but unlike her brother, my mother never sought the limelight. She never signed autographs or felt any entitlement was due

Curtis Roosevelt (right), eldest grandson of Franklin and Eleanor Roosevelt, joined the author for this photograph in Warm Springs, Georgia, in 2009. Now deceased (2016), Curtis and his sister spent a significant part of their childhood years growing up in the Roosevelt White House of the 1930s.

her just because of who her grandparents were." On the other hand and continuing in that vein about her uncle, Fierst emphasized, "Curtis enjoyed it all too much and they used to get into arguments about the history of it all and the things that happened. They always viewed their childhood years through very different glasses. In fact, I think it's different for girls. They grow up, get married, and change their names, and with my grandmother [FDR's and ER's daughter] divorcing Curtis's

Part Four—Descendant Dictates

father when he was relatively young and not remarrying for several years, I don't think my uncle ever had a father figure to look up to other than his grandfather, who just happened to be president."[8]

Meanwhile, Buzzie remained in the limelight in later life by appearing frequently on French television and writing for European publications like *La Figaro, International Herald Tribune, La Tribune, France-Amerique, Marianne,* and even Spain's *El Mundo.* He also wrote and published poetry and served as a visiting professor at the Geneva School of Diplomacy.[9] Upon the divorce of his mother and stepfather years ago, he was encouraged by family not to take the surname of his father (Dall) but to use his famous middle name (Roosevelt) instead, which he did and continued throughout life.[10]

Sistie, meanwhile, although listed as a librarian, educator, historian, and editor by online biographies, has largely retained her reputation of remaining away from the spotlight.[11] Perhaps her most visible achievement, other than involvement with the D.C.-based Democratic women's group, was as editor of a 1994 book originally published in 1817, *Delano's Voyages of Discovery and Commerce,* which revealed the travels and business dealings of one of her more prominent Delano ancestors, Amasa Delano, who traded extensively in China and the Far East.[12] He was an enterprising and adventuresome captain of the *Massachusetts,* an impressive and well-documented sailing ship built in Quincy, Massachusetts. It's a very interesting personal account of travel among the South Sea Islands of the Pacific that took place shortly after the *Mutiny on the Bounty* episode occurred in 1789, when an obviously disgruntled and starry-eyed crew in the service of England's Royal Navy engineered the takeover of the HMS *Bounty.* (That story was eventually made into not one but two motion picture classics, the first starring Clark Gable in 1935 and the second starring Marlon Brando in 1962.)[13]

In fact, one of the book's expansively titled chapters—"Personal Encounters Touching the Mutiny on the Ship *Bounty*; The Fate of the Mutineers; The Settlement on Pitcairn Island; Captain Mayhew Folger Tells of His Discovery of the Lost Colony; Other Accounts"—attempts to answer questions surrounding the aftermath of the rebellious crew and their apparent decision to overthrow the captain, Lieutenant William Bligh, and anyone on board who remained loyal to him. Afterwards, they decide to remain in the South Pacific, allegedly taking beautiful

11. Too Close

The first grandchildren of Franklin and Eleanor Roosevelt, Curtis and Anna Eleanor were better known by their nicknames, Buzzie and Sistie, during their time in the White House with their mother, Anna Roosevelt, FDR and ER's daughter and oldest child. In this 1933 photograph, they are shown playing on gym equipment installed for them on the White House lawn.
LIBRARY OF CONGRESS, PRINTS AND PHOTOGRAPHS DIVISION, HARRIS AND EWING—
REPRODUCTION NUMBER LC-US962–123456.

Tahitian wives and settling on a remote, "unharbored" island after dashing the *Bounty* on the rocks, thus removing any vestige of the ship's existence in the event of future visitors. Two years after the mutiny (1791), the British government attempted to trace the as-yet-undiscovered mutineers by sending another ship, the *Pandora*, to Tahiti, the findings of which (or lack thereof) are detailed along with further discoveries in the 20 or so years that followed, including several speculative reports about a lost colony of their descendants.[14]

It's the kind of tale that makes for very interesting reading, not only in that one chapter, but throughout the book, spicing one's mind

Part Four—Descendant Dictates

with idyllic settings, faraway adventure, and unsolved mysteries. It's also the kind of firsthand narrative that historians depend on, causing bewilderment over its formally limited availability in libraries of the 20th century. That is what prompted Seagraves, in the introduction of her new version, to list "encounters with alien social and natural environments, different habits of culture, religion, and measures of justice that figure in our American genesis down to the present time" as reasons why it was obviously important for her to better record and preserve the historic travels of this adventurous ancestor.[15]

Amazingly, the Delano heritage everyone identifies with FDR as the result of his middle name was also shared by two other U.S. Presidents, Calvin Coolidge and Ulysses S. Grant (ironically, both Republicans), and included ancestors who helped charter the *Mayflower* and at least three family members who signed the Mayflower Compact, the original governing document of America's fledgling Plymouth Colony. Delano was actually derived from the French name De Lannoy, meaning "of a town in France."[16] Of more direct lineage to FDR and his oldest granddaughter than Amasa Delano was the better known Warren Delano, Jr., FDR's maternal grandfather and one of the so-called "Boston Brahmins," the recognized patriarchs of first families of Massachusetts during the 1800s. And it's no secret that the fortune he amassed was largely due to development of the opium trade initially through the Cantonese Province in Southern China and later the entire Far East.[17]

Because Amasa Delano and his brother Samuel eventually migrated to South America and settled in Chile, and because their relocation eventually begat a prominent citizen in that country's major seaport, Valparaiso, by the name of Pablo Delano, there's also a reference in Seagraves' introduction touching on the sheer delight that knowledge of this South American "kinship" must have had for her grandfather. It would have been a reaction that she, having been there, could undoubtedly anticipate. It reads, "FDR must have been delighted when this kinship corroboration was brought to his attention. There is no way of knowing whether or not he had ever heard of the Pablo connection before this. But here was a fact of life not to be ignored. One imagines FDR looking up at his informant, catching the eyes of others surrounding him, throwing his head back, and with a broad grin exclaiming his happiest phrase, 'Don't you love it? Don't you just love it?'"[18]

12

Like Father, Like Son?

It turns out David Roosevelt, one of Elliott's three children by his second wife, was another FDR-ER grandchild responsible for a book. He authored one in 2002 entitled *Grandmére* (pronounced Gran-mier), the term of endearment Eleanor's grandchildren learned to call her in the same way other grandchildren might use more common titles like Grandma, Nana, or Maw-Maw when referring to their grandmothers. In fact, David stated in his preface, "We called her Grandmére, from the French she had spoken since she was a child."[1]

Although he's been to Warm Springs, including as a primary speaker at the Southern Governors 75th Anniversary Conference in November 2009 (an obvious nod to the first such conference originally held there in 1934 at the invitation of his grandfather), David Roosevelt did not attend the family's reunion in Warm Springs four years later. His older sister and brother, Ruth Chandler Lindsley and Elliott, Jr. (also called "Tony"), were there from Dallas, as was the young family of Elliott's great-grandson, the previously mentioned "Thatcher," but David was a no-show despite voicing support in his book for family reunions. In it he wrote: "I am delighted to say that these reunions continue on a fairly regular basis today, usually every other year, at various locales connected with the family. And as my generation and the next become well acquainted, there shall be greater understanding of the legacy of our ancestors and fewer divides between us. In many ways, I think it is a rediscovering of our own roots and the importance of not just the three most prominent family members in our nation's history, but of so many others as well."[2] With publicly expressed sentiments like those, and given the exclusive screening of the Burns documentary, it does seem surprising he wasn't able to attend.

Part Four—Descendant Dictates

At the same time, as a previously mentioned member of the advisory group that contributed directly to the establishment of the FDR Memorial, David might never win a popularity contest among his generation on the Franklin and Eleanor side.[3] Just as his father was often viewed as a troublemaker by his siblings, especially after his tell-all authorship, so too David has sometimes not endeared himself to his cousins. Not only was his reluctance about the statue of FDR in a wheelchair in conflict with a majority of the Roosevelts, his book also proved contentious in a few family circles following its publication in 2002. In the book's preface, he confirmed reliance on the many oral histories, family and otherwise, available at the FDR Library in Hyde Park in addition to his own childhood experiences at Val-Kill, as infrequent as those apparently were following his parent's divorce in 1944, two years after he was born. While his father did reside at Top Cottage for seven years after FDR's death in 1945, David, along with his older brother and sister, was growing up with their mother in faraway Texas. So while appearing to speak for all of Eleanor's grandchildren in his approach to the halcyon Val-Kill days of their collective childhood in the book's Part One, he did so despite the fact many of the others had lived in much closer proximity to her and had been with her much more often, some even on a near daily basis. Unlike the rest of his book, his documentation for this part doesn't credit any oral histories or interviews. Instead it references just two books about ER. One, *Her Star Still Shines*, was compiled by a former FDR Library director, Lynn Bassanese, and was obviously drawn from the oral histories found there. The second, *The Candles She Lit*, would be reprinted by the Eleanor Roosevelt Center in 2000, confirming similar reliance on individual remembrances of the great lady. Understandably, more inclusive documentation or actual comments from his cousins would have been better received within the family, given his limited time at Hyde Park.[4] Ironically, Collier's book, *The Roosevelt's: An American Saga*, referenced David Roosevelt's older brother and sister visiting their father at Top Cottage but did not mention the presence of their little brother (who was affectionately dubbed "Little Texas" by his grandmother) during what Collier says was Elliott's last summer in Hyde Park. David would have been nine years old at the time.[5]

Meanwhile, David's book was important in the way it tied the two

12. Like Father, Like Son?

Roosevelt branches together through Eleanor. After all, his father was named for ER's ill-fated father, his own great-grandfather from the TR side, whom he depicts at one point as "the most loveable of the Roosevelts" and, despite his tragic demons, someone his grandmother always considered "the one great love of her life."[6] Among the connections he makes is ER's confirmed similarity to the famously energetic TR when she commented, "My uncle, Theodore Roosevelt, was known for his remarkable energy. Where did all this energy and capacity for work and for play come from? In fact, he preached the strenuous life. I decided then that back of my Uncle Theodore's family must lie some very healthy, sturdy ancestors and when people say to me that for a woman of my age I have extraordinary vitality and energy I am obliged to point to my ancestors and say ... I must be grateful to them for handing down to me good health and the capacity to acquire good discipline."[7] He later follows that up by establishing ER's exposure to politics, thanks to the TR clan, way before she became the wife of FDR. In fact, none other than her antagonistic cousin Alice alluded to as much in an interview reprinted from an ER biography, which read, "Politics were always being talked about at Sagamore Hill. Eleanor Roosevelt would have heard politics there. She was a do-gooder. She got that from our grandfather (TR Sr.)."[8]

David's book also developed the idea that ER inherited her love of travel and cultural exposure from her father, who, regardless of his personal shortcomings, had enjoyed family travels abroad when he was growing up, which, according to his great-grandson, "created a fascination with foreign cultures, a fascination that was unquestionably inherited by his daughter." To further support this notion, he points out how she traveled extensively "the world over," and in her later years, "whenever possible," she would include one or more of her grandchildren on these trips, "exciting opportunities" for his generation.[9]

Again to David's credit, he did not avoid the damning details of ER's childhood, her "beautiful" mother's seeming indifference towards her; her father's "miss-adventures" and regrettable choices as his alcoholism (and seizures) spiraled uncontrollably towards breakdown and demise (both his and his children's); and Eleanor's unfortunate situation along with her surviving brother, Hall, as they grew up in the stodgy surroundings of their maternal grandmother's home following the

Part Four—Descendant Dictates

shocking deaths of both of their parents at young ages.[10] Nevertheless, in doing so he also reinforced ER's fondness for her Oyster Bay relatives, particularly her uncle TR, which he stated "lasted throughout life." He even contends that in many respects TR became the father figure she so desperately sought "and she another daughter in his already bulging family." Then he admits, "Indeed, her reverence for her uncle would in time cause her to be torn between that devotion and her own husband's political designs."[11]

One area David only touches on, which would have been even more interesting if he had addressed it further, was ER's dedicated but often strained relationship with his father. In fact, while portrayals of Elliott Roosevelt as the most troublesome, headstrong, and controversial of the FDR-ER children are fairly commonplace in the vast volumes of their lives, his own son's description of that relationship seemed contained in just one paragraph, which read, "My dad was often called 'the most loveable,' of the boys. He was, like his grandfather Elliott before him, restless and possessed of personality traits that most assuredly reminded Grandmére of her own father. He was also, perhaps, the most impetuous of all the Roosevelt children. Even before the war he had entered a succession of business enterprises ranging from ranching to radio, [as well as] the fledgling world of television, and writing."[12] It was in those "enterprises" and "worlds" that conflict seemed to arise and divide the middle child from his mother throughout her later years.[13] Although not essential to the ER story, the grandson's take on the reasons and prevalence of this unfortunate dynamic between the two would have been interesting and possibly enlightening.

At the same time, the lead to an article in the *Los Angeles Times* dated October 8, 2000, seemed to confirm any question about the ongoing discordant nature of Elliott's (and by extension David's) Texas branch of the family when it comes to at least some of the Roosevelt legacy. With the hotly contested presidential election of that year as a backdrop, the op-ed article by Roosevelt scholar Susan Dunn was entitled "Roosevelts—Betrayed and Betrayers" and it referenced a significant endorsement for then Republican candidate George W. Bush's proposed plan to partially privatize Social Security. That endorsement came from none other than Elliott Roosevelt, Jr., David's older brother.

12. Like Father, Like Son?

Obviously, FDR's landmark Social Security Act of 1935 involved the very progressive and very public "pooling of interests of tens of millions of Americans into one vast program of mutual support, and," as the opening paragraph made clear, "Mr. Bush's plan betrays that essence."[14] That conclusion also left little doubt as to the equally obvious divergence of at least one FDR grandson—who just happened to be one of Elliott's sons—when it came to what is generally regarded as his grandfather's signature legislation. The irony of that was hard to miss.

13

External Family

Still affixed to the wall of the bedroom in which Franklin D. Roosevelt died at his Little White House in Warm Springs, Georgia, is the photograph of an obviously valued acquaintance. It's one of several framed photos that still adorn the walls of this Georgia State Historic Site, but it's the only one in his bedroom of a person ... obviously someone who had a major impact on the life of one of the most famous Americans ever. What an honor!

To be pictured in the bedchamber of an American giant, a place that has (as far as anyone knows) been left just as it was on April 12, 1945—the date and location of his tragic death in the early stages of his record-setting fourth term as president of the United States, would seem a recognition to be remembered and esteemed in a special way. And so it was for Lynn Garland, the granddaughter of Sam Rosenman (and wife of recent Supreme Court nominee Merrick Garland) when she inquired about why her grandfather was the only individual afforded such a station when she visited FDR's Little White House in 2013, nearly seven decades later.

Shown in his judge's robes as a justice of the State of New York Supreme Court, a position he assumed in 1936 after serving as Governor Roosevelt's chief general counsel for the state and, more important, as his principle speechwriter not only in Albany but throughout FDR's 12-year presidential tenure, is Rosenman in a very distinguished looking, three-quarter length, vertical photo. Probably one FDR obtained from Judge Rosenman as a token of his appreciation and friendship, it echoes the mutual regard and attachment of these two men who spent countless hours working together in the process of evaluating, defining, and enunciating the policies of mid–20th century

13. External Family

America, including most of the ones for which FDR is remembered.[1] In other words, it was history in the making or, more succinctly, history in the wording.

Obviously trusted as few others were by Franklin Roosevelt, Rosenman later returned that trust by becoming a leading proponent and classic example of intimate insider turned valued historian and biographer once his primary subject, FDR, was deceased. In 1950, he was editor of *The Public Papers and Addresses of Franklin D. Roosevelt*, a massive, 13-volume undertaking.[2] Then, two years later, he authored *Working With Roosevelt*, a very personal but documented manuscript that clearly supports its opening statement—that of being "a partisan book ... written by one who believes Franklin D. Roosevelt, with all his faults, ranked with Washington, Jefferson, and Lincoln as one of our greatest presidents, and a very great human being besides."[3]

Just as clearly, Rosenman was one of FDR's inner circle of associates and friends, including only the most intimate of family confidants, who made up his daily retinue throughout his professional career. The often-acknowledged others included Louis Howe, his very savvy political handler and career architect; Basil O'Connor, his law partner and successor at Warm Springs and in the war against polio; Missy LeHand, his devoted personal secretary and gatekeeper throughout recovery from polio, his return to politics, his four-year governorship, and the early years of his presidency; Harry Hopkins, his trusted liaison and "trouble-shooter" during the later World War II years; Daisy Suckley, his very attentive cousin who was with him when he died and with whom he shared a closeness that others were rarely permitted; and, of course, Eleanor, who served him as a political partner the likes of which no other First Lady has ever attained.[4]

To this inner-circle should be added the name Grace Tully, FDR's "other" secretary, who eventually succeeded LeHand as his primary administrative assistant once major health issues forced Missy's early retirement in 1941.[5] Like Rosenman, Tully would later publish her remembrances of those historic days in a 1949 book entitled *F.D.R., My Boss*. After joining the staff of the Democratic National Committee (DNC) in 1928, she first went to work for Roosevelt while he was governor of New York.[6] She later followed him to Washington when he ascended to the presidency in 1933. Following his death in 1945, she

Part Four—Descendant Dictates

returned to the DNC and also spent time in a long clerical career in support of Senate Majority Leader Lyndon B. Johnson, ultimately, of course, another U.S. president.[7] Both the Rosenman and Tully books offer unique perspectives on the FDR persona, with the kind of observations only a professional intimate could make through observing him day in and day out. Although obviously not Roosevelts, one might, in fact, look upon such intimates as external family.

The same could be said for Captain Archibald Butt in terms of his boss, Theodore Roosevelt. For over 20 years, Butt had been a respected military quartermaster when TR tabbed him as his handpicked aide upon entering the White House in 1901. That followed earlier postings to the Philippines and Cuba, where he built a sterling reputation, much of it coming during the Spanish American War.[8] Rather than personally authoring a book, however, Butt's documented takes on the always-colorful TR are to be found in voluminous personal letters he wrote to his mother and sister during his Washington years. Later compiled in book form following Butt's tragic death as one of the most remembered

13. External Family

passengers on the ill-fated luxury cruise liner *Titanic* (famously sunk during its maiden voyage in 1912),⁹ these letters help illustrate TR at his most energetic and all-encompassing. In fact, the title of this historic compilation was simply, *The Letters of Archie Butt*. It was edited by Lawrence F. Abbott, a well-known American author of the time and another good friend of Theodore Roosevelt, who like Rosenman (with FDR) assisted on many Roosevelt speeches of that era, especially during the later years of TR's illustrious career.¹⁰

Opposite and above: At the Little White House State Historic Site in Warm Springs, Georgia, only one individual picture still adorns Franklin Roosevelt's bedroom wall. What an honor that remains for Judge Sam Rosenman, a member of FDR's "external family." PHOTOGRAPHS PROPERTY OF THE AUTHOR.

Examination of these three books provides an up-close look at both FDR and TR in action ... behind-the-scenes glimpses of two men from the same family who probably enjoyed being president more than any others before or since. Taken individually, the books offer unique perspectives on the personalities, opinions, beliefs, and little known facts of FDR and TR brought about by direct daily contact—closer and more constant association with the commander-in-chief than even their families could expect during the apex of their leadership.

From Archie Butt we learn about such obscure details as that the great TR had "absurdly small feet" ("size 4 or 5") and that the nation's 26th and youngest (42) president always carried a pistol in the days before intense security with the Secret Service became so much a part of presidential life (now in place before, during, and even after every administration).¹¹ We also have confirmed the pride TR took in his

Part Four—Descendant Dictates

mother's southern roots (Georgia) and the connection (or near kinship) he often professed for Butt, who was from Savannah, as a result. This was despite the fact that, as we have seen, he always begrudged his father's avoidance of military service for the Union during the Civil War. On one such occasion, when both were enjoying mint juleps in the company of several cabinet members of northern lineage, TR quipped, "But we can't expect the New England Yankees and the Middle West people to drink with us old Southern gentlemen; it would be asking too much."[12]

Such rare instances of TR's drinking in public actually led to what Butt called "often malicious gossip about the President" during the pre-prohibition era of the early 1900s and a libel suit that he actually took time to bring in 1912 against a Michigan newspaper editor who had alluded to Roosevelt's getting "habitually" drunk. With "nothing but hearsay evidence to present" and "a large company of witnesses" testifying to TR's "temperance and abstemiousness," Butt obviously reveled in the fact his boss was "triumphant" in that case with the unscrupulous editor's credibility stained in the process.[13]

One of the more intriguing letters Butt wrote, on June 15, 1908, dealt with TR's personal choice for the American national anthem. Ironically, their discussion of this subject started with talk of the unofficial but still recognized Deep South anthem "Dixie." As for "The Star-Spangled Banner," they agreed that "not even trained sopranos could sing" it properly. Instead, TR acknowledged his favorite was "The Battle Hymn of the Republic," in which Butt concurred, motivating TR to respond, "I am de-lighted to hear you say that Captain and especially so as you come from the South. There is not a sectional line in the whole hymn. The line 'As he died to make men holy, let us die to make men free,' is universal and was as true 100 years ago as it is now. Yes that hymn ought to be our national anthem, but how can we bring it about." Then, after further brainstorming, TR allegedly added, "I have it. I will write to Joel Chandler Harris [the acclaimed Georgia author of *Uncle Remus*] and get him to start the movement in the [*Atlanta*] *Constitution*. Then I will write to others in the West and get them to take it up and we may live to see it our national hymn. The movement must come from the South and it had better come from someone not connected with politics. Would it not be fine to have an anthem that this great nation could sing in unison?"

13. External Family

Butt's letter went on to share how "possessed" TR had been with the idea. Butt even shared how the famous British poet Rudyard Kipling had once told him "the "Battle Hymn" was the greatest hymn ever written" and that it could "never be touched."[14] In the same letter, Butt revealed TR's admiration for not only Abraham Lincoln but also Robert E. Lee when TR said, "This nation is [now] big enough to revere the name of Robert E. Lee without sectional distinctions. He is no longer [just] southern, he is American, and he belongs to the nation, not to the South alone. The two names which will stand out as the great ones of the Civil War period are Lee and Lincoln. The dignity of Lee after the close of the war [was] awe-inspiring."[15] In editing the book, Abbott also stipulated in a later reference that TR "not only liked Southerners but had a deep-seated desire to replace [their] feeling of political solidarity and antagonism" born by the heritage of division and civil war with a newly acquired "sense of national confidence and responsibility,"[16] apparently a dream of his still many decades away.

Among other admissions to be found in Butt's letters was his certainty that TR planned and executed his now famous safari to deepest, darkest Africa immediately after his seven-plus years as president as much for the benefit of newly elected William Howard Taft, his longtime friend and cabinet member (secretary of war), "as for himself." Butt seemed to confirm that long-held suspicion when he revealed the charismatic TR felt he had to distance himself as much as possible in order for the administration of his handpicked and much more sedate successor to have a chance. He wrote: "If he were anywhere near telegraph lines it would [have been] hard for the public not to suspect he [Taft] was not being managed by him [Roosevelt]."[17]

There's also confirmation that TR struggled his entire life with bad penmanship. Hermann Hagedorn, another esteemed literary friend of TR, had already written of his struggle with "illegibility" in a 1921 biography entitled *Roosevelt in the Badlands,* and Abbott referenced a tale from that book in explaining why one of Butt's letters mentioned how the President wrote "laboriously." In that story TR had been corresponding with a well-known hunting guide by the name of John Willis, who he hoped would lead him in pursuit of a mountain goat in the Rockies of northern Idaho for what would eventually become an imposing group of wildlife trophies in his home at Oyster Bay. In his handwritten letter to Willis, TR had concluded with this question: "If I come out, do you think it possible for me to get a goat?" To which the obviously plainspoken guide wrote back: "If you can't shoot any better than you can write, I don't think it will be."[18]

In another fascinating review of a week spent as a guest of the Roosevelt family at Sagamore Hill, Butt's four (almost daily) letters to his mother in late July 1908, offered a glimpse into the home life of Theodore Roosevelt. Amid invigorating hours of tennis, swimming, hiking, discussion of current events, and excursions to places like Coney Island, Butt indicated his greatest surprise was the "utmost simplicity" he experienced. "I am constantly asking myself if this can really be the home of the President of the United States and how it is possible for him to enforce such simplicity in this environment," Butt wrote.[19]

Among his meal-time observations that week: dinner was always at 8 p.m., the only other rule being "there were no other rules or regulations" at Oyster Bay; TR's preference for fried chicken covered with white gravy because his mother always believed "that was the only way to serve fried chicken"; the surprising inclusion of grits for breakfast, yet another example of TR's mother's Georgia roots; the level to which TR enjoyed coffee, so much so, in fact, that he preferred to always prepare the morning brew himself and was rarely satisfied with its taste if it was prepared by anyone else; and finally, the President's "wholesome" appetite, a factor that often had him talking of needing to lose weight. "You think me a large eater; well, I am small in comparison to him," Butt "noted with some hesitancy."[20]

As for the Roosevelt children, all of whom were still at home except Alice (by that time famously married two years earlier in a huge White House ceremony to Congressman Longworth), Butt observed that the oldest son, Ted, "while not handsome" had a "keen face" and was "clever with a splendid sense of humor"; that second son Kermit was "very attractive in manner and appearance" and a favorite of his mother; that third son Archie, the one who like his father had been sickly as a child, although argumentative and "pugnacious" still appeared "delicate"; that "the other daughter," Ethel, unlike her older half-sister (Alice) found grown-up political talk exceedingly dull and would often excuse herself as a result; and that Quentin, the youngest, was a typical "bouncing" boy often seen "scuttling around corners" in his

13. External Family

efforts to avoid parental detection.[21] "But for all of that," Butt wrote, "I should like the roof of this simple home to be removed for 24 hours [so] that 80 million pair of eyes could be focused on Sagamore Hill. What a revelation would be its naturalness, its genuine family life, and above all its united love and happiness![22] What a privilege it is to have seen this household as I have seen it."[23]

Equal transparency can be found in the words of Tully and Rosenman. Their takes on FDR and his immediate family behind the curtain of presidential privacy provide some unique examples of things we otherwise probably wouldn't know about our longest-serving chief executive. Among the examples to be found in Tully's book are FDR's fondness for what she called "gadgets"—probably second only to his beloved stamps, the collection of which biographers have long talked about. Tully even went so far as to draw a conclusion and categorize the accumulation of "gadgets" as an accepted family trait when she wrote, "Wherever you find Roosevelts, you will also find gadgets." Evidently, hundreds of tokens of affection from supporters, including many animal figurines, were typical of these gadgets and something one might expect to find in the Oval Office during the FDR years. Not surprisingly, Democratic donkeys always seemed a key component of this animal menagerie along with bears and dogs (especially those depicting Scottish terriers like FDR's Fala), but Tully also made known that among the earliest of these arrivals at the Roosevelt White House (1933) was a little elephant, the acknowledged Republican mascot and one that became a Roosevelt favorite.[24]

Another example Tully shared was his preference for gray suits. Although FDR was "not particularly interested in clothes—his or other people's," she stated that light or dark gray suits, usually with a "white pinstripe," were always a part of his wardrobe. Also known for his navy blue or black capes, a convenient outdoor layer given his disability and the awkwardness he often experienced when trying to don an overcoat while settling into his wheelchair, FDR did occasionally wear "mixed tweeds" or brown if in a "rough material," according to Tully. However, "dark suits" such as "navies and gun-metal" were "shunned." She also recounted how his ties "ran" with "stripes or polka dots [and] with an occasional red number." Apparently, he was also somewhat "partial to the bow tie." Soft-collar, made-to-order white shirts were another key part of his normal presidential attire and he exceedingly disliked "tails" and the "stiff trappings" of more formal attire. She also told of a particular "gray morning suit" he once wore to a congressional appearance that attained much favorable comment from his staff and questions as to its origin, to which he replied "he had always admired a similar suit worn by TR when he was president, so he made up his mind to own one."[25]

As with any secretary, Tully was also well aware of her boss's innermost thoughts when it came to rivals and enemies. She revealed as much in her book when she addressed the men who opposed FDR for president, the Republican candidates he defeated during four successful campaigns for the White House. These included, in order, presidential incumbent Herbert Hoover (1932), Kansas Governor Alf Landon (1936), corporate lawyer Wendell Willkie (1940), and New York Governor Thomas E. Dewey (1944). "Of the men who opposed FDR for public office, Thomas E. Dewey and Herbert Hoover were the ones toward whom he expressed personal resentment," she stated at the beginning of a chapter entitled "The Only Thing We Have To Fear...," a title obviously chosen to be inclusive of all the opponents FDR had faced throughout his political career, including as a New York state senator; a candidate for both the U.S. Senate and vice president; and while running for the governorship of New York.

FDR's Hoover contempt, which was mutual, has been well documented through the years. In fact, there's virtually no doubt the outgoing president at the height of the Great Depression and his incoming successor were barely on speaking terms by the time Inauguration Day 1933 arrived. That was the case even though Hoover, like Roosevelt, had been once regarded as a progressive disciple of TR, causing FDR to briefly call for a Hoover presidential run as a Democrat before his Republican affiliation was officially announced in 1920. What Tully added to this well-established story of political animosity is the fact FDR never did get over it—even a little bit—and never in the next 12 years did he indicate the slightest change of heart when it came to his White House predecessor. Tully believed the same would have been true for Dewey had FDR not tragically passed away just months after defeating his fellow New Yorker and taking office for a fourth consecutive term in 1944.

Despite similarly progressive leanings early in the careers of the two men, FDR's secretary Grace Tully, in her book, *F.D.R.: My Boss*, confirmed FDR's total disdain for Herbert Hoover by the time FDR succeeded him as president. Needless to say, this was one "cold shoulder" ride on their way to the inaugural ceremony that March of 1933. LIBRARY OF CONGRESS, PRINTS AND PHOTOGRAPHS DIVISION—REPRODUCTION NUMBER LC-DIG-PPMSCA19179.

On the other hand, she confirmed that her boss often referred to Landon as a "thoroughly nice man" in the years following their opposing campaigns and that FDR did, in fact, develop "a genuine affection" for Willkie, who even testified before Congress in support of his controversial Lend Lease Program after losing the 1940 election.[26] Further

Part Four—Descendant Dictates

proof of the latter was offered by a story she told of FDR inviting Willkie to a secret dinner for just the two of them soon after the 1940 election, a dinner for which he had Tully secure the services of an outstanding "outside" chef. Apparently, the recent adversaries dined that night on turtle soup made of terrapin meat that had been sent to the President. Willkie remained until nearly midnight and judging from the sounds of laughter that emanated from FDR's study that night, Tully was convinced the two recent adversaries really enjoyed being together. After that, there was no doubt in her mind that "FDR had genuine regard for Willkie, as a human being and a great American."[27]

A further mending of old Roosevelt animosities that Tully was privy to occurred sometime during the war years of 1941–45 with FDR's predecessor as New York governor, Al Smith, the Democratic presidential candidate and party figurehead largely responsible for his return to politics in 1928 (after polio) and someone who had rather obviously split with all things Roosevelt in the intervening years. When Tully got wind that Smith was in town and staying at the Mayflower Hotel, she alerted the president, who, as she hoped, "invited him over" despite his usual "crowded schedule." And again, she alone was privy to the intra-party rivals sharing an hour's worth of "hearty laughter" behind closed doors before they separated, back on a first name basis for the first time in years.[28]

Another of Tully's chapters deals totally with the First Family. Although its obvious intent was an overview of immediate family interaction, it also provides its share of interesting tidbits Roosevelt readers might not get elsewhere. While confirming the already discussed larger family's political divide and the crossover issues initiated by ER's marriage to Franklin, several quotes by her boss pertaining to family history also made for enlightening copy. For instance, there is FDR's comment on the Roosevelts' religious heritage before coming to America from Holland (or "the Dutch Islands"): "In the dim distant past they may have been Jews or Catholics or Protestants—what I am more interested in is whether they were good citizens and believers in God—I hope they were both."[29]

In addition there is such Roosevelt minutia as the fact that Eleanor was "slightly deaf," what Tully terms her one physical "affliction" in the midst of "good health" and enormous "physical expenditure" but

13. External Family

something she would occasionally use to her advantage when wanting to get past what she considered "irrelevant, extraneous remarks;"[30] that Fala (FDR's celebrated Scotch Terrier) had a Secret Service code name—"The Informer;"[31] and that while FDR dreaded the chore of government budgets and the grueling period it took to produce them each year probably more than any other presidential responsibility, he nevertheless took great pleasure in balancing his own family accounts—to the point of "work[ing] for hours to track down a discrepancy" and "always [being] highly pleased with himself when he found the error."[32]

Later in the book we learn that in Tully's opinion "nobody" knew the exact moment or circumstances in which FDR decided to run for a history-altering third term as president, something clouded by the political enemies of his time who pronounced it "a long-standing intention, planned and plotted in sinister fashion" with "a cruel political disregard for the ambitions of other potential candidates." Obviously, Tully was aware of FDR's ongoing popularity among the electorate and the majority endorsement of most of his policies, so she considered him "most of all anxious that these proven [measures], domestic and foreign, should be carried on."[33] In other words, who better was there to ensure continuity than FDR?

We also learn of her personal, one-word group depiction for the Roosevelts, whom she collectively described as "gregarious,"[34] an oft-used adjective that according to Webster's means: "(1) tending to associate with others of one's kind; (2) growing in a cluster or colony, as with a plant, wasps, or bees; and (3) living in contiguous nests but not forming a colony." Whether or not that aptly applied to her next observation—that "from both sides of the clan they inherited an active interest in people, an inquisitive sympathy for the problems and preoccupations of others, and a delight in good company"—seems debatable,[35] but there should be no disputing of her "firsthand" comment. As a daily witness to history, Grace Tully was definitely in a position to draw such conclusions and make familial depictions, and as she also confirmed near the book's final pages, "It [was] not just a use of words to say that most persons who worked with and for FDR were in effect family."[36]

For the same reason, there should be no disputing the FDR observations Rosenman made in the biography he authored, especially as

Part Four—Descendant Dictates

they related to the huge shadow cast, and that continues to be cast, by this Roosevelt across the pages of 20th century history—not only American but worldwide history. And in no area would Judge Rosenman's observations be more apropos than in regard to FDR's famous political acumen and what made his governing skills so acute when it came to combining public opinion with progress. One such factor had to be his tremendous intellectual retention capacity, which he often illustrated through his excellent recall of names throughout the country. "This was a feat of memory that he displayed on many occasions to the bewilderment of those around him, as well as to the amazement and delight of the person with whom he was talking," Rosenman related.[37] For another example of Roosevelt recall, the judge wrote as follows:

> By the time FDR became governor, his basic philosophies and principles had been pretty well formed. In a general way he had thought [and understood] a great deal about all the subjects on which he later proposed legislative reforms. His ideas became more specific and concrete through assiduous reading and long hours of conversation with experts whom he invited to come to see him—usually for dinner and to spend the night. He used to love, as he put it, to "bat ideas around" with people who were sympathetic to his general philosophy and objectives. And he learned fast—so fast that he amazed the people from whom he learned. He could quickly squeeze every bit of information he wanted from a visitor. And he was able to retain it, although he seldom made notes other than a few words on a pad, which he soon threw away.[38]

This picking of expert's brains that FDR loved to do usually resulted in the confidence he needed to make decisions, no matter how difficult or crucial the choice seemed. Often he interviewed more than one so-called expert or assigned more than one staffer the same issue without their collective knowledge in order to gather contrasting viewpoints. Rosenman acknowledged as much when he wrote, "Sometimes he did [such things], I am sure, in order to have checks and balances without the various persons knowing it." And again, as the author later admitted in disbelief, "I was amazed that he never seemed to worry. After meeting with the right people, he would think a problem through very carefully and having come to a decision, he would dismiss it from his mind as finished business. He never went back to worry about whether his decision was the right one."[39] FDR famously felt that once a decision had been made, there was no use worrying as events would

13. External Family

soon prove whether it had been the right one—and if not, he would simply move on and try something else.[40]

Another factor Rosenman believed contributed to FDR's power of perception by the time he moved to Albany (as governor) was the fact that he had overcome disability. "As you got to know him, it was the first thing you forgot," the judge advised in regard to meeting FDR for the first time and the realization that despite his powerful upper body this was a man "without the use of [his] legs. It was something that he himself [FDR] seemed never to think much about." In fact, if he needed—or wanted—to end a conversation, he would often seem to make light of his situation with the comment, "Well, I'm sorry, I have to run now!"[41] At the same time, Rosenman "never saw a man that worked harder" and illustrated how FDR's polio might have actually served him in a positive way in that regard: "The loss of the full use of his legs deprived him of many of the diversions and amusements of other persons; the time he might have spent [in those] he put largely into work."[42]

This full-time, all-in commitment was also obvious by the pace FDR kept. In Rosenman's words,

> He generally followed the same daily work routine in Albany and later in Washington. He had breakfast in bed at about eight, during which he read papers, talked with his immediate staff, and laid out the work for the day. Then about ten in the morning he would be off to his office, where he worked without stop, with lunch at his desk, until five in the afternoon. Then home for a swim and some tea, frequently with visitors on official or political business. Dinner was often with one or more friends, public officials, or special guests, seldom alone. After dinner—except for a rare social engagement—he was wheeled into his study, where he continued work on papers, speeches, bills; he even carried memoranda and reports to bed from where he frequently continued to discuss business with me or others. And he always had to read several late newspapers before finally turning out the light.[43]

As for his overall political success, even with some Republican voters, Rosenman emphasized how FDR never sought to alienate them or any other group as a whole. Rather, he would limit his attacks to "the leadership" of the Republican Party. In this vein, he once told the judge the following:

> There are thousands of people who call themselves Republicans who think as you and I do about government. They are enrolled as Republicans because their

Part Four—Descendant Dictates

families have been Republicans for generations and that's the only reason. Some of them even think it's an infra dig [apparently his pet phrase for putting someone down] to be called a Democrat. They believe the Democrats in their village are not the socially nice people the Republicans are. So never attack Republicans or the Republican Party—only Republican leaders [by name]. Then, any Republican voter who hears it might say to himself: "Well, he doesn't mean me, I don't believe in the things those guys [Republican leaders] and their reactionaries are saying."[44]

Additionally, according to Rosenman, FDR made it a practice never to mention his presidential opponents by name: "There were reasons for this deliberate practice. Since he was the president running for re-election, an attack by him could only result in giving his opponent more publicity than he would otherwise get. [Plus] it would give his opponent a chance to answer him and the very fact that he was answering a [sitting] president would build up publicity for the answer."[45] Obviously, even in those days, one of the best ways for the opposition party's presidential challenger to make the front page was to say something negative about the sitting president. Unfortunately, it still is.

Of FDR the master politician, Rosenman, the speechwriter also believed that as much as anything "it was the warmth of Roosevelt the man and orator, who knew how to convey his personality and charm to the people either through speeches, in person, or over the air [radio]."[46] At the same time, he had an ability to relax and seem at ease no matter the situation, and to Rosenman this was magnified whenever and wherever he spoke.[47] Like his cousin Teddy, FDR loved crowds and drew strength from them. "Whether in a convention hall or along [city] streets, from them he drew strength and determination," Rosenman emphasized. "Crowds gave him a deep thrill and a comforting feeling that the people were with him in his objectives and methods for attaining a better life and a better world."[48]

In addition, FDR, as most historians have recognized, was a realist, especially when it came to public opinion, and a compromiser when he had to be. Otherwise, his Democratic coalition of western progressives, northeastern liberals, and southern conservatives would have certainly collapsed, and his ability to prosecute daring New Deal legislation during his earliest, depression-dominated days in office or controversial initiatives like Lend-Lease before America was thrust into World War II in 1941 would have been impossible. He was at his best

13. External Family

when reading the tea leaves and knowing which way the political winds were blowing. Rosenman confirmed as much when writing about a particular executive order that FDR was considering during the war (1942), only to ultimately think better of such individual action by sending the issue back to Congress. "The course the President finally adopted was a compromise [and] a compromise in such a situation was not unusual for Roosevelt," Rosenman reminded in his book.[49]

In FDR's doing so, however, Rosenman also made known that he considered FDR and ER distinctly different in that regard. Writing about how Eleanor "never hesitated to express her views to the President," and how "invariably frank" she could be in her criticism, he also noted how FDR "welcomed" and even "invited" her advice, even when he knew they would disagree. As a result, Rosenman made the case that although most of her objectives were the same as his, "she had none of the give that is one of the great essentials of a successful political leader." Continuing in that vein he wrote, "It was hard for [ER] to compromise and she frequently disagreed with the President when he was willing. She advocated the direct, unrelenting approach. If she had her way, there would have been fewer compromises by Roosevelt, but also, I am afraid, fewer concrete accomplishments."[50]

Accomplishments that came despite occasional manifestations of a "vindictive" streak were about the only thing that ever got him into political trouble. "[FDR] was most generous and forgiving about human weaknesses, but he was implacable and vindictive toward those who deliberately were unfair to him," Rosenman stated, "especially in political matters."[51] But incidents of that nature were usually kept to a minimum, especially as FDR looked to avoid personal conflict whenever possible. At the same time, his ability to keep things close to the vest, another Rosenman talking point, has become something his various biographers have embellished in recent times as Roosevelt's personality has undergone more and more scrutiny. In fact, some have gone to great lengths to convey that even his innermost circle didn't know all that he was thinking or considering at any given time. Of this trait, the man on FDR's bedroom wall wrote: "Sometimes the President went to extreme lengths to keep proposed actions secret. He delighted in springing things on people. This was especially true where the press was involved. Most times it seemed to make little practical difference

Part Four—Descendant Dictates

if a leak occurred—but it made a great difference to him. Often he wanted secrecy because he had grown tired of argument and discussion. This was further confirmation of his dislike of unpleasantness, which he knew was inevitable if he had to argue it all over and over again, including with close associates he knew would be opposed to the course he was taking."[52] Fortunately, secrecy like that wasn't so prevalent that the views—and reviews—of Roosevelt external family like Butt, Tully, and Rosenman failed to make their way through the decades as interesting contributions to family lore.

14

Unfulfilled Offspring

Not only did Ken Burns' 2014 documentary, *The Roosevelts: An Intimate History*, bring out many similarities that characterized the political careers of Theodore and Franklin Roosevelt, it also made viewers aware of the similar political beliefs and methods TR and FDR employed despite ascending through different parties. In their case, Progressive, as a label, made a lot more sense than either Republican or Democrat, and could aptly be applied to both of their legacies. The Burns documentary even emphasized that many of the things Teddy hoped to get done while running as a Progressive, third-party candidate in 1912 (only to hand that election to Woodrow Wilson by splitting the Republican vote with incumbent William Howard Taft) were things Franklin would later do during his first and second terms.[1] In an editorial aside from *The Roosevelts: An American Saga*, Collier echoed as much when he noted, "They were using a model TR had provided, for much of [FDR's] New Deal program was a delayed implementation of the 1912 platform of the Progressive Party [what became Teddy's 'Bull Moose' Party]."[2]

As stated earlier, the progressive branch of the Republican Party reached both its zenith and its climax with TR, leaving him (along with his party's other great change agent, Abraham Lincoln), out of step with the conservative mantras so closely identified with Republicans today.[3] In fact, it's as if the two presidential Roosevelts were actually of the same political fabric and would-be adversaries in name only, regardless of the partisan divide that obviously separated their family's individual branches for years. Jonathan Alter, in his *Defining Moment: FDR's Hundred Days and the Triumph of Hope*, stated, "FDR hardly had the pedigree of a populist; he was more in tune with the Progressive

Part Four—Descendant Dictates

Movement embodied by Theodore Roosevelt." Later Alter notes how many "leftover Republican progressives," especially in the western states, joined FDR's coalition (an example is Harold Ickes, who even joined his cabinet).[4]

While FDR idolized, and even voted for, TR as a young Democrat—and Teddy encouraged his young cousin's electoral career—most of TR's descendants (with the exception of his son Kermit) never followed suit.[5] Although party loyalty would come and go among their offspring, familial loyalty was definitely lacking when it came to existing party lines. As Ted and Alice obviously were confronted, and eventually haunted, by FDR's emergence on the national stage, it has always been easy to examine the very open hostility that they enunciated for decades in regard to their interloping, "feather-dusting" cousin from Hyde Park, who seemed to them, at least, to be stealing their very birthright as the eldest children of the late, great TR.[6] Early on, many Americans even assumed FDR was TR's son without drawing any party distinctions and that had to be frustrating for Ted, who returned from World War I a decorated hero (by both France and the U.S.) ready to assume Teddy's political legacy, and his equally aspiring half-sister, who famously went so far in later years as to announce she would rather vote for Hitler than FDR.[7]

On January 9, 1936, at the opening of a separate wing named for TR at Manhattan's Museum of Natural History, strained feelings even surfaced in a very public forum when both branches of the family struggled through a New York snowstorm and were well represented (and seated) on opposite sides of the dais. President Franklin Roosevelt opened with words of praise for the tremendous legacy of his late cousin. Mayor Fiorello LaGuardia followed with words of praise for the entire family and what was currently happening, thanks to the progressive New Deal, throughout the country. Those remarks were then followed by Ted Roosevelt pointedly referring to FDR as "the gentleman you just heard speak" rather than "Mr. President" and with little regard for decorum, making sure those in attendance knew FDR had not supported TR against Wilson in 1912. Included among the "Special Features" with *The Roosevelts* documentary was Ken Burns' quote of FDR's cousin Margaret "Daisy" Suckley. Of Ted's comments that day, her diary entry noted, "It was a very stupid speech." Burns called it simply "an awkward occasion."[8]

14. Unfulfilled Offspring

As mentioned, Ted Roosevelt ran for governor of New York and held several prestigious, appointed positions without ever really succeeding in his father's large political footprints, and three of FDR's sons would also enter the political arena in one form or another (James and Franklin, Jr., as candidates, Elliott as instigator and later mayor of Miami Beach), variously succeeding and failing, switching parties or allegiances or both, staying in the limelight without ever really displaying the innate political sense that had so epitomized their old man. The previously acknowledged congressional career of James—six Southern California terms—would obviously rate as a high-water mark along with the three-term New York representation in the same congressional capacity of the more charismatic Franklin, Jr., who hitched his hopes to the administration of John F. Kennedy in much the same way JFK's father had boarded the FDR bandwagon 30 years earlier, only to find those political coattails cut off by Kennedy's assassination in 1963. He would later run for mayor of New York City and then governor of New York on a third-party ticket without further success.[9]

Meanwhile, John, the youngest and only Roosevelt son to actively avow a desire to avoid profiting from his prominent lineage, did marry into a well-established Republican family and adopted that party as his own.[10] He even seconded the nomination of General Dwight Eisenhower for president at the 1952 Republican Convention, just one of several examples of political disengagement within the family by all four sons during the FDR presidential years and beyond. Other incidents that attracted media scrutiny included Elliott's opposition to his father's seeking a third term in 1940 while actively backing Vice President John Garner, a Texan and mutual friend of oil barons in that state, and James's previously acknowledged support for Republicans (and by then fellow Californians) Richard Nixon and Ronald Reagan in later presidential campaigns.[11]

Michael Hiltzik pointed out in his book *The New Deal* that FDR's obvious "intention [was] to revive the Progressive Movement [of TR and Wilson] after its eclipse under three Republican presidents [Harding, Coolidge, and Hoover]."[12] However, that "path would be rockier than he or anyone else predicted" and none of his or TR's sons ever assumed the progressive wave their fathers had obviously ridden to political prominence. Perhaps their aspiring male political offspring

Part Four—Descendant Dictates

could have learned something from the earlier prominence of Alice Roosevelt, who was described in her biography by Stacy Cordery as "a role model for Progressive Era women because of a fame rightfully earned. She was neither a Victorian woman nor a new woman, but rather something else entirely; a modern celebrity" by the time she married Congressman Nicholas Longworth in perhaps the most celebrated White House wedding ever.[13] Or perhaps they could have better heeded the path blazed by TR at the 1912 Republican Convention, when he famously stated "the parting of the ways has come. The Republican Party must stand for the rights of humanity or else it must stand for special privilege" before leading his delegates out to form the Progressive/Bull Moose Party.[14] Such positive notoriety and progressive leanings had certainly worked for Roosevelts before.

In 2014, an article in *Politico* magazine obviously sought to more fully isolate the reasoning that ultimately led to the political disappointment of FDR's sons. In it Rob Goodman wrote, "It's one of history's puzzles that a political family that looked poised at mid-century to pass from success to success instead fizzled and failed. And it is one of history's ironies that the great beneficiary of dynastic politics, Franklin Delano Roosevelt, also left behind one of the sharpest critiques of dynasties in American life. Even as he reaped the rewards of a famous name, no one spoke for the dignity of the democratic mindset like FDR did. It's worth remembering that message—and the Roosevelt family's consequential failures. It's worth asking [as the article was entitled]: What happened to the Roosevelts?" In going there, however, Goodman attempted to substantiate his premise by focusing only on James. Included in his seemingly too brief synopsis was James's supposed "stigma of influence-peddling," which enveloped him after rumors surfaced that he had used his family's influence to generate huge profits for his insurance agency, as well accusations that he was the young "bootlegging partner" of Joe Kennedy towards the end of prohibition."[15]

From, perhaps, a more realistic viewpoint, the niece of James, Elliott, and Franklin Roosevelt, Jr., John's daughter Nina, offered a much different and admittedly family-driven take on attainments (or lack thereof) on the national stage of her uncles and cousin Ted. In that regard, she recently wrote the following:

14. Unfulfilled Offspring

I do think the idea that none of the sons of TR and FDR-ER lived up to their famous parents' stature has always been an over-simplification. That they were never as much in the limelight and influential in the manner of their parents is really a restatement of the fact the U.S. is a democracy. Chances are none of them would have ever been elected president even if viewed as wonderful as their fathers in every respect. Rarely does a child walk directly in their parents' footsteps. It is a testament to our culture that even if your family is famous, each member of that family remains an individual and develops in his or her own way. America, thankfully, doesn't cling to only a few families for its development.[16]

15

Stretching Limits

Perhaps the most unique article to expose the extended limits of the Roosevelt family legacy in recent years was a *New York Times* story by Joseph Berger in 2005. While concentrating on the FDR-ER side of the equation, it shed new light on the freedom of expression that branch of the family obviously believed in and encouraged by their undeniable support for the common man regardless of race, religion, gender, social standing, or any other traditional barrier.

In it, Berger features several FDR-ER descendants who certainly missed the aristocratic mindset of earlier Hyde Park generations, opting instead for lives that took them completely outside the mainstream to such surprising and divergent positions as that of Jewish rabbi, communist sympathizer, Texas oil man, and concert violinist. All grandsons, great-grandsons, or great-granddaughters, they attest to the example FDR biographers like James MacGregor Burns and Doris Kearns Goodwin considered "a kind of permission to descendants to move as widely as they wished." In Berger's words, "Eleanor's example particularly encouraged many of her children and grandchildren to find friends in a variety of circles and to do battle with social inequities."[1]

While many from both sides of the family still study at prep schools, run charities or law firms, and marry among the modern elite, Berger's article exposed the fact that "others have veered from those paths, sometimes sharply." The previously noted Hall Delano Roosevelt, an adopted grandson raised in later life by James as part of his fourth (and final) marriage, became a city councilman and later an environmental consultant. Berger quotes him as learning one important lesson from his adopted Roosevelt father: "When you get to a point in life where you've worked hard and gotten yours, [there's] an

15. Stretching Limits

absolute obligation to help somebody else get theirs."[2] On the other hand, Camilla Cushing "Lulie" Haddad, a well-known New York-based documentary producer in her own right—whose mother, Kate Roosevelt Whitney, was one of the two daughters of James's first marriage who would take on the last name of their equally prominent stepfather, John Hay "Jock" Whitney—was also quoted with a succinct and surely representative comment for succeeding Roosevelt generations. She said, "There is this legacy to live up to, but I'm never going to win a world war."[3]

And speaking of just such a war, the previously mentioned rabbi, Joshua Boettiger, grandson by Anna's second marriage (and Jewish by virtue of his mother), has rationalized FDR's reluctance to rescue Jews from Nazi Germany during World War II, believing instead that the President's focus on victory first was indeed truly essential to the overall Allied effort. This view helped Boettiger overcome any doubts he could have otherwise had in the matter and allowed him to maintain a pride that seems fairly unanimous among later Roosevelts when it comes to their famous forebearers. This pride was especially true for Eleanor, whom Berger credited as someone who always recognized individual promise no matter what an individual's background or leanings.

The very detailed "Roosevelt Family in America: A Genealogy" makes apparent an unexpected profusion of professions among Early American Roosevelts, including hardware merchant, carpenter, liveryman, cigar maker, insurance broker, homeopathic physician, builder of church organs, and even a "fishmonger" in addition to the more expected director of banks, lawyer, etc. Even the listing for FDR's own grandfather, Isaac Roosevelt, a graduate of the College of Physicians and Surgeons of New York, elicited some occupational surprise with its revelation that his decision to leave the medical profession following medical school was due to the fact he "could not stand the sight of blood."[4] None, however, come close to the alternate paths listed for the previously exposed Robert Barnwell Roosevelt, TR's eccentric but obviously multi-talented uncle, who comes down to us as a "writer, conservationist, diplomat, newspaper editor, humorist, lawyer, and novelist" in that order.[5]

Although acknowledged in the *Wilderness Warrior: Theodore Roosevelt and the Crusade for America* as something of a black sheep

Part Four—Descendant Dictates

because of his previously noted "streak of lechery," Robert Barnwell Roosevelt's "wayward morals" were also deemed his "least interesting aspect," the result of his amazing capacity for diverse roles throughout life. According to author Brinkley in that voluminous, 800-plus-page narrative, "he could be a barroom enthusiast, a romantic adventurer, a barrister, a rousing orator, a husband, an adulterer, a sage, an animal protection advocate, a gourmet cook, a humble farmer," and even a writer "capable of memorable prose as a novelist and satirist."[6] His middle name, too, was "unconventional," as he supposedly changed it from Barnhill to Barnwell to avoid "manure" jokes. Even now various bios of the man list both.

It's easy to see how such a "self-styled man of letters" as RBR could influence and appeal to the equally erudite TR, especially in his role (yet another one) as charismatic uncle. In fact, his must have been the same kind of appeal that Cousin Teddy exerted upon FDR. Although not quite the same great-man syndrome (or legacy), the early notoriety attained by RBR through published works like *Five Acres Too Much*, an 1869 satire, and the novels *Progressive Petticoats* (1874) and *Love and Luck* (1880), as well as his already-established crusading efforts on behalf of conservation and every-man politics had to have made an indelible impression on his aspiring nephew, especially one as energetic and constantly motivated as Theodore Roosevelt. Indeed, as the young and maturing TR entered Harvard in the fall of 1876, his irrepressible uncle was already well known by faculty and students alike, including as a pioneer and crusader in biological circles.[7] Indeed, because this Roosevelt's life would have made for such interesting reading, it really is a shame he has been overshadowed by "those who came after."

Among other Roosevelts since then who also make interesting copy is FDR's half-brother James Roosevelt Roosevelt. Most people don't know that Franklin D. Roosevelt's father had another, much older son by a previous marriage. This son, known as "Rosy," briefly served as secretary of the U.S. legations to both Vienna and London before his death in 1927.[8] He also married into another prestigious and extremely wealthy New York-based clan, the Astors, and his wife's brother, John Jacob Astor, would, in fact, be the richest passenger to die on the ill-fated *Titanic* of 1912[9] (the same tragic fate as the previously featured Archie Butt).

15. Stretching Limits

Two others of note were the brothers Joseph and Stewart Alsop, grandnephews of TR who both became well-known columnists and political commentators at the *New York Herald Tribune*, *Saturday Evening Post*, and *Newsweek*. In fact, they publically took Elliott Roosevelt to task in 1946, just one year after his father's death, over his book *As He Saw It*, the controversial exposé that purportedly made known FDR's attitudes and secret diplomacy from the war years.[10] One of their own, Stewart Alsop's daughter Elizabeth Winthrop, followed their example to become an accomplished writer in her own right, one who has produced over 60 published works with the promise of others to come at the time of this writing.[11]

In addition, there was a French-born Roosevelt by the name of André who won a Gold Medal in rugby at the 1900 Summer Olympics and went on to become a well-known filmmaker and resort

Other influential Roosevelts have included international filmmaker André Roosevelt (left) and early conservationist Robert Barnhill Roosevelt, TR's uncle. LIBRARY OF CONGRESS, PRINTS AND PHOTOGRAPHS DIVISION, BAIN NEWS SERVICE AND BRADY-HANDY COLLECTION—REPRODUCTION NUMBERS LC-DIG-GGBAIN-36669 AND LC-DIG-CWPBH-00644.

Part Four—Descendant Dictates

entrepreneur. A grandson of TR, Kermit Roosevelt, Jr., was responsible for initiating a Middle Eastern coup two generations later.[12] Another who married into the family was Bruce Kerry Chapman, who followed in ER's footsteps by serving as ambassador to the United Nations as well as head of the U.S. Census Bureau and secretary of state for the State of Washington.[13] There was also a Midwestern mayor in the family, William Albert Roosevelt of La Crosse, Wisconsin; a family historian at the FDR Library in Hyde Park who married into the family, George William Roach; another five-time married descendant, the previously mentioned Stewart Spencer Elliott; and, if you think TR was the only Roosevelt to serve in the Spanish American War, think again, thanks to the legacy of Lloyd Cartwright Roosevelt. In other words, there exists potentially endless subject matter when it comes to other, unexplored members of this great family.[14]

Part Five—Extended Family

16

True Heirs

While sons of Theodore and Franklin Roosevelt obviously never lived up to their famous fathers' enormous influence, there were two brothers in the Roosevelt clan who verged on that coveted legacy despite coming at it from a totally different direction—the "Fourth Estate"—although not to the level expressed by Doris Kearns Goodwin in *The Bully Pulpit* when she referenced the early 20th century phenomena of "the hand that rocks the pen is the hand that rules the world" to illustrate the influence so-called muckrakers of that time were having via the printed press,[1] American media did begin to wield real power during the Progressive Era. And while two of FDR's sons, James and Franklin, Jr., and TR's eldest, Ted, all pursued political glory and inherited paths to prominence through the ballot box, it would be two of TR's grandnephews, the previously mentioned Alsop brothers, Joseph and Stewart, who would come closest to the national and even international influence FDR, TR, and ER achieved. But they did it through journalism. As renowned columnists and writers for outlets like the *New York Herald Tribune* and *Saturday Evening Post* in the midst of post–World War II and Cold War America, they would both become household names at a time when television was just getting started and the Internet hadn't been conceived.[2]

Just as TR and FDR knew how important the use of the media could be in affecting public sentiment, as exemplified by Theodore Roosevelt's recruitment of reform-minded writers like Lincoln Steffens and Ray Stannard Baker due to their significance in *McClure's* magazine[3] and Franklin Roosevelt's effective use of the new medium of radio for his presidential "fireside chats,"[4] so too the Alsop brothers were among the most widely read and respected journalists of their, or any

Part Five—Extended Family

other, American era. Like their iconic kin, the Alsops were products of the aristocratic eastern establishment, graduates of Groton and later Harvard and Yale, and firm believers in the same U.S. worldwide leadership that TR, FDR, and ER all espoused.[5] Like their great-uncle Teddy and the entire Oyster Bay side of the family, they were lifelong Republicans, but also like TR's avowed progressivism, many of their stands on issues were much more in line with Democratic doctrines of the day, and, tellingly, among their most lasting and influential relationships were those developed with the other side of the political aisle, in particular the Kennedys.[6]

Like TR, a master at utilizing the available media of his era to get whatever message he wanted out to the nation, FDR developed the idea of "fireside chats," taking advantage of radio, which most Americans had in their homes by the 1930s. LIBRARY OF CONGRESS, PRINTS AND PHOTOGRAPHS DIVISION, HARRIS AND EWING—REPRODUCTION NUMBER LC-DIG-HEC47156.

16. True Heirs

This was especially true in the international sphere, where the Alsops covered firsthand all of the major conflicts of the 20th century after World War I. In fact, the doctrine of American leadership in the ideological contest of democracy versus communism that emerged from World War II had no greater advocate in the written word than Joseph Alsop, who remained firmly committed to that American ideal throughout the Korean War, the Berlin Wall, the Cuban Missile Crisis, and the Vietnam War, even when the rest of U.S. society was very obviously trending in the opposite direction.[7] Doggedly assertive and even combative in his beliefs, especially as he got older and more recognized, Joe was both the best friend and worst nightmare of many politicians, depending on where they fell on the issues. He was the elder brother and decidedly elder statesman in the brothers' relationship, the one who had first made a journalistic name for himself before inviting his younger brother to partner with him in his already established world of syndicated column writing.[8] Stewart became the "kinder, gentler Alsop," but a devotee of Joe's self-proclaimed "WASP Ascendency [the rise of White Anglo-Saxon Protestant males]" nonetheless, despite having started out as a "Marxist liberal" in the way he viewed himself while still in college.[9]

Working for the now-defunct *New York Herald Tribune*, a bastion of upper crust values, their syndicated column, "Matter of Fact," was a collaborative effort for a dozen years, with Joe primarily traveling abroad to cover the international hot spots of the day while Stewart became ingrained in the Washington scene, started a family, and made a name in his own right as a very astute, connected observer of domestic policy. Much more feature-oriented in his approach than his hard-hitting, scoop-driven brother, Stewart was nonetheless equally influential in the thought-provoking messages he conveyed and together they developed a recognized brand, not just in this country but in foreign capitals as well.[10] Along with the *Herald Tribune* and a syndication that included most of the nation's foremost newspapers (papers like the *Washington Post, Los Angeles Times, Louisville Courier-Journal, St. Louis Post-Dispatch, Pittsburgh Post-Gazette,* and *Boston Globe*), their early collaborative efforts also extended to the equally values-driven and influential *Saturday Evening Post* before its decline as a general interest magazine in the 1960s.[11]

Part Five—Extended Family

Like so many of the national intelligentsia who emerged after experiences in World War II, both of the Alsops had unique stories to share following the war. Although not of the career launching character of Theodore Roosevelt's rough-riding entrance and complete, gung-ho emersion in and out of the Spanish American War, or Franklin Roosevelt's understanding and sheer will to succeed as the result of having overcome polio, the two elder Alsop brothers (younger brother John would have a more localized political career in their home state of Connecticut) played atypical but nonetheless noteworthy roles in the "big war."[12]

By the time Japan bombed Pearl Harbor on December 7, 1941, putting the kibosh on any lingering American isolationist tendencies in the midst of world war, Joe, a Harvard graduate like both TR and FDR, had already cast his lot with China. Six months earlier he had left his life as a 34-year-old preparedness leaning columnist (he originally partnered with *Herald Tribune* economics expert Robert Kintner); a sympathetic though Republican confidant of the Democratic administration; and even, sometimes, a favored guest of his White House cousins, Franklin and Eleanor Roosevelt.[13] Instead, anxious to be part of the developing global conflict, he utilized his familial connection with the First Lady to acquire a commission in U.S. Naval Intelligence. Before heading to the Far East, he even treated himself to a very personalized uniform, much as his great-uncle had done before heading off to his own conflict at the head of the Rough Riders in 1898.[14]

Like that TR-recruited, all-volunteer force of the Spanish American War, Joe became infatuated with the American Volunteer Group (AVG) of former U.S. aviator Claire Chennault, the so-called "Fighting Tigers" who had aligned themselves with Nationalist Chinese leader Generalissimo Chiang Kai-shek in an attempt to provide aerial support against the Japanese in 1941 and 1942. Due to ill health, Chennault had been forced out of the army in 1937, but he had won the trust of the desperate generalissimo after making his way to invasion-torn China.[15]

Meanwhile, after starting in Hong Kong, Joe made his way to Chongqing the summer of '41, the improvised Chinese capital (the establishment of which had been necessitated by the Japanese invasion) at the confluence of the Yangtze and Chia-ling rivers. While there he finally met Chennault and learned more of the American pilots (and

16. True Heirs

Shown here with his first column partner, Robert Kintner, Joseph Alsop (standing) was a great nephew of TR who influenced both national and international affairs during the Cold War as a syndicated columnist for the *New York Herald*. LIBRARY OF CONGRESS, PRINTS AND PHOTOGRAPHS DIVISION, HARRIS AND EWING—REPRODUCTION NUMBER LC-DIG-HEC-23636.

their "battered" P-40 fighter planes) who had been allowed to relinquish their enlistments in order to join him and the AVG in China. He decided upon the same course, submitting his Navy resignation in order to become Chennault's aide and advisor.[16]

As such, Joe was soon back in Hong Kong that December, having flown there as part of a foraging mission at the same time as Japan's surprise attacks on Hawaii and the Philippines. Along with every other visiting Westerner of the time, he quickly found himself trapped there by the nearly immediate Japanese siege of the totally unprepared British colony. Two weeks later he and the others were incarcerated, but not before he had destroyed all clues of his connection to the AVG, passing himself off as a visiting newsman.

Seven months in prison would follow, a wretched existence that included overcrowding, meager rations, and dilapidated facilities, but by July of '42, amidst entreaties from the families of those "innocents" who had been detained, including Eleanor's "irrepressible" first cousin Corinne Robinson Alsop (Joe's anxious mother), diplomatic channels produced a prisoner exchange that evolved into a Japanese ship carrying them to Portuguese East Africa and from there a Swedish hospital ship bringing them home.[17]

After his fortuitous return stateside, Joe sought immediate reunion with Chennault and the AVG, which by that time had both been assimilated back into the U.S. Army. That's when the White House and its acknowledged "fix-it man," Harry Hopkins, again interceded on Joe's behalf, putting him in charge of Lend-Lease in China, the American program FDR had rammed through Congress in order to provide much-needed equipment and supplies to both Britain and the Soviet Union before official U.S. entry into the war. It was a position that reported directly to Hopkins and it was in that capacity that he became involved in the increasingly contentious relationship of Chennault with the U.S. general in charge of the Allied effort in China, Joseph "Vinegar Joe" Stillwell. In fact, it was Stillwell's lack of faith in Chiang and his perceived encouragement of the insurgent Communist Chinese that led to Joe actively lobbying his distant cousin FDR for Vinegar Joe's recall, something that would transpire before the war was over, much to the chagrin of top army brass, including General George Marshall, FDR's wartime head of the Joint Chiefs.[18]

It was one of what would become many successful "nudges" by Joe Alsop on the institutions of American power, an influence that would continue long after "family" was no longer in the White House. As Robert W. Merry made clear early in his book *Taking on the World: Joseph and Stewart Alsop, Guardians of the American Century*, "he was, after all, a Roosevelt as much as an Alsop" and no one better exemplified the traits Joe brought to daily life than his maternal grandmother, Corinne Roosevelt Robinson. In fact, TR's youngest sister has been deemed the family member Joe most closely emulated. One of her

16. True Heirs

favorite family maxims held that two things would determine lifelong success: "effectively climbing to the top of whatever tree you pick" and "by becoming part of the larger world." Throughout his journalistic career Joe Alsop would strive for both of those "very Rooseveltian initiatives."[19]

Meanwhile, Stewart Alsop would experience his own unique World War II odyssey. After graduation from Yale, his first real job came as a copy editor at Doubleday Books, working under his Uncle Ted, who was still on the rebound from his unsuccessful bid to be New York's governor in 1924 and politically retaliated removal by FDR as governor-general of the Philippines in 1933. As was to be expected, TR's oldest son by that time had recovered handsomely, first by becoming chairman of the board of American Express and later by moving on to the vice presidency of Doubleday's esteemed publishing house.[20]

It was while Stewart was in the editing role and before America's entry into the war that he decided to join the preparedness effort and enter the military. However, when high blood pressure and asthma (ironically, the oft-mentioned childhood malady of his great-uncle Theodore) conspired to deny him entrance into the U.S. Army, he opted instead "to test the British service's reputation for being less demanding on physical standards," ultimately attaining entry with his 20/20 vision into the King's Royal Rifle Corps, a leftover infantry unit dating to the days of colonial America. So after taking a train to Halifax, Nova Scotia, a port city in eastern Canada, he was soon bound for England on a freighter in the midst of a protected convoy constantly on the alert for prowling German submarines in the North Atlantic.[21]

Four years younger and always in Joe's shadow, Stewart was anxious by 1942 to establish his own wartime legacy, but he was sobered by the sight of war-ravaged London, something he witnessed firsthand with fellow Ivy Leaguer Tom Braden of Dartmouth College and Dubuque, Iowa. Another volunteer in the same unit, Braden would become Stewart's lifelong friend. Based in Winchester, Hampshire, in the very Victorian, red-brick barracks of the Sixtieth Rifles, they would endure a strenuous basic training, but one that offered lots of opportunities to experience the English people and countryside. On one such excursion, he met his future wife, Tish Hankey, a member of a large family of nine children from the village of Eton in the south of England.

Part Five—Extended Family

Although considerably younger than Stewart, she provided "that moonlight and roses feeling" he would not forget.[22]

With morale in Great Britain improving, especially after the defeat of German general Erwin Rommel (aka "The Desert Fox") at El Alamein in North Africa and the accompanying capture of the ports of Casablanca and Algiers, Stewart was one of five "Yanks" (as their British hosts termed the Americans) recently commissioned as lieutenants who were allowed to volunteer for active duty. That finally came in July of 1943, but after seeing little action, except for a few skirmishes that proved less dangerous than the Saharan heat, their unit was ticketed for Italy, where the war was "heating up." By the time Stewart arrived in November, however, the Allied armies were held up and he experienced firsthand mortar attacks, dive bombing, and machine-gun fire, as well as many nights out in the open enduring torrential rains. Fortunately, his first "all-out battle" resulted in no casualties for his platoon.[23]

Soon thereafter he again crossed paths with his Uncle Ted, who, as previously portrayed, was recommissioned a brigadier general when World War II began, primarily because of his exemplary World War I record. It was their first meeting since Doubleday and it would be their last, as Theodore Roosevelt, Jr., died following D–Day, about a year later. Long before that, however, Ted found time to write his younger sister Corinne and assure her that her middle son was adjusting well and the war "had done one thing for him: he knew now he could take care of himself no matter what the conditions."[24] Several weeks later, Stewart's unit was ordered "out" of the Allied line and despite a harrowing drive "out," during which the truck he was riding in turned over, he was soon off to headquarters back in Algiers, hoping, by then, to be able to transfer to the U.S. Army he had been denied two years earlier. Disappointingly, once again, his own country's army informed him no transfers were being accepted "except doctors, dentists, and flyers."[25]

Following this second rebuff, Stewart put in for leave and returned to London to continue his courtship of Tish. At the same time, he learned of a highly classified joint mission of British and American soldiers designed to provide arms and aid to underground forces in occupied France. Known as Operation Jedburgh, it was taking volunteers and the still-undeterred, legacy-seeking patriot from Avon, Connecticut,

16. True Heirs

signed up to learn how to parachute into occupied France and join the French Resistance. Before they were through, in fact, "the Jeds," as they were called, became one of the most successful secret missions of the Office of Strategic Services (OSS), America's first full-fledged intelligence service.[26]

Despite extensive parachute training, Stewart's eventual jump into France the following July (1944) was a harrowing, mistake-prone experience that landed him nowhere near the place he was supposed to be and in extreme danger of being captured and shot. In fact, Adolf Hitler had mandated that any captured Resistance fighters were to be treated as spies. Luckily, his first contact came with sympathizers and not undercover Gestapo, and the time he and the other "Jeds" spent behind enemy lines was more often as military advisers, not spies. The Allied invasion, which had begun a month before (June 6, 1944), was gaining momentum at a much more accelerated pace than even the most optimistic pre-D-Day experts had deemed possible and by October Stewart had reemerged in London to file his OSS report.[27]

Briefly, he and Braden, who had joined him on the secret mission, would be sent back to assist along the increasingly "ragged" German lines, but for the most part his dangerous days were in the rearview mirror and he was free to chart a homecoming with his by-then pregnant bride (over the strenuous objections of her parents, he and Tish had been married June 20, 1944—prior to his Jedburgh jump). Before returning stateside, however, Stewart Alsop was awarded the French Croix de Guerre by none other than Charles De Gaulle, the reborn French Republic's eventual president.[28]

About a year later after agreeing to partner with Joe, Stewart's first big journalistic coup would come on a three-month trip in 1946 to Greece, Turkey, and other parts of the Middle East, where he uncovered and confirmed British intentions to withdraw from their dominions in that part of the world, creating an obvious void that the Truman administration would feel compelled to fill. As a result, his report of the situation seemed to set the stage for the Truman Doctrine and ultimately the controversial Marshall Plan (of by then Secretary of State George Marshall) that followed.[29]

Obviously, to say both Alsop brothers came out of World War II a lot more worldly than they went in would be an understatement, but

Part Five—Extended Family

the experiences they had endured and the changes they lived through, including the death of FDR (April 12, 1945), brought both them and America to a new place, a place neither brother had been before.[30] Seizing the initiative, with America suddenly cast as leader of the free world, they embraced their kinship more than ever through partnership.[31] It was a partnership that would not only make headlines on a regular basis but also continue to influence much of American policy in the second half of the 20th century, much as those other, earlier "Roosevelts" had always done in the first half.

17

Embracing Influence

> It was at this moment in history, when America's Anglo-Saxon elite emerged as the custodian of world peace and stability, that the Alsop brothers thrived. As men of words, they joined the era's men of deeds who struggled with profound geopolitical forces unleashed by the greatest war of all time. At every crisis and critical juncture, they were there to give expression to the principles and impulses that guided the nation's foreign-policy leaders and shaped America's role in the world. They operated at the margin of big events, and at the margin they often wielded crucial influence, leading the way toward what they considered the proper outlook of unfolding developments.[1]

So wrote Robert Merry in the epilogue of his previously mentioned book, *Taking on the World*. It was only one paragraph in a 500-plus-page synopsis of Joe and Stewart Alsop's very interesting, event-filled lives. They really did see themselves as defenders of a time when the America of their youth and very prominent breeding became the last, best hope of a historically Western-led world trying to recover from the global chaos of World War II. Just as TR, FDR, and even ER were completely comfortable in moments of leadership during the first half of the 20th century, so too the Alsops eagerly embraced their opportunities to influence policy in the latter half. Although history was certainly not impacted by these two men to the extent it was by their famous family predecessors, the brothers' always aggressive and interpretive writing style for over 40 years educated, influenced, and at times altered public opinion, as well as entire legacies. At least one fellow journalist of the times confirmed this by acknowledging the Alsop brand of reporting was intended "not only to enlighten but to affect, to move the principal players on decisions."[2] To accomplish this, the brothers claimed two basic journalistic rules in everything they wrote: (1) never express opinions not supported by good reporting and (2)

Part Five—Extended Family

always have at least one new item of information that had never appeared elsewhere.[3]

Following their separate wartime exploits, Joe's invitation to Stewart to join him as a replacement for Bob Kintner in the rebirth of his popular, prewar syndicated column was a brotherly offer of regard and affection and a rather obvious gamble. He himself already well established journalistically, Joe offered his younger brother a new and exciting career path but one that would require a significant learning curve and Stewart's complete buy-in when it came to his brother's primacy in the partnership, both editorially and in their "60–40 split" of all earnings. Nevertheless, working in concert, their new column, "Matter of Fact," appearing as it did in newspapers coast to coast for a dozen years, would become a national staple at a time when America's acknowledged leadership in the 20th century became established fact.[4]

Joe's fashionably decorated bachelor home (with live-in butler and maid) became the usual setting for weekly gatherings remembered as the "Sunday Night Suppers" of what Gregg Herken entitled *The Georgetown Set.*[5] In his book, Herken explored the elite thinkers and policy makers left over from FDR's New Deal and the war years, who settled in Georgetown, one of D.C.'s oldest and more prestigious neighborhoods.[6] With TR and the portraits of other honored family members starring down from the walls of his dining room and other locales throughout the house, Joe would invite and hold court over a plugged-in contingent of reliable sources who provided the brothers' columns with many of the tidbits, rumors, and scoops they would become famous for.[7] Other news would be garnered through globe-hopping trips, often privileged access, and near constant contact with the power brokers in their capital city and the world—what Stewart termed "not only the news-behind-the-news but the news-before-the-news."[8]

Almost every day after individual rounds and contacts had been made, they would come together either in person or via the telephone for an all-important session of give and take, which allowed their joint, four-times-a-week columns to take shape. This back and forth, although sometimes dominated by Joe's senior status, made for the kind of collaborative effort that normally kept them out front in a very competitive media atmosphere, especially where politics and policy were concerned.[9] Two things would dominate their writing: the Soviet

17. Embracing Influence

Union and the atomic threat.[10] In the midst of the Cold War, no one advocated deterrence, communist containment, and military superiority more than the Alsops. Among the nicknames they received from rivals were "Doom and Gloom" and "The Brothers Cassandra." One suggested the name of their column should be changed to "For Whom the Bell Tolls." Even *Pravda*, the Soviet Union's state-run newspaper, portrayed them as "militarists" and "war mongers."[11]

Regardless of these barbs, they professed to be "with and for" if not actually "from the people," and Herken noted times when they were "prepared to scare hell out of the country in order to awaken the American people to the dimensions of the growing Soviet threat."[12] Among these were the Berlin crisis, the debate over continued development of a hydrogen bomb, and the formation of the CIA.[13] According to Herken, "their provocative column blended erudite background" with "calculated opinion and yeasty gossip."[14] Merry wrote of how the "fundamental question" for the Alsops was always how Soviet expansionism and desired control of vital areas like the Middle East posed a "moral threat" to America and "the West," meaning the U.S. must step into any void left by British and French imperialist decline to contest ever-increasing communist outreach and outright aggression.[15]

Such stands, without the hint of any desired diplomacy, obviously set the stage for their consistent and unconditional support of the Truman Doctrine and Marshall Plan; the Berlin Airlift; the H-bomb; the Korean War; all things Kennedy, including JFK's "line-in-the-sand" handling of the Cuban Missile Crisis; and the United States' eventual sustainment of South Vietnam.[16] Major milestones of the second half of the 20th century, these and many others incidents, including the Alsops' total disdain for the communist witch-hunts of Senator Eugene McCarthy, were impacted by the influence these brothers wielded when it came to public opinion.[17] Only in such things as Truman's ability to win reelection, Eisenhower's ability to maintain popularity, and Nixon's ability to survive impeachment were they wrong, and only when the late 1960s and '70s had given rise to unrest and mistrust of government because of such things as civil rights, Watergate, and the prolonged Vietnam conflict did their influence begin to wane.[18]

This was especially true for Joe, who even became the target of a Soviet sting operation (while in Russia during one of his numerous

Part Five—Extended Family

global trips) designed to reveal his gay lifestyle to an unsuspecting and, in those times, what could have been a largely unaccepting readership. In going after their perceived No. 1 American journalistic nemesis, the Soviet KGB arranged photographs of Joe in compromised situations, photos that would eventually show up in the hands of media rivals in the years ahead. Luckily, it was not something anyone, rival or not, ever exposed and a situation that was monitored closely by the FBI.[19]

Nevertheless, both brothers had their demons, and these frequently led to policy rifts, even at the presidential level, where Truman, Dwight Eisenhower, Lyndon Johnson, and even Richard Nixon in his final days on the job all had occasional choice words when it came to the Alsops.[20] Their influence was such that, regardless of their stance, they were able to maintain access and what sometimes seemed preferential treatment to the rest of the press corps. To deny or openly criticize either Alsop was to cultivate an adversarial relationship that most politicians and government officials wished to avoid.[21]

Gradually, however, the critical approach that had always made them and their column relevant because of the interest and name recognition it ensured began to wear on many of the Middle America publishers their syndication relied on.[22] One example was Joe's acknowledged contempt for the military cutbacks and perceived inept administration of former General Eisenhower, who remained immensely popular as president. As a result, "Ike" was often the target of what those publishers felt was undeserved criticism and any such recurring negative theme in their writing often drew complaints and the threatened loss of subscribers. This forced the brothers, and especially Joe, to attempt to "tone down" the very style that had made the column so hard-hitting and successful.[23]

At the same time, Joe's bombastic domination of their relationship finally began to wear on Stewart as well and by 1958, the younger brother, who had never really possessed Joe's "instinct for the jugular," was ready to set out on his own when an opportunity to pursue a different kind of journalism presented itself on the staff of the *Saturday Evening Post*. After all, it offered the creative style Stewart preferred and he felt it played to his individual strengths and offered a much better chance for the further development of his career.[24]

The split came just a few short months after *Newsweek* labeled

17. Embracing Influence

them "the most influential and provocative newspaper columnists in the business" because of an ability to "browbeat, cajole, and otherwise pry timely exclusives out of high-level places." Understandably, their breakup was the subject of much speculation. Most of the so-called experts felt the column's influence would remain unscathed because Joe had always been "its heart and soul." Other insiders weren't so sure, since Stewart provided a counterbalance they felt would be missed.[25]

Over the next decade, in addition to their regular assignments, both would write and publish a number of books. Stewart would finish with six and Joe nine, including a biography of distant cousin FDR and a labor of love on art collecting.[26] At the same time, while Joe's influence (and subscribers) waned during the 1960s in large part because of his unyielding support of the Vietnam War, Stewart's career was on the "uptick"—so much so, in fact, that by 1968, *Newsweek*, the new challenger to *Time*, was actively recruiting him for a regular weekly column while the *Saturday Evening Post* was in obvious decline due to the proliferation of television. Needless to say, it was another opportunity he couldn't pass up.[27]

Both men would witness and write about what they perceived as the demise of the "establishment" over the next four years—years of tragic assassinations, Nixon's surprising resurgence into the White House, and his reelection in 1972.[28] That would also be the year Stewart was diagnosed with leukemia, a family tragedy that would leave him struggling the next two years to stave off the disease's progression while also trying to maintain his career against all odds. It was a fight he couldn't win, and he passed away at the age of 60 in 1974, the same year Watergate would finally catch up with Nixon, forcing his history-making resignation.[29] Meanwhile, Joe would live and work on until 1987, when cancer of another kind (lung) began silencing the man who more than any other had been the Cold War establishment's bellwether. Like his brother, he battled on for two more years before succumbing to his disease at the age of 78 in 1989.[30]

By that time, the age of America's Anglo-Saxon elite of which the Alsops and their famous Roosevelt predecessors were a part was truly expiring. In his epilogue, Merry referenced a moment in time that signaled the beginning of this expiration. In so doing, he used a statement TR made as president about the ever-increasing waves of immigrants

Part Five—Extended Family

coming to this country as the 20th century was getting started. Addressing that situation TR stated, "We freely extend the hand of welcome to every man, no matter his creed or birthplace, who comes here honestly intent on becoming a good United States citizen like the rest of us, but we [also] have a right to demand that he shall indeed become so and not confuse the issues."[31] It was the same kind of stance Joe, or even Stewart, would have taken ... and written.

18

Secretly Significant

Unbeknownst to most Americans, another Roosevelt contemporary of the Alsops played an equally significant if far less apparent role in the mid–20th century. In fact, his was a very secret part without fanfare. That would be Kermit Roosevelt, Jr., eldest son of TR's second son, whose secret mission for the fledgling Central Intelligence Agency (CIA) in 1953 would become the first example of American-engineered international regime change and contribute directly to the destabilization of the Middle East that continues to frustrate (and threaten) the United States and other Western nations today.[1]

In his 2003 national bestseller, *All the Shah's Men*, Stephen Kinzer unmasked once and for all this tale of espionage, intrigue, and destabilization during the Cold War world the Alsops were so much a part of. In fact, one wonders if they, as the ultimate behind-the-scenes journalists and provocateurs they were, might have had any inkling or knowledge of just what their second cousin was up to when his entry into secret foreign service in the 1950s positioned him to alter the course of Iranian and thus world history. Even if they did, it stands to reason this is one family secret they would have supported and never divulged in the midst of U.S. competition with the Soviet Union for worldwide influence. After all, that would be the justification eventually attached to U.S. involvement in the toppling of Mohammad Mossadegh, perhaps Iran's best hope for democracy in place of the Shah and before the Ayatollah.[2]

Once it all came out—after decades of English colonialism had made Iran a world leader in petroleum production and a prop for the post-World War II British economy; after Mossadegh, a national icon and prime minister for 26 months, had for all intents and purposes replaced the Shah as Iran's leader and nationalized his country's oil and gas resources; and after the Truman administration had for several years ignored British entreaties to support its desire to replace Mossadegh in response to its own energy and economic needs—that's when the Eisenhower administration, led by the Dulles brothers, John Foster as secretary of state and Allen as head of the CIA, finally embraced the necessity of Iranian regime change. But this occurred only after the argument of continued Soviet containment achieved priority.[3] That's when and how the U.S. agent in Iran (America's spy in Tehran), Kermit Roosevelt, or KR as we shall refer to him, became a major perpetrator of revolutionary history.

Thirty-seven years old and chief of the CIA's Near East and Asia Division, KR was what Kinzer termed "an acknowledged master of [the] clandestine trade." Like his famous grandfather, he had a "penchant for action and was known to be decisive in times of crisis."[4] Unlike his father (of the same name)—who as we have indicated was the only member of TR's brood to exhibit any affinity for their distant cousin

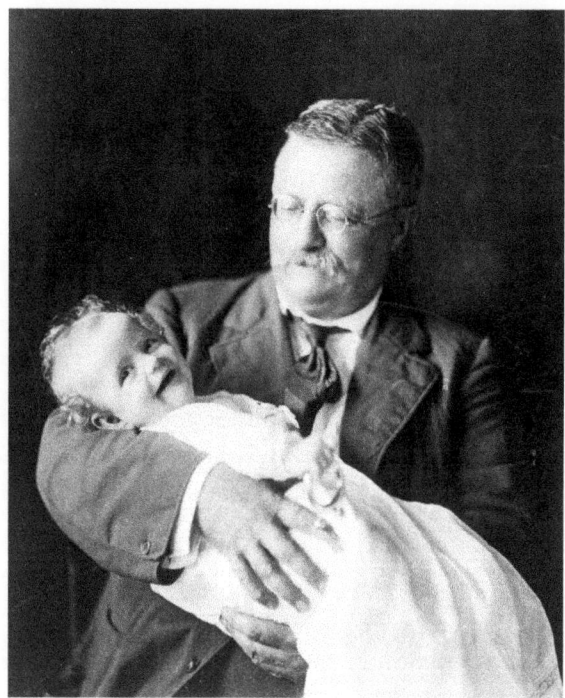

A proud grandpa, TR is pictured holding his infant grandson Kermit Roosevelt, Jr., in 1916. Known later as Kim, this Roosevelt baby would grow up to secretly influence the overthrow of Iran's civilian government in 1953, securing the Shah's power for 26 more years and setting the stage for the Iranian Hostage Crisis of 1980. LIBRARY OF CONGRESS, PRINTS AND PHOTOGRAPHS DIVISION.

18. Secretly Significant

FDR—KR was much more like his Uncle Ted or Aunt Alice in terms of his Republican passion and the way he actually considered that other Roosevelt president "a curse."[5]

Although born in Argentina, where his father had business interests, "Kim" Roosevelt, as he was also known, was reared near the family base at Oyster Bay and, like his illustrious grandpa, educated at Harvard. Later, while a junior faculty member in the Harvard History Department, his doctoral thesis on the use of propaganda during times of civil war came to the attention of the fledgling OSS when the U.S. entered World War II. As a result, it wasn't long before he followed his first cousins Archie Roosevelt, Jr., the only son of TR's third son (Archibald) and Cornelius and Quentin Roosevelt, Ted's two sons, into the new undercover service. Officially known as the Office of Strategic Services and forerunner of the CIA, it was so little understood at first that many assumed its initials stood for "Oh So Secret." Made up primarily of what Kinzer termed "Ivy Leaguers," sons of the eastern establishment, KR immediately settled into an existence shrouded in secrecy. It is believed he spent his initial overseas tour of duty in Egypt and Italy, but no one in the family knew for sure and his wife later admitted, "That was spook talk and he didn't talk spooks to me."[6]

Going by the dual code names Rainmaker and James Lochridge, KR was "clever, well trained," and certainly confident of the "immense international power" that supported his every move in the Middle East. Once the Eisenhower administration bought into the necessity of a coup in Iran, KR's efforts on behalf of the Shah, the restoration of British control over Iranian oil, and the overthrow of the Mossadegh government became very focused and precise.[7] Needless to say, KR did his homework. To compare him to the supremely confident, made-for-movie spies that have become such a part of American culture would not be off base. Just as James Bond or *Mission Impossible* movies leave little doubt as to the astute ability of their "everything under control" main characters, KR orchestrated the necessary Iranian dominoes to such an extent that even when the original coup attempt failed on August 15, 1953, he still had the necessary groundwork (and guts) to pull it off four days later despite repeated pleas from his superiors in Washington to just get out.[8]

On August 19, 1953, it all came together for Kermit Roosevelt, Jr.

Part Five—Extended Family

The secrecy that had been his hallmark, even to the extent of never allowing his main Iranian collaborators know the identities of each other; the chaos he created by making a majority of the Iranian people believe Mossadegh planned to depose the Shah when nothing of that sort had ever been contemplated; and the psychological warfare that he and his operatives engaged in, including tricking Mossadegh into withholding police oversight of the budding, national demonstration until it was too late to stem the tide—these were all in evidence that fateful day.[9]

By the time it was over and Mossadegh had been falsely arrested, the Shah, who had fled the country after the coup's initial failure and knew nothing of its successful restart and resolution, found out along with the rest of his royal family during their anticipated exile in Italy. At about the same time, KR, whose confidence was never shaken, was able to telegraph his superiors in Washington: "Happy to report the Shah returning to Tehran in triumph. Love and kisses from the entire team." And best of all from the American standpoint, President Eisenhower would leave office having never had to acknowledge American involvement.[10]

Following the operation's remarkable success and on his way back to America, KR stopped off in England for a congratulatory meeting with none other than Winston Churchill. It was then that the aging British prime minister indicated he would have "loved nothing better," had he been younger, than to have been a part of what he termed "this great venture." Then, about a month later in a very private ceremony at the White House, KR was presented with a National Security Medal by his president. In writing about this in his wide-ranging 1993 classic, *The Fifties*, the late, great David Halberstam noted that Eisenhower's diary entry that day read as follows: "Our agent there [in Iran], a member of the CIA, worked intelligently, courageously, and tirelessly! I listened to his detailed report and it seemed more like a dime novel than an historical fact."[11] That such an international undertaking had been carried out behind the scenes of world exposure was an initial trophy for the CIA and fed similar U.S. adventures later in Cuba and Guatemala. KR was even offered the chance to lead the proposed Central American coup but respectfully declined to begin espionage retirement in 1958. Following six years with Gulf Oil and a series of what

18. Secretly Significant

Kinzer termed "moderately successful consulting and lobbying ventures," he died in 2000 "still considering August 1953 to have been the highlight of his life" and "fervently" believing what he engineered in Iran had been "right and necessary."[12]

Whether it was and whether this little-known grandson of the great TR should be regarded as hero or villain by history will probably always be open to debate. While both administrations were seeking containment of Soviet intervention in the Middle East, the change from the Truman administration's belief in nurturing emerging democratic governments like the one Mossadegh was attempting to put in place in Iran to the Eisenhower administration's acceptance of espionage to ensure regional status quo was a pretty dramatic shift that immediately elevated the role of an operative with the obvious talents of KR.[13] One has only to read Kinzer's book to understand the strings he so astutely tied up and later pulled (even in the face of initial adversity), orchestrating and ensuring what was by then America's Cold War desires on the Persian Gulf. There's no denying this Roosevelt did his job well.

For 26 years thereafter, the Shah's rule continued unabashed and unthreatened, but not without some oppression of the Iranian people. Unfortunately, this ill-advised monarchial over-extension would prove the Shah's undoing, opening the door to Islamic fundamentalists who ultimately took advantage of the people's anger in 1979 by orchestrating their own revolution. Perhaps equally ill-advised was then President Jimmy Carter's decision to offer sanctuary to the Shah America had embraced and previously propped up, resulting in student anger and the takeover of the U.S. embassy in Tehran—the now famous Iranian Hostage Crisis that lasted nearly 15 months.[14]

These developments, in turn, would end governmental relations between the two countries and crystallize America's initial support for neighboring Iraq and its dictator, Saddam Hussein, when that country went to war with Iran in a horrific struggle that gave rebirth to such inhumane weapons as poison gas for the first time since World War I. Needless to say, this Iraqi support would further erode any foreseeable renewal of American relations with Iran and prove disturbingly ironic when later wars were initiated to both contain and then ill-advisedly overthrow Saddam—all while an isolated Iran became a base for international terrorism.[15] In fact, the familiar verse "oh, the tangled web we

PART FIVE—EXTENDED FAMILY

weave when first we practice to deceive" may have never been more applicable than when applied to America's initial intrusion into Iran and its implications for the generations that have followed. Yes, the secret's out. There can be no argument: this Kermit was another Roosevelt of immense significance.

19

The Unknown Brother

In looking back at all the many columns, articles, and books authored by the Alsop brothers, there was one in *Life* magazine in 1940 entitled "The Roosevelt Family Album," which profiled something of another secret member of the then President's Hyde Park side of the family, the so-called "in-season Roosevelts." In it, Joe Alsop (again while teaming with Robert Kintner) broke down the "vanished race of Hudson River aristocrats" from which FDR had sprung. One example he gave was Helen Roosevelt, the daughter of FDR's half-brother who married one of TR's nephews, Theodore Douglas Robinson, thus rendering the children of Franklin and Eleanor and those of the Robinsons "simultaneously sixth cousins, second cousins, and half first cousins once removed."[1] Such was the kind of mindboggling intermingling for which Roosevelts and other "upper crust" families of the eastern establishment were known for in those days. It was the same kind of in-breeding the upper classes of Europe had long been involved in, especially at the royal level, where kings and queens, czars and kaisers, and many of the lords, ladies, princes, and princesses were all distant cousins of one or another when it came to the courts of Europe before World War I. In fact, at one time and in one way or another, it's hardly a stretch to believe they were all descendants of England's Queen Victoria—at least that's what many books make it seem like.[2]

One direct descendant was Edward VII, Victoria's son and successor who became Great Britain's king right after the turn of the century, about the same time an American contemporary of his (and some would say look-alike) was, in fact, moving up the social ladder himself by marrying into the Astor family of New York. His name was James Roosevelt Roosevelt (JRR), an ironic double entendre thanks to the fact

Part Five—Extended Family

that his father, James Roosevelt I, didn't care for the use of "Jr." as a means of establishing a difference between fathers and sons with otherwise identical names. As for his immediate family, they would refer to JRR as "Rosy" (the preferred spelling, but the name also appeared as "Rosey" in some early publications, including *Life*).[3]

In fact, his father was the same James Roosevelt of the Hudson River Valley who would lose his first wife (and second cousin), Rebecca Howland, Rosy's mother, in 1876 before remarrying four years later. That was his union to the much younger Sara Delano that would produce the 32nd and only "quadrupley"-elected president of the United States, Rosy's half-brother, Franklin Delano Roosevelt.[4]

You see, not only was FDR disabled by polio and forced to rely on braces and a wheelchair, a fact most Americans of the time (and since) have never seemed to realize, he also had a little-known half-brother who unfortunately died a year before FDR's return to politics in 1928.[5] As a result, unlike the over-publicized brothers of some U.S. presidents (examples being the outrageous Billy Carter, brother of Jimmy; the scandal-plagued Neil Bush, brother of George W.; and more recently the controversial Malik Obama, half-brother of Barak), there was really no chance for the general public to ever get to know Rosy Roosevelt despite some interesting connections to his much younger half-brother. For instance, it was Rosy's private family box at Madison Square Garden that provided Franklin and Eleanor with an initial meeting place when they renewed their friendship as young adults after not seeing each other since childhood. And it was Rosy who was the first family member Eleanor notified upon FDR's contracting polio at the family's Campobello Island summer home off the coast of Maine in 1921. Ironically, part of the money left from Rosy's estate would also provide the available cash FDR needed when he made arrangements to purchase an old, rundown resort in Warm Springs, Georgia, and turn it into what would become a world famous polio treatment center.[6]

All that to say there was a section in Joe Alsop's *Life* article about Rosy entitled "The President's Brother: Edwardian Gentleman." In it we learn that not only was James Roosevelt Roosevelt a Columbia University graduate married to Helen Astor, daughter of Caroline Astor, the "Lady Astor" of social register fame, but also that he liked to drive a four-in-hand, a very imposing type of carriage in which the reins

19. The Unknown Brother

were arranged in such a way that a single, accomplished driver could manage a team of four horses rather than just one horse or two.[7] We also confirm (as previously mentioned) that Rosy served as first secretary of the U.S. Vienna and London embassies under President Grover Cleveland as the result of his father's obviously impactful support for that lone Democratic winner between 1860 and 1918. It turns out that Cleveland, the only president to serve nonconsecutive terms, originally offered those same diplomatic posts to James, the father, who, in turn, asked that they instead be conferred on his eldest son. In fact, it was after his first wife, Helen, died in 1893 and during his diplomatic term in England that Rosy, according to Alsop, married "a pretty Englishwoman" named Elizabeth Riley.[8]

In writing about another of his distant Hyde Park cousins, Alsop described Rosy as "a man of the world, witty, agreeable, intelligent, and kind." He also pointed out how unfortunate it was that Rosy died a year before seeing his brother ("whom he reportedly cherished") return to politics in 1928 and capture the governor's race in the State of New York.[9] In fact, consider how unlikely that course was for a person with polio and FDR's social standing to pursue. At least one FDR biographer, Geoffrey Ward, in his book *Before the Trumpet: Young Franklin Roosevelt*, even compared the two brothers and the fact it would have been easy for FDR to follow in Rosy's footsteps as a well-positioned but reclusive member of the landed gentry,[10] especially once he had polio—in other words, to simply retire to his Hyde Park estate without accepting the many challenges and effort required of a politician and government official faced with a crippling disability.

Alsop also made this point: "By rights he [FDR] should have been like his half-brother Rosy, an Edwardian American.... Rosy Roosevelt beautifully completes the curious contrast between the President and his background. He was one of the privileged people who maintained themselves so handsomely in the happy years before the First World War against the backdrop of prosperity and peace." In fact, both could have easily exemplified "the Federalist burgher, the country gentleman in easy circumstances" that Alsop obviously sought to contrast with the assertive, influential, and very progressive way FDR turned out.[11] He did so to then make the point that "prosperous and foolish people" have long considered FDR a "traitor to his class." Alsop called that

Part Five—Extended Family

preposterous and untrue because his "real lesson" of the Roosevelts was that they had no entitled class. Instead, he advocated their "family album" should contain the "subtitle, 'Picture of a Vanished Race'" with country gentry like FDR's father and half-brother adrift amidst the burgeoning and self-confident merchants and entrepreneurs of a newly industrialized America following the Civil War. Only a few, Alsop maintained, like Rosy, "managed to accommodate themselves" comfortably in this new and dramatically changing era. Meanwhile, FDR, despite his prep school (Groton) and Harvard education, found himself cut off from other sons of the rich with whom he never developed typical schoolboy friendships and who even excluded him from their most elite collegiate club (Porcellian). As a result, Alsop believes FDR was truly "liberated" and able to chart his own course, a progressive course, to an even greater extent than his cousin TR had—and one faulted by the nation's most conservative, ultra-rich ever since.[12] No such enduring legacy could have possibly attached itself to the brother almost no one really knew he had. Like his father before him, James "Rosy" Roosevelt Roosevelt obviously preferred the nondescript lifestyle of a Hudson Valley country gentleman, a lifestyle so foreign to the world-changing events of which FDR would become a part that no one, even now, might ever surmise them descended from the same family tree.

20

Overcoming Class

While it would have been easy for both Theodore Roosevelt and Franklin Roosevelt to adhere to their lofty social standing and like "Rosy" live a very contained lifestyle amidst the trappings of established privilege on their New York estates, it was not in their DNA to do so. Instead, their abandonment of class, so intrinsically attached to FDR's (and by extension ER's) Democratic legacy, was actually adopted by TR, the Republican, first and more completely. The 2001 book *The Three Roosevelts: Patrician Leaders Who Transformed America* probably looks at this aspect of their combined legacies more than any other part.

In it, coauthors James MacGregor Burns and Susan Dunn spend the early chapters establishing the political transformation of Theodore Roosevelt that occurred between his early career as a New York assemblyman and his final campaign. That, of course, was the famous 1912 presidential contest between William Howard Taft, his handpicked successor, Republican incumbent, and longtime friend; Woodrow Wilson, the former Princeton University president turned New Jersey governor and promising Democrat; Eugene Debs, the union leader and socialist candidate; and TR himself, the previous U.S. president and one of the most universally popular Americans ever. Although TR's transformation from class-conscious state representative had actually begun almost as soon as he entered the New York legislature, his progressive tendencies became much more apparent after becoming governor of that state. Then, with his ascension from vice president to the presidency upon the assassination of President William McKinley (September 1901), his opportunity to rise above established party principles by making government bigger, more involved, and influential in the

Part Five—Extended Family

lives of all Americans took root.¹ But it wasn't until his ill-fated Bull Moose candidacy in 1912 that his transformation was complete and clearly defined.² Burns and Dunn established where they were headed in revealing this transformation in the book's early pages when they wrote: "It would take TR decades to realize and to act forcefully on the realization that government had a central role to play in creating equality and social justice for all, fostering real civilization rather than merely permitting lawless individualism."³

To get to that point, however, TR had to relinquish the lofty, class-conscious attitudes so ingrained in the eastern elite of which the Roosevelts were a part. "This was the New York leisure class in all its resplendent, self-admiring, stifling glory," according to Burns and Dunn. The authors also establish how New York's "Knickerbockers" had been somewhat displaced by the suddenly ascendant tycoons of the city's new, entrepreneurial elite. Certainly there was overlap in their ranks, especially as marriages took place, but there's no denying the historical differences between old money and new within the city's high society, the so-called "Four Hundred."⁴

In fact, "nagging" TR were feelings his Knickerbockers were "a dying class," along with their "graciousness, code of honor, and misplaced belief in their own superiority and entitlement." The "secure, elegant, and interesting" New York lifestyle that he had inherited, a security based on "birth and breeding" not wealth, was for him passing away as the result of inaction. Instead of lofty examples like his own father ("the best man he ever knew"), who espoused and exhibited "public service and moral virtue" by his involvement and contributions in civic affairs, most of New York's old-money elite were content to remain in what they viewed as a "state of grace, uncontaminated by anyone or anything as "vulgar" as politics, philanthropy, or public welfare. Actually, "as a group, the new plutocrats" would prove "far more philanthropic." To TR, the Knickerbockers were indeed "languishing at the margins of a dynamic country."⁵

In this regard, Burns and Dunn established how "the Roosevelts counted themselves among the country's most socially prominent citizens" and how TR possessed the family background and social status to be "utterly secure" and above the fray if he had wished. The fact that he became "part of the governing class, where he had to associate with

20. Overcoming Class

political rascals by stepping down" to their level, confirmed that the "life of a non-productive gentleman bored him" and that he considered his "fellow patricians' unwillingness to assume civic responsibilities nothing less than a moral failing."[6]

All this said, the rest is history, beginning with his joining a political party "to fight corruption"; his desire to be a "hero in an age without heroes" by fostering a new breed of leadership; and his understanding of "the collusion between business and politics" that was taking place. In the earliest days of his political career, the *New York Outlook* called him "a specially notable figure because he represents the American citizen of position, culture, and means devoting himself to public affairs," and further said, "Mr. Roosevelt has developed energy, independence, and zeal for reform that seems incredible."[7] Needless to say, he did seem out of place and one of a kind at the boss-driven, graft-plagued dawn of the American 20th century. He was a new breed of socially significant politician "disgusted by the idle rich," people who had become "irrelevant and displaced by a new class of capitalists." Indeed, these authors leave little doubt that TR was equally repelled by the do-nothing attitudes of his own "passive aristocracy" and by the arrogant disregard for fellow Americans of the so-called new barons of finance, whom he would famously seek to "regulate and restrain" once he became president.[8]

The young and aspiring FDR was witness to this phenomenon, this class abandonment and moral high ground assumed by Theodore Roosevelt. A "fervent admirer who wished to emulate" his cousin Teddy, as we have seen, Franklin Delano Roosevelt had entered New York politics and married "the President's niece" despite the way "other Oyster Bay Roosevelts," held him in "contempt." As established, TR was "more than a model" for FDR. He became "an absentee mentor" and marrying into the Oyster Bay clan didn't serve to make him any less a hero—"rather the opposite." In the words of Burns and Dunn, TR "always loomed" on the young FDR's "horizon, symbolizing moral leadership, political energy, and Rooseveltian vigor." On one rare occasion before his marriage, FDR even defied his domineering mother while at prep school in order to accept an invitation to visit his paternal kin at Oyster Bay, "so enamored" was he with his famous cousin.[9]

By 1912, Franklin Delano Roosevelt's own class-conscious transformation was in the works. Challenged by TR's moral leadership as well as similar reform initiatives by his soon-to-be boss, President Woodrow Wilson (who appointed him assistant secretary of the navy), the social world to which he and his wife belonged didn't seem nearly so important given these new, competing visions, both of which applied conscience to politics. Even when FDR came along, politics was still an unusual career choice for a young man of his status and background, especially, as *The Three Roosevelts* emphasized, when "they were educated and socialized to understand the difference between us and them." TR's passion, however, helped inspire a turning point in FDR as well—a turn from his own "high society" upbringing. Like TR, his "new theory" was "liberty for the community rather than liberty of the individual" and once, early on, their political connection was illustrated when he voted for his cousin despite their party differences. FDR rationalized his ballot at the time by stating, "I just thought he was more democratic than the Democrat."[10]

As for Eleanor, her transformation was longer in coming. Surprisingly, Burns and Dunn indicate it took ER "decades to transcend the prejudices of her class." Although she would claim her Uncle TR "had a feeling for social justice that was ahead of his time" and "instead of traitor to his class he should be remembered as a pioneer pointing the way for his country," the fact social life had been so important in her "grandmother's world" and the fact her "social code demanded a great deal of self-discipline, especially among women," made her own conversion a painstaking process. The authors maintain she was actually "haunted by her upper class upbringing."[11]

Perhaps, as they speculate, this was because she "could not reconcile her enjoyment of work with her image as the patrician lady she had been brought up to be," something that led to her always minimizing her contributions to society. Nevertheless, ER would eventually break with the leisure class culture she had been born into. Much as her uncle and husband before her (although FDR's "repudiation of aristocracy and privilege," while resembling TR's "campaign against privilege" was always done in a more politically expedient way), Eleanor Roosevelt would eventually seize her newfound opportunities to "quit the narrow social universe of the upper class" and allow herself to invest in whatever cause or social inequities she encountered for the remainder

20. Overcoming Class

of her life.[12] In fact, while FDR remained ever the astute (or "realistic") politician "who could easily move between the Hudson River aristocracy" of his heritage and the real world objectives of his political career,[13] ER would become recognized as the leading voice of the downtrodden during her time as First Lady and for the remainder of her life.[14]

By 1932, well on their way to becoming the most effective political partnership in the history of American presidential couples (the Clintons being their only conceivable rivals), the "genius of the Roosevelts," FDR and ER, was such that the Grand Ole Republican Party, the GOP, "had no answer" for the kind of socially conscious solutions they would advocate over the next 12-plus years.[15] Indeed, just as TR acknowledged that he had been thoroughly repudiated by his social class over what was deemed his "radical (even revolutionary) beliefs,"[16] so too Franklin and Eleanor were ostracized countless times by their own establishment peers when they resuscitated the same ideas and programs that TR had championed 20 years before, including Social Security.[17]

In the end, if social justice and the greater good at the expense of the most privileged has long been an American metaphor for political class warfare then they were all guilty of being traitors to their class. Being labeled as such obviously didn't bother any of the three one iota.

21

French Born

As much as their departures from purely class-conscious, eastern-establishment denizens helped define their transformation to progressive national leaders, and as much as their political career paths were eerily similar, Theodore and Franklin Roosevelt should also be eternally linked by their whole-hearted support of America's fledgling national parks. While TR as president has long been connected with conservation and the National Park System, to the point of being considered its unofficial father (although not its founder, a little-known distinction that belongs to Woodrow Wilson, in 1916), his distant cousin proved almost equally influential in the continued development of what modern documentary maker Ken Burns has labeled "America's Best Idea" when FDR reached the White House a quarter of a century later.[1]

While TR was the president responsible for the further protection and development of the premier parks Yellowstone and Yosemite; for initial safeguards of the awe-inspiring Grand Canyon; and for passage of the 1906 American Antiquities Act, he would also set aside Crater Lake, Wind Cave, and Mesa Verde as national parks during his time in the White House, as well as designating ten national monuments and a host of other national preserves. Similarly, FDR would continue the Roosevelt tradition of national park creation with the establishment of Olympic, Kings Canyon, and Great Smoky Mountains national parks during his tenure as president, as well as expansion of Grand Teton National Park; the setting aside of four national monuments, all of which have since become national parks (Joshua Tree, Capitol Reef, Dry Tortugas, and Channel Islands); and even the placement of our historic national battlefields under the auspices of the National Park Service instead of that of the Army.[2]

21. French Born

Such emphasis on the preservation of natural and cultural resources "for the enjoyment, education, and inspiration of future generations" obviously became a recognized Roosevelt trait throughout the first 40 or so years of the 20th century. Echoing TR's earlier commitment, FDR famously said, "There is nothing so American as our national parks … the fundamental idea [of which] is that the country belongs to the people."[3] Ironically, that same concept nearly manifested itself internationally in the life of another Roosevelt from the same era, a first cousin once removed of TR who was born in France in 1879 and lived until 1962, eventually dying in Port-au-Prince, Haiti, at the age of 83.

In fact, it seems appropriate that the previously mentioned André Roosevelt, who like his cousin has been described as "an adventurer" and whose father married a French actress while living in Paris (where André was born), passed away on an island after much of his life's work had been spent trying to preserve as an international park the exotic island of Bali in the extensive archipelago lying between Australia and the Asian continent.[4] Although one of the smaller islands in Indonesia's multi-island makeup, Bali in the early 1900s had one of the bigger reputations. Tourism, that modern driver of economies in so many places, was what André was trying to promote as an "entrepreneur, and filmmaker" following a divorce and a second marriage to a woman in Haiti around 1924.[5]

Also remembered for his Gold Medal participation on the French national rugby team at the 1900 Paris Olympics, André's earliest involvement with the infant film industry came via his production of a French propaganda piece entitled *For France* during World War I. Almost a decade later, his cinematic experience would come back into play during a visit to Bali in 1928. It was then that he joined Belgian documentary maker Armand Dennis in the shooting of footage for a planned melodrama centered around the romantic story of a prince and a servant girl. Finally released in 1932, this historic venture would be known as *Goona-Goona* and would create what the IMDb online film library now terms "a Bali craze."[6]

Rarely used today but at one time a slang term with sexual connotations, the hyphenated moniker *Goona-Goona* actually came from a Southeast Asian belief in aphrodisiacs, or "love powders," among native cultures in that part of the world, and such ideas obviously played into the Western world's earliest impressions of Bali. Before the 1920s, these impressions had been largely built on tales and images of beautiful, dark-skinned, native women with bared breasts living in simplistic isolation on an exotic island paradise untouched by the hands of civilization. And visions of such a place in the minds of mostly Western men obviously inspired travelogues and "*National Geographic*-style films,"[7] of which the Dennis and Roosevelt production became the most prominent and remembered.[8] In addition, this Roosevelt would manage a resort hotel on Bali and left clear indications of his hope the island would eventually become an Indonesian national or even international park under the auspices of several supporting nations as a means of preserving its unique culture.[9] That idea actually sounds similar to the shared responsibility the United States and Canada now have in administering Roosevelt Campobello International Park off the coast of Maine in New Brunswick.[10]

Five years after *Goona-Goona* in 1937, a book by well-known Mexican painter and caricaturist (turned student of anthropology) Miguel Covarrubias, *The Island of Bali*, attempted to set the record straight and limit some of the runaway speculation and rampant tourism that had befallen Bali as a result of the Roosevelt production and other entrepreneurial efforts of the period. Covarrubias resided with his wife on the island for three years and developed an extensive text to go along with 90 drawings, 114 photographs, and five full-color paintings as a means of illustrating the unique culture of the place and how, although exotic and somewhat erotic in their dress, religion, and mores (at least in the remote, mountainous interior), the vast majority of the population were poor, unaspiring, rice-growing people who would have preferred to be left alone to live and let live as they always had.[11]

Instead, what the colonial Dutch had started there, most of the other incoming, entrepreneurial Europeans were glad to perpetuate. In his introduction, Covarrubias wrote, "To some it was simply a smart place to go. To others, it was brown-skinned girls with beautiful breasts, palm trees, and rolling waves, the truly romantic notion of a South Sea island paradise."[12] At the same time, the author maintained, it was quite obviously "a living culture that was doomed to disappear under the merciless onslaught of modern commercialism and standardization."[13]

21. French Born

As evidence of this, he talks about the "myth of Bali"; the hardworking villagers with their ancient, terraced rice fields; native women being forced to wear "clumsy blouses"; the necessity of escaping the tourist-riddled capital for the mountainous countryside in order to collect data about the traditional Bali lifestyle; and the depressing state of two dozen Balinese being transported to France as "specimens" for a world exposition of the 1930s, only to be trapped there, "cold and miserable," in "more civilized surroundings" until finally allowed to return home.[14] Covarrubias claimed, "Today, the beauty of the Balinese has been exploited in travelogues and by tourist agencies from as far back as 1619."[15]

Was he speaking specifically of *Gonna-Goona* when he made such a claim? Probably, but then again, what if André Roosevelt's dreams had come true? What if his stated goal of an island park had proven the best way to preserve and continue the unique culture that attracted worldwide attention? Too bad the evolutionary forces of Western civilization would have never allowed it, especially in the 1930s. Maybe if writers like Covarrubias had adopted the same theme rather than a repudiation of the "travelogues" enough interest in the so-called "Bali craze" would have eventually led to national or international commitment and cultural preservation. Like so many other lost civilizations: too bad.

22

Intriguing In-Laws

Of obviously more recognizable literary significance was Upton Sinclair's historic, muckraking novel, *The Jungle*, a 1906 classic that exposed the unsavory policies and unsanitary conditions that surrounded America's meatpacking industry and particularly Chicago's Big Three—Armour, Morris, and Swift—at the start of the 20th century (leading directly to the Pure Food and Drug and Meat Inspection Acts that same year). Posing as just another indigent worker in the city's stockyards and meatpacking plants of 1904, Sinclair gathered information for seven weeks for a series of articles he would write for the socialist-leaning newspaper *Appeal to Reason*. First released on the public conscience between September and November 1905 and published in book form by Doubleday early the next year, it aroused intense indignation. While the main story line was a depressing tale of one immigrant family descending into the mire of the industrial revolution, the novel's lasting legacy was the impact it had socially, politically, and even morally on American industry and its leadership.

As a result, the 16th page of the 2013 Roosevelt Reunion Address and Information List as well as pages 29, 30 and 31 naturally attracted attention. The first family listed at the top of page 16 was Mr. and Mrs. Abbott Lawrence Reeve of Manchester-by-the-Sea, Massachusetts, who, it turns out, were not only Roosevelt progeny (specifically the line of TR's uncle James Alfred Roosevelt) but also descendants of Swift Meats founder Gustavus Franklin Swift, the man credited for *The Jungle*'s authentic phrase, "they use everything about the hog except the squeal" when alluding to the early packers' alarming capacity to include every conceivable body part in their production processes.[1] Equally compelling, the next seven listings on that page were all Reeves as well,

22. Intriguing In-Laws

an eye-opening connection to Swift & Company, one of America's early industrial giants.[2]

In addition, the name Lowell surfaced numerous times among that particular segment of the Roosevelt brood with their roots obviously in Massachusetts, where America's early textile industry was centered around a water-powered city of the same name on the Merrimack River. That city was named for Francis Cabot Lowell, who founded the "Lowell Experiment" in 1821.[3] Thus, it seemed only natural to assume this segment of the Roosevelt family had an even earlier tie (mid–1800s) to yet another bastion of the industrial revolution in this country. When that assumption proved correct, making for a unique historic triangle, the case had been made for one of the nation's most famous families being linked directly to not one but two of its earliest industrial successes—Swift Meats and the Lowell mills. Who said the Roosevelts never did well with big business?

Other Roosevelt descendants with a share of this unique tripartite lineage included Mr. and Mrs. Alfred Reeve and J. Stanley Reeve of Prides Crossing, Massachusetts, Arlana Reeve of Albuquerque, New Mexico, Cintra Lowell Reeve of Ipswich, Massachusetts, Daphne M. Reeve of Paris, France, Mr. and Mrs. Gustavus F. Taylor of Equon, Wisconsin, Mrs. and Mrs. Reeve B. Waud of Lake Forest, Illinois, Victoria Reeve Spaulding of Hamilton, Massachusetts, Cassandra Reeve Stone of Newport, Rhode Island, Mr. and Mrs. Cornelius B. Waud, also of Manchester-by-the-Sea, and Katherine Roosevelt Reeve and Lawrence Roosevelt Reeve, both of Vero Beach, Florida. From one direction on their family tree, Josiah Stanley Reeve married Katherine Lowell Roosevelt, James Alfred Roosevelt's granddaughter. Tracing back the other way, Abbott Reeve's father was Lawrence Lowell Reeve and his mother, Eleanor Swift Reeve, was the daughter of George Hastings Swift and the granddaughter of Gustavus F. Swift, the fellow already acknowledged for the meat-packing empire that Sinclair's legendary novel targeted. But he was also so ahead of his time that he would be credited by Henry Ford for his assembly line idea of production, the one for which Ford would actually become famous several decades later. In fact, to G.F. Swift should also go the credit for the first refrigerated railcar.[4]

The Reeves, however, are just one example of the intriguing in-laws who often married Roosevelts. Another would be the Jacksons,

PART FIVE—EXTENDED FAMILY

as in the Jacksons of Supreme Court justice Robert H. Jackson. In fact, as an upstate Democrat from New York like FDR, Jackson developed into a disciple of the future president while Roosevelt was serving as assistant secretary of the navy and in a position to help the younger man (ten years his junior), who was already serving on the Democratic State Committee at only 21 years of age. Indeed, FDR proved an invaluable contact for Jackson at the federal level when it came to patronage issues and specifically postmaster appointments within the young man's district, a situation that fostered their initial connection in a relationship destined for the national stage.[5] Later, as an up-and-coming lawyer who had forsaken politics for the bench, Jackson would relocate his family to Washington, D.C., during FDR's first term as president after being named chief counsel for the Bureau of Internal Revenue. That position, in turn, would lead to their renewed relationship and ever-expanding roles for Jackson within the Roosevelt administration as solicitor general, attorney general, and eventually associate justice of the U.S. Supreme Court. Jackson remains the only person to hold all three of those offices and after serving as FDR's attorney general he once rather astutely observed, "The President had a tendency to think in terms of right and wrong, instead of legal and illegal. Because he thought that his motives were always good for the things he wanted to do, he found difficulty in thinking that there could be legal limitations on them." In fact, such audacious Roosevelt initiatives as FDR's Lend-Lease Act to help the British and Russians with American-made naval destroyers before U.S. entry into World War II and TR's bold decision to send America's "Great White Fleet" around the world as a show of naval strength in 1907 seem proof Jackson's observation was another of the shared traits of the two Roosevelt presidents.[6]

Later Jackson would be considered possible vice-presidential material and then, most famously, serve as lead prosecutor for the victorious Allies at the Nuremberg Trials of alleged Nazi war criminals following Roosevelt's death and the end of World War II.[7] Assisting him in that hugely hyped undertaking was his son, William E. Jackson, by then a Yale University and Harvard Law School graduate and a very promising attorney in his own right who would go on to establish an impressive client list as touched on previously.[8] William, in turn, would eventually marry Nancy Roosevelt, a daughter of TR's third son,

22. Intriguing In-Laws

Archibald (or Archie), and together they would have five daughters.[9] The two would also witness the downward spiral of the senior Jackson's illustrious career in a wave of disappointing developments, all traced back to his time in Nuremberg, Germany.

According to Noah Feldman—whose 2010 book, *Scorpions: The Battles and Triumphs of FDR's Great Supreme Court Justices*, details the lives and careers of the four Supreme Court appointees of "the second Roosevelt's presidency"—the Nuremberg tribunal offered "the act" for a justice "who did not want to lose the chance for a permanent place in history." At the same time, it also set the stage for a series of missteps and misguided ambition that would leave the Jackson legacy tarnished rather than one of lasting achievement only. This result, which occurred after Jackson's controversial appointment to the Nuremberg mission by then President Harry Truman in 1945 despite his ongoing place on the Supreme Court, was brought about by a series of events in this country, many of which Jackson had no control over while away in Europe, and many of which he only made worse during his absence.[10]

Feldman writes of Chief Justice Harlan Stone's disapproval at the time, not only because of the time Jackson would be away from his duties at the Supreme Court but also due to his belief that the whole trial was a mistake given the fact, in his words, "that it [was] a political act of the victorious states dressed up with a false facade of legality." Stone felt that although "morally right," it was an enterprise not really worthy of an operation of law.[11] Later in 1946, when Stone's unexpected death from a cerebral hemorrhage provided what appeared a clear path to the chief justiceship for Jackson, his absence from Washington allowed rivals on the court (William O. Douglas and, even more so, Hugo Black) to torpedo any consideration Truman might have given his candidacy and kept him from any effective countermeasures.[12] Instead, Truman made an old political ally, Fred Vinson, the next chief justice.[13] Already shaken by some surprising roadblocks to his initial prosecution at Nuremberg, this loss of the chief justiceship was a blow to Jackson's ambition from which he never recovered and, in fact, compounded when he defended himself and past positions by submitting a cable to the House and Senate Judiciary Committees that made front page news. It exposed internal conflict on the Supreme Court as had never before occurred.

Part Five—Extended Family

"The reaction to Jackson's disclosures and tirade was shock," Feldman confirmed. Predictably, the resulting damage to Jackson's previously impeccable reputation was significant. "Far from home, far from reliable advisers, trapped in the paranoid mode of a man prosecuting the greatest criminal conspiracy in human history, Jackson's faculty of practical wisdom deserted him when it came to his own personal affairs," the author continued. Strained and overworked in the trial of the German war criminals, he irretrievably damaged his image by taking "dirty laundry" to the press, a devastating lack of judgment, particularly by a judge.[14]

Meanwhile, 12 of the 24 Nazi defendants at Nuremberg received death sentences and seven others got ten years to life. There were only three acquittals, one medical dismissal, and one suicide before the proceedings even began.[15] But eight years after what remains one of the world's most famous judicial proceedings, Jackson, 62, went to an early grave in 1954 still focused on a destiny he felt was undeservedly denied.[16] It's too bad he wasn't around to appreciate at least one of those previously mentioned granddaughters, Melissa Carow Jackson, following in his footsteps as a trial lawyer and jurist of international repute, known especially for presiding over and denying initial bail for International Monetary Fund director Dominique Strauss-Kahn when he was arrested for allegedly assaulting a maid in a New York City hotel in 2011. And it's also too bad he wasn't around to experience that ongoing family-related part of his legacy, a legacy still maintained and recognized at the Robert H. Jackson Center in his hometown of Jamestown, New York.[17]

These families—the Reeves and the Jacksons—are just two of many intriguing in-laws Roosevelts added through the years. Perhaps no family linked to the Roosevelts by marriage, however, is more intriguing than the previously mentioned Du Ponts (or, more correctly, du Ponts) of Delaware, the first family of gunpowder and explosives and the one the marriage of Franklin Roosevelt, Jr., to Ethel du Pont so improbably brought together in June of 1937. Imagine what that wedding, which was so prominent it made the cover of *Time* magazine, must have been like for both families.

Imagine how uncomfortable it had to have been for Franklin and Eleanor Roosevelt to travel to Greenville, Delaware, for the wedding

22. Intriguing In-Laws

After being sworn in as an associate justice of the Supreme Court in 1941, Robert Jackson receives congratulations from fellow New Yorker FDR, accompanied by his wife, Irene, and their daughter, Mary. Jackson's son would later marry into the TR side of the Roosevelt family. LIBRARY OF CONGRESS, PRINTS AND PHOTOGRAPHS DIVISION, HARRIS AND EWING—REPRODUCTION NUMBER LC-DIG-DS-0136.

of their third son to a daughter of one of the leaders of the erstwhile American Liberty League, which had come into existence three years earlier for the expressed purpose of denying FDR and his New Deal policies a second term in the White House[18] (only to see him prevail once again in a landslide in 1936). Imagine what a revolting development it must have been for Eugene du Pont, Jr., Ethel's father, and his entire family to host the Roosevelts that day and come to grips with the fact that not only would they have to put up with FDR's progressive tendencies (many of which they considered socialist) for at least three more years, but also that they had to welcome his namesake as a new member of their family. "He's a good egg, but it would be better if he had a different name," the father of the bride reportedly uttered when asked about his new son-in-law.[19]

Three decades later, writing about the wedding in his book *Eleanor and Franklin,* ER confidant Joe Lash also confirmed the groom's mother "didn't know whether to be happy or sad," which probably summed up the feelings that day on both sides of the aisle.[20] For the mother of the groom, the nation's First Lady, it was "all rather hard to swallow."[21] But what had to make it even harder for the du Ponts to swallow was their obvious history of striving to keep their marriages among themselves, so to speak, as much as possible. In fact, as much as the Roosevelts were guilty of "inter-marriages" among cousins, with Franklin and Eleanor an obvious example, the du Ponts took such things to another level, especially for this country. That is to say, much as the nobility (and, of course, royalty) in Europe had for centuries conspired to pick and choose marital partners from "their own kind," the du Ponts, since arriving with their French roots in the early 1800s and establishing one of the most successful businesses known to mankind, had also gone to great lengths to keep things "all in the family" whenever (and for whomever) a marital partner was needed. Going outside the family to find a mate or, more specifically, outside the ever-expanding list of du Pont cousins, was not only considered "in bad taste" but also to risk a certain amount of familial ostracism, both socially and professionally.

Just as the du Ponts would prove among the best ever at promoting from within when it came to business and keeping what would become fantastic wealth—greater than that of any other family in America by the 1920s—theirs was also a very restricted gene pool when it came to how their sons and daughters were brought up to, as expected, pick and choose husbands and wives from among each other. As British-born correspondent Leonard Mosley so thoroughly revealed in one of several du Pont family exposés between the late 1970s and the 1990s, *Blood Relations: The Rise and Fall of the du Ponts of Delaware,* some mothers were even known to plot future marriages within the family from birth.[22]

However, that was just one of a multitude of interesting dynamics covered by Mosley and others in regard to the amazing family with whom Franklin Roosevelt, Jr., tied the knot that much-publicized day

22. Intriguing In-Laws

in 1937. For another, consider that perhaps no other family in history, American or otherwise, derived so much financial benefit from the suffering of others as did the du Ponts of Delaware. As incriminating as that statement may sound, remember the root of their great wealth was black powder, as in gunpowder—and not just gunpowder for small firearms but gunpowder leading to all things explosive for the armies and navies of the world and all their weapons of mass destruction. Indeed, the ammunition used by most of the major powers of the Western world in most of the conflicts between the War of 1812 and at least World War II, including the Crimean War, the American Civil War, the Spanish-American War, and, of course the other big one, World War I—the war that was supposed to end wars but to the financial benefit of the du Ponts, it didn't.[23] Although their business was also beneficial to mankind through their development of products like dynamite, nylon, and neoprene, the fact remains that this great family's greatest bonanzas, at least in the beginning, were derived from armed national and international conflicts.[24]

By the time Pierre Samuel du Pont de Nemours, his two sons, and the rest of their family set sail for America in 1799, following both the American and French revolutions, the seeds of their new life and new business had already been sown, without their realizing it, before leaving France. That was due to the second son with the unique family name of Eleuthere Irenee (a name that would reappear in family circles for generations much like Roosevelt given names) having studied under the famous French chemist Antoine-Laurent de Lavosier, from whom he learned the rudiments of making gunpowder. After all, somebody had to do it. That became increasingly apparent to Irenee, as he was called, while hunting in his new country and discovering after several misfires that the American-made gunpowder he was using was of a much poorer quality than what he knew he could make. That fact became even truer after he returned to France for a seven-month refresher course. On April 21, 1801, while still in Paris, he "incorporated a company for the 'manufacture of military and sporting powder in the United States of America,'" E.I. du Pont de Nemours and Company. Afterwards, the French government made it possible for him to buy powder-making machinery and even helped in his recruitment of experienced powder workers to take back to America upon his return.[25]

Part Five—Extended Family

In another du Pont book, *Alfred I. Du Pont: The Man and His Family* (1990), author Joseph Frazier Wall, in the first chapter, gives all the credit to "the first Eleuthere Irenee," "to whom" the du Ponts "owed their fortunes and place in American society." And while it would have seemed Irenee's eldest son would have assumed leadership upon Irenee's death in 1834, such would not be the case and would remain not the case throughout the du Pont's remarkable rise. Instead, it was an assertive aptitude (and attitude) that always seemed to trump birthright and became an accepted characteristic of the family's very corporate existence.[26] So it was that the du Pont family property on the Brandywine River, just north of Wilmington, Delaware, and within easy distance of Philadelphia, became a perfect water-powered home for the very lucrative manufacture of black power.[27] Although dangerous to produce, gunpowder would prove a most marketable product for a centrally located industry in the early stages of our nation's development and for many generations to come.[28]

By 1870, the so-called Powder Trust, which the du Ponts had been instrumental in founding, controlled over 90 percent of the nation's business in "gun and blasting powder."[29] Adding to the preposterousness of any future Roosevelt-du Pont wedding was Theodore Roosevelt's attacks on the nation's largest corporate trusts while president the first decade of the 1900s, including suits and guilty verdicts against the likes of Standard Oil and American Tobacco, but also versus the DuPont company (the official, corporate spelling) for its "illegal association to dominate the explosives industry and regulate prices not according to any law of supply and demand, but according to the will of the parties of the said contract." In fact, Mosley indicated that had TR's administration continued much longer, it was "unlikely" DuPont would have remained intact.[30]

That suit occurred during the early reign of "the three cousins," a trio of third- and fourth-generation American du Ponts who assumed control and leadership of the company in 1902, when leadership was at its most tenuous and a few aging family members even considered selling out. Along with Wall's leading character, Alfred I., the one who knew and had actually embraced the company's loyal workforce, this triumvirate included Coleman, the oldest and most politically astute, and Pierre Samuel II, better known simply as P.S. and the one who

22. Intriguing In-Laws

would become the real powerbroker at the height of DuPont influence throughout the first half of the 20th century (he died in 1954).[31]

Soon enough, however, their promising start after uniting financially to take control would sink into disagreement, with Coleman ultimately blamed for the federal suit due to his political entanglements. And if you think the Roosevelts' political feud between the branches was contentious, it was nothing compared to the "down and dirty" tricks fashioned among du Ponts during those tumultuous times. Ultimately, P.S. convinced Coleman to sell out to him in a two-thirds versus one-third arrangement without Alfred's knowledge, setting off a wave of animosity that achieved new heights in family circles already strained by such things as extramarital relationships, divorces, litigations, and everyone taking sides.[32] Wall broke this part of the story into three distinct chapters, all with the same title—"Du Pont vs. Du Pont"—but differing subtitles: "The Family," "The Company," and "The State."[33] At the same point in his writing, Mosley labeled the period "sinners versus saints," as divided camps were established along the Brandywine and at corporate headquarters in Wilmington as well as in courtrooms and legislative chambers all the way to Washington, D.C. As Mosley emphasized, du Pont money really did become "thicker than blood."[34]

This, however, is a far different story of a totally different family that just happened to cross paths (and purposes) with the Roosevelts at various times and in various ways during the first half of the 20th century. Suffice it to say these in-laws were perhaps the most influential or significant of any with whom they intermarried (and that's saying a lot) when taking into consideration such things as their pre–1920s bailout of General Motors—that's right, nearly 90 years before the one in 2009—and their contributions to the building of both Oak Ridge, Tennessee, and Hanford, Washington, as part of the Manhattan Project and development of the atomic bomb. Each was on DuPont's resume along with all the other events and products this unique company and family had a hand in worldwide.[35] As mentioned earlier, theirs was indeed a business dynasty that rivaled, and even surpassed, the political one the Roosevelts were building at approximately the same time.

23

Northwest Branch

Ironically, intriguing in-laws, idealistic qualities like national park preservation, and even transformation from class-conscious Roosevelts to class-conscientious leaders can still be found in modern-day family representatives like Rabbi Joshua Boettiger. Part of a little-known branch of the family based in the Pacific Northwest that originated when his grandmother, Anna Roosevelt (FDR's and ER's only daughter), and her second husband, John Boettiger, a veteran reporter for the *Chicago Tribune*, were given a surprising and no doubt "ulteriorly" motivated opportunity to manage the struggling *Seattle Post-Intelligencer* by owner William Randolph Hearst. Making this dual promotion somewhat less surprising was the fact that Hearst was at one time owner of the largest chain of Democratically leaning newspapers in the United States.

Rabbi Boettiger's father, Anna's third and the only child of Boettiger lineage, John Roosevelt Boettiger, was named for his father and would have a distinguished career as a professor of psychology and an author. He lives now in California's Bay Area. His four children by two marriages, Adam, Sara, Paul, and Joshua, also reside on the West Coast. Only one of them, Sara de Noyelles Boettiger, an adjunct professor at the University of California–Berkley who now works with the Bill and Melinda Gates Foundation, attended the Roosevelt reunion in Warm Springs. Joshua had attended one several years before with his father at Hyde Park and made note of the fact he will someday probably attend another as one of those "Roosevelts who have taken alternate paths" (as in the *New York Times* story of 2005).[1]

Actually, prior to the last five years, the Boettigers were much more scattered, but happily, especially for John, now in his late 70s,

23. Northwest Branch

Flanked by his sons Paul (left) and Joshua, John Boettiger has returned along with his children to the Pacific Coast. Another grandson of Franklin and Eleanor Roosevelt, Boettiger is the half-brother of Curtis Roosevelt and Eleanor Seagraves. COURTESY RABBI JOSHUA BOETTIGER.

they have lately all resettled within a few hours of each other between Northern California and Seattle, Washington. Perhaps it was in that previous effort, that rare and heady opportunity to lead a major metropolitan newspaper, that seeds of this branch of the family's attachment to the Pacific Northwest were sown. Undeniably one of the country's most beautiful corners, it could certainly have a way of pulling one, or even a whole family, back once roots had been put down by a previous generation. John remembered it as a true launching pad for his parent's fledgling marriage when "Hearst had the shrewd idea" of offering his father the publisher's position and "giving his parents editorial freedom"—their one condition for acceptance.[2]

John's earliest memories as a toddler include the family home outside Seattle on Mercer Island. Actually inland to the east of Seattle, where it is surrounded by a lake also called Washington (and not among

PART FIVE—EXTENDED FAMILY

the more famous San Juan Islands that dot Puget Sound), it is a totally separate, incorporated town in King County.³ John was born in 1939 and was too young to understand the security concerns prevalent for family of the President living on the West Coast at a time of mounting fears over the prospect of possible Japanese "fifth column" terrorism. He was, nonetheless, aware of the strain that enveloped his family once his father (despite being in his forties) suddenly decided to follow the example of his younger brothers-in-law, FDR's sons, by joining the Army following Pearl Harbor.⁴ In fact, John and his disconsolate mother traveled to Virginia to be with his father while he was involved in basic training at Charlottesville and up until the time he shipped out for North Africa and eventually the invasion of Sicily. Once her husband was headed overseas, Anna, with her youngest child still in tow, returned to Seattle to try to hold together their aspirations and dreams at the *Post-Intelligencer* during his absence, but to no avail. Within months, a new publisher was appointed and her own input removed from consideration by the new management.

Even at such a young age, "Johnny," as later referenced by his half-brother Curtis, obviously sensed the disillusionment this set of unexpected circumstances caused his mother.⁵ In looking back now as an adult, John commented, "Although she was terrific throughout, their dream of building a great Western newspaper together had been brought to a screeching halt. She had been the women's editor at the paper and really a partner in both marriage and business to my father's aspirations. I have no doubt his departure during the war, when he really didn't have to go, left a void in their professional lives and marriage."⁶

Soon afterward, she left the newspaper and after several months spent getting their home at Mercer Island ready and listed for sale, she, Johnny, and Curtis (by this time Sistie was away at school) moved back East, taking up residence once again at the home of her parents, the White House, the place they would call home for more than two years, until FDR's death in April 1945.⁷ It was a place John now recounts as "both exciting and very confusing" for someone as young as he was. At the same time, it allowed his mother to become her aging and, by then, illness-prone father's "right-hand person" at a time when she really needed the sense of worth and fulfillment such a role warranted

23. Northwest Branch

on a bigger stage. As a result, young Johnny's life was "monitored by a bewildering succession of nannies," creating "a three-year loneliness" that he will never forget.[8]

Although he reached the rank of major by the time he returned from the war, John's father never attained or enjoyed the decorated status achieved by the president's sons, two of whom, Elliott and Franklin, would accompany FDR as aides to the important international conferences at Casablanca and Tehran. Anna would later do the same in a much more intimate capacity, as his personal assistant, during history's famous "Big Three" conference (along with Great Britain's Winston Churchill and the Soviet Union's Joseph Stalin) at Yalta.[9]

After the elder John's return, the Boettigers attempted to renew their marriage and their dream in the Arizona desert (1947) by sinking much of their savings into an advertising supplement known as the *Phoenix Shopper*, with the hope of turning it into another major Western newspaper, the left-leaning *Arizona Times*. Unfortunately, in a much more conservative city and state than what they had experienced in Seattle, they were up against an even more established and conservative daily, "whose owner had much deeper pockets," according to their son. He added:

> They jumped into something that was not particularly wise, especially given the conservative resolve of the competition, the *Arizona Republic* and its publisher, Eugene Pulliam. Phoenix was a rock-ribbed Republican town and he was able to undercut their advertising rates. By the time I was seven, we were living in a nice home on the edge of the desert near Camelback Mountain, but all they succeeded in doing with the *Arizona Times* was going into more and more debt. And when it failed, it had a tragic impact on my parent's marriage. My father felt it was all his fault and left, and my mother had to soldier on by herself, selling off the residue of a paper they never should have invested in. After their divorce in 1949, my father spent the last year of his life wandering from place to place, trying to find himself both physically and mentally.[10]

His son also confirmed he was offered jobs in public relations but was never able to get over what he had given up in Seattle and failed at in Arizona. He took his own life in October 1950.

Gradually, Anna was able to pay off the family debt while working a variety of jobs and living in Los Angeles with her two sons. As soon as he was old enough, Curtis left home to "enter the world of advertising," leaving only John with his mother. The two of them would eventually

Part Five—Extended Family

settle in Berkeley, California, where, as a teenager, John remembered being able to see the bay bridges from their home. "For a couple of years, I had mother virtually to myself and I'm grateful for that time together—just the two of us," he said.[11]

In November of 1952 Anna married for a third time. This time to a physician with the Veterans Administration, Dr. James Halsted,[12] who would be reassigned twice before John left home for college. The first was back to Los Angeles, where John started high school, and the second to Syracuse, New York, where he graduated. From there John went on to Amherst College in central Massachusetts and a double major in psychology and political science. Like several of his famous forebearers, he went to graduate school at Columbia University in New York City, followed by postgraduate work in Cambridge, England.

Thus began an accomplished teaching career that saw him relinquish political science in favor of the more personally satisfying psychology, mostly at Hampshire College, where he started the program. Jokingly, he readily admits to having "the Roosevelt social gene that doesn't do marriage very well," which resulted in four of his own, the last of which ended with the tragic death of his fourth wife due to ALS, better known as Lou Gehrig's disease.[13]

Along the way, he also never got over the unfortunate breakup of his parents' marriage and the ill-advised circumstances that surrounded it—so much so, in fact, that in 1978 he authored a book entitled *A Love in Shadow* that tells their story. Like others of his generation, as we have seen, it is yet another account of Roosevelt lives and the spotlight that for years in the 20th century seemed to trail (and sometimes taint) their every turn.[14]

On a happier family note, John Roosevelt Boettiger, like so many others of his generation, proudly sounded off about his illustrious grandmother and the obviously meaningful period in his life he once shared with her. It happened while he was a student at Amherst and several years after the family tragedies of debt, divorce, and suicide. It turns out that while he was in college in the East, so far from home, his grandmother advised him, "Johnny, I want you to consider my home yours during the last three years of your college life." And with that as his standing invitation, he spent summer vacations and holidays in Hyde Park and New York City with ER. Of that period, he recalled,

23. Northwest Branch

"She became my mentor during those years. They were the years of my real maturation and as the graduating class president at Amherst College in 1960, I will always be proud of the fact that the special guest speaker at my graduation was none other than Eleanor Roosevelt, my grandmother. What an honor."[15]

What an honor, indeed!

24

Writer's Roots

For all that is remembered about Theodore Roosevelt, very few Americans realize what a prolific writer he was. Most of more than 35 nonfiction books, to be exact, came from the energetic mind of our 26th and youngest president, an amazing number considering how active and involved he always was in countless other endeavors. Three were biographical—a political memoir on America's leading 19th century expansionist, Senator Thomas Hart Benton of Missouri; a companion to that on possibly our least-known founding father, Gouverneur Morris of New York; and a later, less developed text on one of the most controversial leaders in British history, Oliver Cromwell. Remarkably, the first two still rank among the most significant studies ever done on Benton and Morris, two underappreciated American statesmen from different generations.[1]

In an introduction to a 1999 reprinting of TR's earliest book, *The Naval War of 1812*, which he wrote while only 23 and a college senior at Harvard in 1881, military historian Caleb Carr termed Roosevelt's initial volume revealing of "the prodigious intellect, irrepressible character, and remarkably entertaining style of this future president, who consistently made a good part of his income through writing." At the time it was first published in 1882, the *New York Times* remarked, "An excellent book in every respect, and shows in so young an author the best promises for a good historian."[2]

Actually, "historian" was probably putting it mildly, as his hard-hitting style, even at such a young age, was reminiscent of modern political pundits with their outspoken reviews on the issues and leaders of the day. Only in this case, his takes were applied through the looking glass of history. For instance, the final chapter of that first book dealt

24. Writer's Roots

with the Battle of New Orleans, which, while not a naval confrontation, he felt compelled to include for its importance in the overall outcome of the conflict. At the chapter's start he wrote as follows:

> While our Navy had been successful, the war on land had been for us full of humiliation. The United States then formed but a loosely knit confederacy, the sparse population scattered over a great expanse of land. Ever since the Federalist Party had gone out of power in 1800, the nation's ability to maintain order at home and enforce respect abroad had steadily dwindled; and the 12 years' nerveless reign of the Doctrinaire Democracy had left us impotent for attack and almost as feeble for defense. Jefferson, though a man whose views and theories had a profound influence upon our national life, was perhaps the most incapable executive that ever filled the presidential chair; being almost purely a visionary, he was utterly unable to grapple with the slightest actual danger, and, not even excepting his successor, Madison, it would be difficult to imagine a man less fit to guide the state with honor and safety through the stormy times that marked the opening of the present century. Without the prudence to avoid war or the forethought to prepare for it, the Administration [of Thomas Jefferson and later James Madison] drifted helplessly into a conflict in which only the Navy, prepared by the Federalists 12 years before, saved us from complete and shameful defeat. True to its theories, the House of Virginia [the presidential succession of Virginians Jefferson, Madison and James Monroe] made no preparations.[3]

Tellingly, TR's take on Thomas Jefferson and James Madison was not of the esteemed variety usually reserved for those founding fathers, at least not when it came to our nation's war readiness before 1812. His references to their Federalist predecessors was an obvious endorsement of what has traditionally been viewed as the more Republican-like of the parties during our two-party system's earliest stages—in fact, more Republican than the party that was actually called Republicans at that time, which was led by none other than Jefferson and Madison[4] (just another example of how political monikers and leanings have changed or dramatically shifted several times over the past 200 years).

It's also only one of many examples of the historic evaluations TR made in this book and others, a tell-it-like-it-was approach of which his great-nephews, the Alsop brothers, would have heartily approved. At the same time, simply the prodigious amount of authorship that he accomplished is worthy of a share of the TR legend and a dose of the family pride that remains obvious through such things as the Oyster Bay-based Theodore Roosevelt Association, which expressly

Part Five—Extended Family

preserves "his memory and ideals" and of which the previously mentioned Tweed Roosevelt served as president and Elizabeth Roosevelt as treasurer at the time of this writing.[5]

Pride in TR's writing legacy has also had its place in Elizabeth Winthrop's 35-plus years as a writer. A New York City resident, she recognizes that her writer's gene came mostly from her father, Stewart Alsop, and to a lesser extent her Uncle Joe, but she has always referred to her great-great-uncle Teddy and his writing prowess in the presentations she's given to school groups. It's one family tie sure to get attention, a lot more so, in fact, than her more obvious connection to the Alsop bothers, who most of today's young people have never heard of.

One of Stewart's six children and his only daughter, Winthrop wasn't able to attend the 2013 Roosevelt reunion, but one of her brothers,

In this White House photograph from the 1960s, Stephen Alsop—one of the two Alsop brothers columnists, great nephews of TR and among the most influential journalists of the Cold War era—introduces his daughter, Elizabeth, to then-president Lyndon Johnson. Today, Elizabeth Winthrop is a recognized writer in her own right. COURTESY LBJ PRESIDENTIAL LIBRARY; ALSO THANKS TO ELIZABETH WINTHROP.

24. Writer's Roots

Nick Alsop of Little Rock, Arkansas, did, along with his family. In fact, one of his daughters, Katie, who was 19 at the time, experienced the onset of epilepsy while in Warm Springs, suffering her first seizure the evening of the Ken Burns documentary screening, a brief but traumatic occurrence for everyone in attendance. Since then, following proper diagnosis, she has been on medication to control the illness and, according to her aunt, continues to do very well.

While most of Winthrop's 60-something books have been for children (two others are adult novels), there is one personal memoir with the provocative title *Don't Knock Unless You're Bleeding: Growing Up in Cold War Washington*, a takeoff on one particularly personal episode with her father while growing up in the household of two ultimate D.C. insiders. Because of that upbringing and her proximity to a writer's daily existence, including the advantage of seeing one earn income while working from home, she concluded, "My family never struggled financially, so I understood at a fairly young age that it was possible to earn a decent living as a writer and best of all, you didn't have to go to an office to do it."

After college, Winthrop began her writing career as a reporter for the *Berkshire Eagle* in western Massachusetts, but not wishing to ever invade, compete, or conflict with the world of her father and uncle, she decided to move away from journalism to fiction for children, which she did between 1972 and 1988. In that latter year, she also authored her first adult novel, *In My Mother's Home*, which was based on the life of her grandmother on the Roosevelt side, Corinne Alsop, daughter of TR's youngest sister and a trusted first cousin of both Eleanor Roosevelt and Alice Roosevelt Longworth.[6]

In 2001, she also participated in the Dear Mr. President series, an early interactive, web-connected group of books in which various authors took on the challenge of writing letters from a totally fictitious character of a particular time and place in history to the sitting president of that time. It also required equally fictitious return letters from that president. The time and president Winthrop selected was the Great Depression of the 1930s and FDR, a distant cousin but one she admired and could relate to from all her father and uncle had shared about that period and the New Deal White House. The book was entitled *Dear Mr. President: Franklin Delano Roosevelt Letters from a Mill Town Girl*.

Part Five—Extended Family

FDR's fictitious but very personal correspondent, Emma Bartoletti, was derived from Winthrop's time in the Berkshires and previous residency in North Adams, Massachusetts, a textile mill town like Lowell, Lawrence, and others of that area and era. What is interesting about that choice (other than the fact another author had already done one connecting TR with a young coal miner) was her admission that while she was growing up her parents, uncle, and even her beloved grandmother had all made a point of "not playing up" their Roosevelt heritage too much around Winthrop and her brothers. She even indicated that except for a few obvious examples to the contrary, such as Uncle Joe's prominently displayed family portraits, their Roosevelt lineage was mostly "downplayed."[7]

However, the times and place where she did learn about the Roosevelts were mostly after-school hours spent in the company of her great-aunt Alice at her D.C. home—yes, TR's famously irrepressible first daughter and by then Washington's notorious "Mrs. L,"[8] who for a time was responsible for hosting not only her own granddaughter, Joanna Sturm, but also Stewart's daughter, Elizabeth (Winthrop), on weekday afternoons when their school day was finished and the young Ms. Alsop needed a place to stay before her parents picked her up prior to supper. Of that period, she remembers vividly having afternoon tea at Alice's home and the D.C. matron's intense interest in any inside scoop she may have picked up from her obviously well informed father and uncle. Winthrop stated, "I can remember always feeling like she picked my brain for any gossip that I may have picked up on from the conversations I overheard at home. Even at her advanced age, you could tell how much she enjoyed staying on top of what was going on in the world and the Washington scene, and she was always interested in any tidbits I might provide. It made me feel special and I adored her." In fact, with her grandmother Corinne Alsop living so far away in Connecticut, Aunt Alice was like a substitute, providing an intimacy that made Winthrop aware of the Roosevelt heritage she didn't learn much about at home.[9]

That heritage would have undoubtedly included some discussion of TR's many contributions as a writer, a connection to her immediate family likely reinforced by Alice. Whether or not knowledge of these more distant but illustrious writer's roots also contributed to her later

24. Writer's Roots

literary leanings and career is not a conclusion she's necessarily willing to draw, especially with her father's and uncle's work being so much more obvious to her development, but there can be little doubt her affinity for the written word and ability to turn out mass books is a trait shared and perhaps inherited from Teddy. As John Allen Gable, former executive director of the Theodore Roosevelt Association has written:

> It seems amazing that Roosevelt (TR) was able to accomplish so much, both in his personal life and for his career in such a short, crowded period of time [having died at age 60]. But Theodore Roosevelt was one of the most amazing Americans of all time. The author of over 35 books and hundreds of essays on a dazzling variety of subjects; hunter, naturalist, explorer and conservationist; Dakota rancher and police commissioner of New York City; colonel of the Rough Riders and winner of the Nobel Peace Prize; founder of the NCAA [National Collegiate Athletic Association] and president of the American Historical Association; man in the arena of countless political battles; trustbuster and builder of the Panama Canal; advocate of the strenuous life and the Square Deal; creator of the U.S. Forest Service and the Fish and Wildlife Service, governor of New York State, vice president, and then president at age 42. TR was, in short, an American Renaissance man.[10]

So it goes without saying that such a renaissance man was bound to have rubbed off on many a proud descendant, including a young writer-to-be who learned much about him in the company of another Roosevelt legend.

25

Inclusive Legacy

Speaking of family legacies, one name did not appear on the latest reunion roster, sparking questions about his arrival among the host Warm Springs staff. However, there was no denying his commanding presence and impressive credentials once his identity and connection were established. Such was the entrance of the tall, distinguished gentleman in the company of Kate Roosevelt Whitney, who also brought along a teenage grandson that November weekend in 2013 to afford them both the opportunity to experience firsthand what being a Roosevelt was all about.

Their arrival a day later than most of the attendees was nonetheless in plenty of time to catch one of the guided tours of the historic Warm Springs Quadrangle planned for the Roosevelt family that morning. Indeed, Roosevelt Warm Springs tour guide Linda Creekbaum was quick to pick up on the intense interest Kate Whitney's companion exhibited as she detailed the story of FDR's coming to Warm Springs in 1924 in search of a cure for polio; of his landmark decision to purchase the old mineral springs resort because of its rehabilitative potential for not only himself but other polio victims; and of his founding of what would become a world famous treatment center, the Georgia Warm Springs Foundation, an early catalyst for the March of Dimes and ultimately the vaccines of the 1950s that effectively eradicated the crippling disease.[1]

Franklin A. Thomas, former longtime president of the Ford Foundation and a man *Fortune* magazine once dubbed one of America's corporate "kingmakers" by virtue of his affiliation on the boards of companies like Citicorp, Lucent Technologies, and Pepsico, was obviously impressed. Creekbaum could sense it in the way he hung on her

25. Inclusive Legacy

every word with attention rare among a large tour group of 20 or more, where individual distractions and stragglers can often become the norm as the assemblage transitions from one tour stop to the next.

Instead, his was an obvious interest and appreciation of the information that impressed the veteran tour guide, probably the same reaction Thomas has exerted on people throughout his life. How else could one interpret a personal bio that details his growing up in the tough Bedford-Stuyvesant section of Brooklyn, New York, the youngest child of a poor West Indian family whose father died when he was only 11; who was raised with the mindset "that there were no limits" to what one could accomplish even while growing up in a gang-infested neighborhood; who would nevertheless excel in grade school as both a student and a basketball player; and someone who would turn down major college athletic scholarships in order to pursue an Ivy League education at Columbia University. It was there, where he did star and captain the basketball team, that he also built relationships in the fields of business, law, and politics, and to where, after graduating and a four-year hitch in the U.S. Air Force, he would return for a law degree. His return to Columbia, in fact, served to launch his career into a series of "high-powered government jobs." The first was as attorney for the Federal Housing and Home Finance Agency in 1963 followed by assistant U.S. attorney for the Southern District of New York in 1964; New York City deputy police commissioner in charge of legal affairs in 1965; and, finally, president of then New York senator Robert Kennedy's newly created Bedford-Stuyvesant Restoration Corporation in 1967, a role in which he was responsible for raising $63 million to help improve living conditions in his home community.[2]

Because of that meteoric rise, the same online bio points to his budding reputation as a man who always got "the job done" as the reason he was chosen in 1979 to head the prestigious Ford Foundation, a vast trust initially endowed by legendary car manufacturer Henry Ford and his son Edsel. Validation of his selection as that foundation's president would certainly come 17 years later at the time of his resignation, when assets had reached $7.7 billion.[3] In other words, his was (and remains) a dynamic legacy devoid of any qualms about how such an accomplished individual would fit into the equally dynamic world of a family like the Roosevelts. For that matter, the same could be said of

PART FIVE—EXTENDED FAMILY

the Whitneys—as in the New York Whitneys of John Hay "Jock" Whitney, former U.S. ambassador to the United Kingdom, publisher of the *New York Herald Tribune,* and, during the course of his life, one of the wealthiest men in the world.[4]

Thomas, the second husband of Kate R. Whitney (her first was William Haddad, Jewish son of a Russian mother and Egyptian father, a top investigative reporter with the *New York Post* and later a Kennedy administration appointee)—daughter of James Roosevelt and his first wife, Betsy Cushing, and granddaughter of legendary neurosurgeon Harvey Cushing, stepdaughter of Jock Whitney,[5] and one of ten FDR-ER grandchildren at the reunion—became an immediately welcomed and accepted member of the Roosevelt family at large in Warm Springs. Not surprising for a family so unprejudiced and historically accepting of multiple marriages, it would have also been something TR, FDR, and ER could have been expected to endorse.

You see, Franklin A. Thomas is a tall, distinguished, and obviously very accomplished African American. From legendary educator-orator Booker T. Washington's being invited to dine at the White House by TR (1901) through world famous contralto Marian Anderson's being invited to sing on the steps of the Lincoln Memorial (1939) by ER and FDR's establishment of the George Washington Carver National Monument in Missouri (1943), this family's connection to early civil rights advancement was consistently obvious.[6] "Pushed by Eleanor, the Army agreed to induct colored units into each major branch of the service," according to Jonathan Jordan in his 2015 book, *American Warlords,* over the rather significant objections of critics like Secretary of War Henry Stimson, who termed it "Mrs. Roosevelt's intrusive and impulsive folly."[7] And with so much assigned credit, it's too bad they weren't around to see their inclusive efforts (especially hers) begin to bear fruit in the 1960s before finally reaching what would have surely seemed unfathomable dimensions during their lifetimes with the presidential election of Barack Obama in 2008.[8] Nevertheless, there is no disputing that their individual moments and outright efforts towards inclusion were evident long before the three departed this earth, and like the rest of their progressive ideals would have undoubtedly received their blessing within the family even back then.

Maybe by the next family reunion even more will be known about

25. Inclusive Legacy

those West Coast Roosevelts, the Boettigers, and other far-flung descendants of ER, TR, and FDR—branches of the family like the Elliotts, Alsops, or Reeves. Maybe by then, more interesting connections and observations will have surfaced from their collective in-laws or via the descendants of dearly departed colleagues, and undoubtedly more will have been written about them and theirs as it has been now for more than a century. Maybe some of the better ideals they espoused, hopeful things like social justice and inclusion, will also continue to be manifested, especially by their own family. Maybe "Thatcher" really will grow up to be the next Roosevelt president and maybe another Roosevelt enclave like the Badlands, Campobello, or Warm Springs will be revealed to friends and family alike in a way that hasn't happened before, as it was because of the Ken Burns documentary in 2013. When it happens, however, it might have trouble measuring up to what many have since called their "best reunion ever" in little Warm Springs and chances are, if it does, the next generation of Roosevelts will have to lead it. But regardless of who's ultimately in charge, the family's place in the overall scheme of things doesn't figure to change. No matter whose day it is to "be a Roosevelt," their place and status in the American past doesn't figure to ever go away.

Epilogue
Roosevelt Reminders

Count 'em. There are at least nine national, state, or international homes, birthplaces, parks, or historic sites preserved in honor of Theodore, Franklin, and Eleanor Roosevelt. There is Theodore Roosevelt Birthplace National Historic Site in New York City; Theodore Roosevelt Inaugural National Historic Site in Buffalo, New York; the three units of Theodore Roosevelt National Park in western North Dakota; and Sagamore Hill National Historic Site, TR's preserved home at Oyster Bay; Franklin D. Roosevelt's Home (Springwood) National Historic Site at Hyde Park; FDR's Little White House State Historic Site in Warm Springs, Georgia; the recently reopened double brownstone Roosevelt Home in New York City; the previously noted Roosevelt Campobello International Park on the Canadian isle of the same name just off the American mainland near picturesque Lubec, Maine; and, as discussed in detail earlier, the Eleanor Roosevelt National Historic Site, Val-Kill, also at Hyde Park.

Add to that list on the TR side of the ledger the Theodore Roosevelt Bridge over the Potomac River in Washington, D.C., as well as the Theodore Roosevelt Memorial on Theodore Roosevelt Island in the middle of the Potomac at Washington; the Theodore Roosevelt Dam on the Salt River in Arizona; and Theodore Roosevelt Memorial Hall at the American Museum of Natural History in New York City. For FDR, we have the Franklin D. Roosevelt Four Freedoms Park on Roosevelt Island in New York City; the previously mentioned Franklin D. Roosevelt National Memorial in D.C.; F.D. Roosevelt State Park (and statue) atop Pine Mountain in Georgia; Franklin D. Roosevelt Lake in

Roosevelt Reminders

Washington State; and both New York's Franklin D. Roosevelt Mid-Hudson Bridge connecting Poughkeepsie with Highland, and the Franklin D. Roosevelt Bridge connecting the U.S. mainland to Campobello. Also, in ER's honor, there are the Eleanor Roosevelt Memorial in New York City's Riverside Park and a small bridge more recently named for her as you enter the town of Warm Springs—just to name a few.

And if that's not enough major remembrances for one family, don't forget that TR is one of the four presidents famously depicted on Mount Rushmore (South Dakota), as well as the subject of a host of other monuments at natural wonders throughout the country, places like Roosevelt Point at the North Rim of the Grand Canyon, and the iconic Roosevelt Arch and Roosevelt Lodge at Yellowstone National Park. In fact, it's not surprising—and only fitting—that there are more national park reminders of TR and the role he played in development of the National Park System than anyone else.

There's even a well-known and much-loved memorial to FDR overseas—in London, England—a rendition of him standing with the aid of only a cane in Grosvenor Square. As physically impossible as that would have been for him to do with his polio, it provides an appropriate depiction of how tall he stood in the eyes of the British after leading America to their rescue during the Second World War. At the same time, some might argue that major accomplishments like the Panama Canal, Social Security, and the United Nations Charter are the best monuments of all to the Roosevelt Big Three—lasting achievements for mankind that remain unassailable reminders of their iconic legacies.

At least one other little-known but nonetheless iconic Roosevelt home has already been lost due to fire—the tragedy that was McCarthy Cottage, the first home away from home FDR built in Warm Springs while governor of New York and the place he resided for four years before his more famous presidential getaway, the Little White House, was finished. Another in the same town could be lost if measures are not taken to preserve Pierson Cottage, the first home FDR rented and eventually owned in Georgia. Like McCarthy, which bore the name of its second owner, Canadian ambassador Leighton McCarthy, whose son had polio, Pierson Cottage mostly housed staff once its namesake,

Epilogue

Elizabeth Pierson (another polio survivor who followed FDR to Warm Springs), departed years ago. It now sits largely unused (and unpromoted), along with numerous other historic cottages in even further states of decay in a National Historic Landmark District at the center of a 900-plus acre Roosevelt Warm Springs campus that still exists primarily for state-managed vocational rehabilitation.

When the McCarthy fire occurred in 2009—reportedly due to fierce overnight storms and the possibility of faulty wiring that could surely be prevalent among other old, heavily paneled, "tinderbox" homes built during the 1920s—responses came from as far away as Australia, Russia, and India because of whose house it had been. Although virtually unknown outside the immediate area before it happened, the fact it had been built and lived in by FDR at one time even attracted enough attention for the *New York Times* to send a writer and photographer to Warm Springs to report on its smoldering ruins. During that visit, the writer commented that it was a shame, with its location among so many other aging cottages left from the resort and polio eras,

Left and opposite: **Among many monuments and historic sites dedicated to the memory of TR, FDR, and ER is this outdoor bust of Franklin Roosevelt, displayed at his home and library in Hyde Park, New York. In Arizona, a North Rim marker at the aptly named Roosevelt Point recalls the contributions of Theodore Roosevelt in preserving the Grand Canyon.** PHOTOGRAPHS PROPERTY OF THE AUTHOR.

that it had to be the one FDR lived in that caught fire. "Of course, if it had been any of the others, we wouldn't be here," he correctly concluded. Whether or not such historic influence will ever attach itself to any of the Big Three's descendants enough to warrant similar memorialization remains to be seen. At this writing, no monuments to any succeeding Roosevelts have surfaced.

At the same time, there is one other home of earlier Roosevelt vintage and significance verging on collapse at last report (2014). That's the one ER grew up in near Tivoli, New York: Oak Terrace. Like Springwood, it's situated alongside the Hudson River between New York City and Albany along with a host of other mansions from bygone eras. Although there is still a nice view of the Hudson from its windows, it appears barren and austere to anyone—including the National Park Service, which took pictures there just a few years back—given clearance by its current, private property owners. Its age and deterioration at present creates a very haunting aspect, but it is easy to imagine an equally cold and forbidding appearance when Eleanor and her younger

Epilogue

brother Hall were sent there—following their mother's untimely death at age 29 in 1892—to live with their maternal grandmother and some unmarried aunts and uncles. In fact, the Hall family vault, which was added in 1894 to the St. Paul's Episcopal Church Cemetery about three miles away, is yet another reminder of a bygone time when no matter how much "blue blood" flowed through a family's veins, urchins were sometimes suddenly fostered due to the tragic deaths of both parents in an era before modern healthcare, rehab, and more structured placement procedures.

Just 20 miles north of Hyde Park as the crow flies and on the same side of the river, Oak Terrace appears to be light-years from the preserved tranquility of Springwood or even Val-Kill. Those National Park Service photos of 2014 were true in their Halloween quality. In fact, haunting might be the best way to describe its appearance and perceived history— or at least the perceived history when little Eleanor and her younger brother, as Hudson River orphans, were left to live there with a very pious grandmother and her own, still-at-home older children—aunts and uncles who would never be mistaken for role models. The house is also referred to as Oak Hall, and Eleanor's time there has been described as "very solitary." Although she learned to enjoy outdoor pursuits like biking and horseback riding, she was without friends or playmates her own age and reportedly spent most of her childhood years feeling very much alone. In her autobiography, she wrote the following:

> We stayed at Tivoli in the summer with a nurse and governess, even [when] the others were away, and [I remember] hot, breathless days when my fingers stuck to the keys as I practiced piano, but I never left off any garments. Even in summer, we wore a good many. I would roll my stockings down and then be told that ladies did not show their legs and promptly have to fasten them up again! The house at Tivoli was big, with high ceilings and many rooms, most of them large. We had neither gas nor electricity. We had lamps, but often went to bed by candlelight. The library was filled with standard books. Besides my grandfather's religious books, a good deal of fiction (also) came into the house by way

Opposite: **A Roosevelt-related historic site that has not been preserved like most of the others, Oak Terrace at Tivoli, New York, was the home where ER and her younger brother Hall were kept by their maternal grandmother after their parents died. Although in disrepair, its second and third floor windows still offer views of the Hudson River.** PHOTOGRAPH NATIONAL PARK SERVICE, BILL URBIN.

Epilogue

of my young aunts and uncles. There were just two bathrooms in [that] large house, but it never occurred to us that it was an inconvenience or that it really made much work to have to use basins and pitchers in our rooms. We children had to take two hot baths a week, [but I was also] expected to have a cold sponge every morning. My grandmother let me follow her about in the early mornings when she was housekeeping and I carried supplies to the cook. Today, few servants would be content to cook in the semidarkness which reigned in that big, old-fashioned kitchen [and] the laundry was little better.

Built in 1872, Oak Terrace was constructed in the Second Empire Style, with such distinctive features as a mansard roof and asymmetrical square tower. Modeled after the Paris home of Napoleon III, it possessed similarities to Italianate architecture, including bracketed eaves. Officially listed on the National Register of Historic Places if not the more hallowed landmark list of other Roosevelt sites, it nevertheless remains a part of this remarkable family's story, a reminder, just like the other locations, of an American dynasty that echoes to the present day.[1]

Pictured at the FDR Library and Museum in Hyde Park in 2014, the author alongside statues of Eleanor and Franklin Roosevelt.

Appendix
Eleanor's "My Day" Observations

While FDR's extensively edited speeches, fireside comments, and quick-witted quips have been quoted and reprinted for decades, and while there's no disputing the prolific historian and published writer that Teddy was, probably no Roosevelt left more information about personal convictions and what we know of this dynastic, multi-layered family than Eleanor did. While Franklin and Theodore have been the constant subjects of books ever since their respective eras as president, and while TR was himself a surprisingly prodigious nonfiction writer (again, how did he have the time?), it was Eleanor who surely documented the most about being a Roosevelt through her autobiography, the several books she authored later in life, and, perhaps most important, her syndicated "My Day" columns that ran nationwide for more than a quarter of a century.

In 2001, David Emblidge did us all a favor by editing a book containing these timeless points of view under the same title—*My Day*. In it, what Emblidge termed "the best" of ER's columns are grouped by the years in which she wrote them, beginning with a section entitled "Up from the Depression" and continuing through "The War Years," "Building the Peace," and "First Lady of the World." They basically ran from 1936 until her fatal illness and death in 1962, an insightful resource from her last 26 years. As might be expected, many deal with world problems of the time or major causes she championed, but others offer very personal glimpses of her and her family, and it is these that were given special attention as a fitting finale. Who is this extraordinary

Appendix

family—these Roosevelts who so dominated much of the 20th century and whose legacies continue to surface, repeatedly, in so many ways. What better way to conclude what started with a Roosevelt reunion? A sampling follows.

* * * *

One of ER's 1944 columns was particularly revealing when it came to her sincere belief in TR "as an inspiration for young Americans":

> Theodore Roosevelt never failed to convey to young people that he believed they should take an active part in the public affairs of their community and of their nation. He thought every man and woman faced first their family responsibilities, but he was quick to point out that these could not be faced fully without recognizing the tie that the family had to the community. Theodore Roosevelt made you feel that every act in your daily life was a part of your citizenship. I am sure that today he would preach to young people their obligation to participate in the government of their community, the nation, and the world, and the necessity of bringing their influence to bear as individuals and as members of any groups.

Later in that same column she added, "He had very little patience with those who wished to advance their own personal fortunes, regardless of the fortunes of the American citizens as a whole."

* * * *

The very next month, ER's message turned to a play she had just witnessed called *Lovers and Friends* when she touched on what were obviously very personal views of romance, love, and marriage developed during a lifetime of loss, betrayal, recovery, and seemingly constant disappointment, including the many divorces she had to endure involving her own children. Unlike her own marriage, their efforts to stay the course and work things out appear repeatedly nonexistent and undoubtedly influenced these words:

> It is obviously true that the first flush of being "in love" may change into something deeper and calmer, or more superficial. I have known only a few very happy marriages. By that I do not mean just people who get along together and live contentedly through life, but people who are really excitedly happy. These people have somehow preserved the ability to rejuvenate their love so that neither the man nor the woman need wander off to find the romance they long for somewhere else.

According to her, the play showed that "it is not the people who happen to attract each other temporarily who really matter," a lesson she believed worth learning for obvious reasons and repeated examples.

* * * *

Written shortly after FDR's death, funeral, and burial on April 24, 1945, another column revealed something of ER's introspection and determination to move on when she and her sons returned to Hyde Park a week after his interment in the rose garden there. It began with a seeming desire to return to normalcy:

> We came back to Hyde Park yesterday morning, just one week from the time we all gathered here for the committal service in our hedge-surrounded garden. My sons and I went to look at the grave. If two soldiers had not been on guard, and the beautiful orchids flown up from the South had not covered the spot where the sod had been put back so carefully, we would hardly have known that the lawn was not as it had always been. Before very long, the simple stone, which my husband described very carefully for us, will be in place. But in the meantime the children and the dogs will be quite unconscious that here a short time ago a solemn military funeral was held, and they will think of it as a place where flowers grow and where the hedge protects them from the wind and makes the sun shine down warmly. And that is as my husband would have it. He liked children and dogs and sunshine and flowers, and they are all around him now.

Almost poetic in its approach, it's also a good example of the Roosevelt maxim of maintaining a "stiff upper lip" with little or no room for sentimentality in the midst of loss.

* * * *

Nearly two years later, in early 1947, ER lost her driver's license as the result of a traffic accident she caused (as previously established, she was a notoriously bad driver) and although admittedly sad about this loss of independence she at least recognized the advantages of having a chauffeur afforded her over others her age (62) not similarly blessed. Her glass-half-full approach to this personal dilemma was again revealing of very Rooseveltian expectations—core beliefs that called for making the best of adversity. In that column she confided:

> Perhaps at my age, in any case, it is wise to curtail one's activities. One thing is sure—that if you give up any activity, it is much more difficult to start in again. And since the accident, I have done no long-distance driving, not even from Hyde Park to New York City. It will be distinctly awkward to have to walk everywhere around the Hyde Park place, instead of driving. However, at all

Appendix

times and as long as one lives, life administers disciplines, and it is in accepting and obeying them that one learns.

As already established, such beliefs had been a constant in the lives of TR and FDR, allowing them to work through overwhelming adversity, as illustrated by their Badlands' and Warm Springs' examples.

* * * *

ER later authored another column that touched on her feelings for family and home during one of those idyllic Val-Kill summers. "Never happier than when her house was full of children," according to the editor, this particular issue of "My Day" dealt specifically with the exuberant lifestyle to be found in her home at that time, which she documented in the following statement:

> This is working out as a very successful summer, but to most people it might seem as if we were running a children's camp at Hyde Park, for we have had an average of nine children steadily since early June! When one or two leave, others arrive. However, they all fall into the routine very quickly, and it seems to be enjoyable for them. At least I have heard no complaints. Those who ride take care of their own horses. The littlest ones play in the sandbox and swing in the swings by the brook, and swim in the pool. All the youngsters spend hours of every warm day in the pool. The two children who are not quite three years old have to wear life belts, but they go through all the motions of swimming and evidently learn from just watching the others. We picnic by the pool for lunch every day and that seems to be a perfect idea because the children do not have to take off their bathing suits, which always creates sadness and controversy.

For those children, life was always fun at Grandmère's house.

* * * *

In fact, despite ER's somewhat dour upbringing, fun was something she could enjoy, as illustrated by another summer column three years later. While not the life of the party her late husband had been, she did have her fun-filled, tongue-in-cheek moments, as she must have had when she addressed the world of men's fashion in the following way:

> I never have understood why every member of the male sex had to dress in the same way. I always like to look at pictures from the era when gentlemen wore breeches of beautiful materials and colors, long silk stockings and beautiful shoes with a variety of buckles. Coats and waistcoats rivaled any lady's finery and, if they so wished, men wore powdered wigs tied with gorgeous ribbons. How they came to be so restrained later on I don't know, unless the difficulty of

> obtaining this finery in the early days of the country was too great. Perhaps the Quakers and some of the other religious sects had a quieting effect. I'd like to see our gentlemen follow the rules of nature that govern our animal friends. Almost always the male animal is the showoff while the female remains demure and is less startlingly clad. Perhaps someday we will have the courage to strike a good medium and let the men have a little self-expression in their clothes.

While often the target of fashion critics herself, she was clearly unafraid when irreverently confronting a topic she supposedly knew little or nothing about.

* * * *

At the same time, ER's more common, rational thinking was normally prevalent in her writing, as it was following the death of her longtime secretary of 29 years, Malvina "Tommy" Thompson, in April 1953:

> One does not weep for those who die, particularly when they have lived a full life. And I doubt, in any case, whether the gauge of love and sorrow is in the tears that are shed in the first days of mourning. People who remain with you in your daily life, even though they are no longer physically present, who are frequently in your mind, often mentioned, part of your laughter, part of your joy—they are the people you really miss. They are the people from whom you are never quite separated. You do not need to walk heavily all your life to really miss people.

Such deep, contemplative thinking must have certainly eased the loss of a valued coworker and companion, for not only herself but the entire family, who were accustomed to Tommy's being a part of her life and, by extension, theirs.

* * * *

The causes, policies, and topics of the day—the national and international happenings ER almost always had an opinion on—continued to find their way into her columns even after her years as First Lady, near the seat of power, were over. Examples can be found throughout *My Day* the book, but several of her prophecies from the late 1950s still up for debate include the following:

> A reassessment of Social Security (started by FDR) benefits should be made. The cost of living has gone up. Of late, prices always seem to be going up and never coming down. Perhaps there should be a sliding scale for pensions to meet the changes in living costs.

Continuing along that line of thought, she said:

Appendix

> Most of these people are old, and perhaps Congress will not think their votes amount to much. But this group is certainly getting larger in this country and, therefore, even from a political standpoint, this situation should receive consideration from both Republicans and Democrats.

On another still ongoing discussion, she opined:

> I wonder if others throughout the country feel strongly enough about this situation to do something about campaign expenses. I have long felt that the same amount should be spent by both parties, that both should be given free radio and television time, and that an equal amount of advertising and travel should be allowed in the different categories and paid for by the public.

In regard to how America is viewed by the rest of the world:

> No country in our position is loved, but we should make ourselves respected and better understood. Our policy of giving military aid to foreign nations instead of actually raising the living standards in those countries has been a big mistake.

It is debatable whether TR or FDR would have said any of those things, but as her favorite uncle and husband there is no doubt they would have been proud of her for saying them. After all, was that not what a Roosevelt would be expected to do?[1]

Chapter Notes

Prologue

1. The following sources were used in the research and writing of this prologue: Jonathon Alter, *The Defining Moment*; H.W. Brands, *Traitor to His Class* and *T.R.*; Douglas Brinkley, *The Wilderness Warrior*; Ken Burns, *The Roosevelts: An Intimate History*; Peter Collier, *The Roosevelts: An American Saga*; Hugh Gregory Gallagher, *Splendid Deception*; Doris Kearns Goodwin, *No Ordinary Time* and *The Bully Pulpit*; Nathan Miller, *F.D.R.*; Edmund Morris, *The Rise of Theodore Roosevelt* and *Theodore Rex*; Eleanor Roosevelt, The Autobiography of Eleanor Roosevelt and her recorded comments in *FDR*, an American Experience documentary; Edith Danby Williams' interview in *TR*, also an American Experience documentary.

Chapter 1

1. Winston Skinner, "Descendants Hold Reunion," *Newnan Times Herald* (10 November 2013).
2. Chris Roosevelt, interview with the author (1 November 2013).
3. Elizabeth Roosevelt, interview with the author (1 November 2013).
4. Timothy Field Beard and Henry B. Hoff, ed., "The Roosevelt Family in America: A Genealogy," *Theodore Roosevelt Association Journal*, 7–122; David Roosevelt, *Grandmère: A Personal History of Eleanor Roosevelt*, 238–239; Joseph Berger, "Roosevelts and the Quirks of Destiny," *New York Times* (16 March 2005).
5. Chris Roosevelt, interview (1 November 2013).
6. Peter Collier, *The Roosevelts: An American Saga*, with David Horowitz, 481–482.
7. Stacy A. Cordery, *Alice: Alice Roosevelt Longworth, from White House Princess to Washington Power Broker*, 376; Jonathan Alter, *The Defining Moment: FDR's Hundred Days and the Triumph of Hope*, 24–25.
8. Cordery, *Alice*, 261.
9. Peter Collier with David Horowitz, *The Roosevelts*, 86–87.
10. Cordery, *Alice*, 26, 28–29; Ken Burns, *The Roosevelts: An Intimate History* (documentary); Edmund Morris, *Theodore Rex*, 251, 344.
11. Cordery, *Alice*, 165, 219–220, 376.
12. *Ibid.*, 312–313; Peter Collier with David Horowitz, *The Roosevelts*, 286–290; Laton McCartney, *The Teapot Dome Scandal*, 85–86.
13. Elizabeth Roosevelt, interview with the author (1 November 2013).
14. Tweed Roosevelt, interview with the author (2 November 2013).
15. Chris Roosevelt, interview with the author (1 November 2013); H.W. Brands, *Traitor to His Class: The Privileged Life and Radical Presidency of Franklin Delano Roosevelt*, 51; Ken Burns, *The Roosevelts*.
16. Jonathan Alter, *The Defining Moment: FDR's Hundred Days and the Tri-

umph of Hope, 32; Chris Roosevelt, interview with the author (1 November 2013).
   17. H.W. Brands, *Traitor to His Class: The Priviledged Life and Radical Presidency of Franklin Delano Roosevelt*, 322–323; Frank Freidel, *Franklin D. Roosevelt: A Rendezvous with Destiny*, 85, 240.
   18. *Ibid.*, 482.
   19. H.W. Brands, *Traitor to His Class*, 3; Anna Eleanor Roosevelt, *The Autobiography of Eleanor Roosevelt*, 49–50; Nathan Miller, *F.D.R.: An Intimate History*, 51–52; Peter Collier with David Horowitz, *The Roosevelts*, 17–23.
   20. *Ibid.*, p. 76.

Chapter 2

   1. Roosevelt Reunion Address/Information List, Courtesy Roosevelt Warm Springs (accessed August 2013).
   2. F. Martin Harmon, *The Warm Springs Story: Legacy and Legend*, 83.
   3. Winston Skinner, "Descendants Hold Reunion," *Newnan Times Herald*, November 10, 2013.
   4. F. Martin Harmon, *The Warm Springs Story*, 42, 82–83.
   5. Roosevelt Reunion Address/Information List, Courtesy Roosevelt Warm Springs (accessed August 2013).
   6. *Ibid.*
   7. "Robert T. Gannett, Jr.," www.press.uchicago.edu (accessed July 2013).
   8. "Emily Allen, Samuel Hornblower," *New York Times* (13 June 2009); Internet Movie Database, www.IMDb.com (accessed July 2013).
   9. "Anna Curtenius Roosevelt," www.en.m.wikipedia.org (accessed July 2013).
   10. Ken Christian,"Goodwill NNE CEO Anna Eleanor Roosevelt Speaks at Greater Portland Chamber's Eggs and Issues," www.goodwillnne.org (accessed December 2014).
   11. "Mark Roosevelt," www.en.m.wikipedia.org (accessed July 2013).
   12. "Warren Zimmerman," *Guardian*, February 9, 2009; J. Cushman Laurent and Ambassador Thomas Melady, "The Seven Nation States of the Former Yugoslavia: An Evaluation," www.iwp.edu (accessed February 2016).
   13. Laurie Bennett, "Money, Brains, and the Roosevelts," www.news.muckety.com, September 3, 2013; Jeff Blumenthal, "Teddy Roosevelt's Great-Great Grandson Talks Documentary, Family," *Philadelphia Business Journal*, September 19, 2014.
   14. "William S. Cowles: Honorary Life Member, Board of Directors," School for Advanced Research (SAR), www.sarweb.org (accessed July 2013); "William S. Cowles," www.en.m.wikipedia.org (accessed July 2013); "William Sheffield Cowles, Jr.," Find A Grave, www.findagrave.com (accessed July 2013); "William Sheffield Cowles, Teddy Roosevelt's Nephew and Ex-Legislator Dies at 88," *Los Angeles Times*, May 5, 1986.
   15. "Running Weld," www.nymag.com (accessed July 2013).
   16. "William E. Jackson: Biographical Information," www.archives.law.virginia.edu (accessed July 2013); "William Eldred Jackson," www.rootsweb.ancestry.com (accessed July 2013); Peter Dale Scott, *The Road to 911*, 312; Gholam Reza Aflkham, *The Life and Times of the Shah*, 694.
   17. Roosevelt Reunion Address/Information List, Courtesy Roosevelt Warm Springs (accessed August 2013).
   18. *Ibid.*

Chapter 3

   1. *Ibid.*, 17; David Roosevelt, 17; Edmund Morris, *The Rise of Theodore Roosevelt*, 429–31, 439–441, 474.
   2. David Roosevelt, *Grandmère: A Personal History of Eleanor Roosevelt*, 105.
   3. Anna Eleanor Roosevelt, *The Autobiography of Eleanor Roosevelt*, 9; David Roosevelt, *Grandmère*, 59.
   4. *Ibid.*, 61; Peter Collier with David

Horowitz, *The Roosevelts*, 85; Anna Eleanor Roosevelt, *The Autobiography of Eleanor Roosevelt*, 18.

5. *Ibid.*, 18–19; H.W. Brands, *Traitor to His Class*, 27; H.W. Brands, *T.R.: The Last Romantic*, 392.

6. Anna Eleanor Roosevelt, *The Autobiography of Eleanor Roosevelt*, 20; Eleanor (Ellie) Roosevelt, *With Love, Aunt Eleanor*, 10.

7. Joseph P. Lash, *Eleanor and Franklin: The Story of Their Relationship*, 74–87; Anna Eleanor Roosevelt, *The Autobiography of Eleanor Roosevelt*, 21–35.

8. *Ibid.*, 36.

9. *Ibid.*, 37; Ken Burns, *The Roosevelts* (documentary); Nathan Miller, *F.D.R.*, 46–47.

10. Anna Eleanor Roosevelt, *The Autobiography of Eleanor Roosevelt*, 44–47.

11. *Ibid.*, 48.

12. Ellie Roosevelt, *With Love, Aunt Eleanor*, 14; Jonathan Alter, *The Defining Moment*, 30.

13. H.W. Brands, *Traitor to His Class*, 34–35; Nathan Miller, *F.D.R.*, 52–54.

14. *Ibid.*, 57–58; Joseph P. Lash, *Franklin And Eleanor*, 154, 193–194.

15. Peter Collier with Michael Horowitz, *The Roosevelts*, 10–11; David Roosevelt, *Grandmère*, 238–239.

16. *Ibid.*, 366–374; H.W. Brands, *Traitor to His Class*, 129–130, 231; Jonathan Alter, *The Defining Moment*, 30–31; Doris Kearns Goodwin, *No Ordinary Time: Franklin and Eleanor Roosevelt and the Home Front in World War II*, 178–179.

17. H.W. Brands, *Traitor to His Class*, 39–41, 52–53.

18. Anna Eleanor Roosevelt, *The Autobiography of Eleanor Roosevelt*, 63.

19. H.W. Brands, *Traitor to His Class*, 50–56; Nathan Miller, *F.D.R.*, 92, 100–101.

20. John Milton Cooper, *Woodrow Wilson: A Biography*, 163; James Chace, *1912: Wilson, Roosevelt, Taft, and Debs—The Election That Changed the Country*, 7.

21. *Ibid.*, 179–180.

22. *Ibid.*, 8.

23. John Milton Cooper, *Woodrow Wilson: A Biography*, 179–180; Ken Burns, *The Roosevelts* (documentary).

24. Anna Eleanor Roosevelt, *The Autobiography of Eleanor Roosevelt*, 72, 90.

25. Jonathan Alter, *The Defining Moment*, 41–42.

26. Anna Eleanor Roosevelt, *The Autobiography of Eleanor Roosevelt*, 162–163.

27. Doris Kearns Goodwin, *No Ordinary Time*, 19, 28, 379, 396, 617.

28. Ellie Roosevelt, *With Love, Aunt Eleanor*, 72–79.

29. *Ibid.*, 68; Anna Eleanor Roosevelt, *The Autobiography of Eleanor Roosevelt*, 283–284.

30. Ellie Roosevelt, *With Love, Aunt Eleanor*, 95–98, 106, 111, 154–155, 162, 170, 172; Eleanor Calkin, Haven Roosevelt, Lauren Elliott, Nina Roosevelt Gibson, Stewart Elliott, interviews with the author (2 November 2013).

Chapter 4

1. Anna Eleanor Roosevelt, *The Autobiography of Eleanor Roosevelt*, 224; Doris Kearns Goodwin, *No Ordinary Time*, 226–227; Ellie Roosevelt, *With Love, Aunt Eleanor*, 50.

2. *Ibid.*, 86–172.

3. H.W. Brands, *Traitor to His Class*, 126–127; Anna Eleanor Roosevelt, *The Autobiography of Eleanor Roosevelt*, 143–145.

4. *Ibid.*, 284; Ellie Roosevelt, *With Love, Aunt Eleanor*, 42–45; Peter Collier with Michael Horowitz, *The Roosevelts*, 315.

5. National Park Service Tour Notes, Eleanor Roosevelt National Historic Site, Hyde Park, New York (28 July 2014).

6. *Ibid.*

7. Anna Eleanor Roosevelt, *The Autobiography of Eleanor Roosevelt*, 143–144; Doris Kearns Goodwin, *No Ordinary Time*, 107–108; Bill Urbin, National

Park Service Tour Notes (Top Cottage), Home of Franklin Roosevelt National Historic Site (28 July 2014).
8. Ellie Roosevelt, *With Love, Aunt Eleanor*, 42; Nina Roosevelt Gibson, interview with the author via e-mail (27 August 2014); Peter Collier with Michael Horowitz, *The Roosevelts*, 315, 438–439.
9. National Park Service Interpretive Tour (28 July 2014).
10. Nina Roosevelt Gibson, e-mail response to the author (August 27, 2014).
11. Peter Collier with Michael Horowitz, *The Roosevelts*, 315, 438–439.
12. David Roosevelt, *Grandmère*, 198.
13. Ellie Roosevelt, *With Love, Aunt Eleanor*, 42–43.
14. Eleanor Calkin, interview with the author (2 November 2013).
15. Stewart and Ted Elliott, interviews with the author (2 November 2013).
16. Nina Roosevelt Gibson, interview with the author (2 November 2013); Ellie Roosevelt, *With Love, Aunt Eleanor*, 96–98.
17. Lauren Elliott, interview with the author (2 November 2013).
18. Nina Roosevelt Gibson, interview with the author (2 November 2013).
19. Haven Roosevelt, interview with the author (2 November 2013).
20. Nina Roosevelt Gibson, interview with the author (2 November 2013).
21. Haven Roosevelt, interview with the author (2 November 2013).
22. Stewart Elliott, interview with the author (2 November 2013).
23. Haven Roosevelt and Nina Roosevelt Gibson, interviews with the author (2 November 2013).
24. Haven Roosevelt and Stewart Elliott, interviews with the author (2 November 2013); Ellie Roosevelt, *With Love, Aunt Eleanor*, 106–107.
25. *Ibid.*
26. Haven Roosevelt, interview with the author (2 November 2013).
27. Nina Roosevelt Gibson, interview with the author (2 November 2013).
28. *Ibid.*; Ellie Roosevelt, *With Love, Aunt Eleanor*, 162–164.
29. Peter Collier with Michael Horowitz, *The Roosevelts*, 468.

Chapter 5

1. Nina Roosevelt Gibson, e-mail response to author inquiry (10 May 2015).
2. *Ibid.*
3. *Ibid.*

Chapter 6

1. Theodore Roosevelt IV, interview with the author (2 November 2013).
2. *Ibid.*
3. *Ibid.*
4. *Ibid.*; H.W. Brands, *T.R.*, 802–804; David Pietrusza, *1920: The Year of the Six Presidents*, 65–66.
5. John Milton Cooper, *Woodrow Wilson*, 5; Barbara Tuchman, *The Guns of August*, 440; Dorothy Clark Wilson, *Alice and Edith: The Two Wives of Theodore Roosevelt*, 330–331; Theodore Roosevelt IV, interview with the author (2 November 2013).
6. Jack Beatty, *The Lost History of 1914: Reconsidering the Year the Great War Began*, 9.
7. Charles Brinkley, *The Wilderness Warrior: Theodore Roosevelt and the Crusade for America*, 576; H.W. Brands, *T.R.*, 661, 528–540.
8. *Ibid.*, 661.
9. Rick Atkinson, *The Day of Battle: The War in Sicily and Italy, 1943–1944*, 95.
10. Theodore Roosevelt IV, interview with the author (2 November 2013).
11. Rick Atkinson, *The Guns at Last Light: The War in Western Europe, 1944–1945*, 59–60.
12. *Ibid.*, 61–62.
13. Peter Collier with Michael Horowitz, *The Roosevelts*, 424; Edmund Morris, *The Rise of Theodore Roosevelt*, 654.
14. Rick Atkinson, *The Guns at Last*

Light, 60; "Theodore Roosevelt Jr." and "Quentin Roosevelt," www.en.m.wikipedia.org (accessed September 2014).
   15. Theodore Roosevelt IV, interview with the author (2 November 2013).
   16. *Ibid.*
   17. Chris Roosevelt, interview with the author (1 November 2013).

Chapter 7

   1. "Du Pont Family," www.en.m.wikipedia.org (accessed March 2014).
   2. Peter Collier with Michael Horowitz, *The Roosevelts*, 363.
   3. Chris Roosevelt, interview with the author (1 November 2013).
   4. "The Franklin Delano Roosevelt Memorial," www.en.m.wikipedia.org (accessed March 2014).
   5. Chris Roosevelt, interview with the author (1 November 2013).
   6. Associated Press, "Debate Over FDR Memorial Grows" (5 July 1996).
   7. David Stout, "Clinton Calls for Sculpture of Roosevelt in Wheelchair," *New York Times*, April 24, 1997.
   8. Doug Struck, "Other FDR Descendants Support Wheelchair Statue," *Washington Post*, April 24, 1997.
   9. Chris Roosevelt, interview with the author (1 November 2013).
   10. *Ibid.*; David Roosevelt, *Grandmère,'* 231.
   11. *Ibid.*; Chris Roosevelt, interview with the author (1 November 2013).
   12. *Ibid.*
   13. Stephen Jeffries, interview with the author by telephone and e-mail (8 April 2014); Robert Barnwell Roosevelt, "How to Pronounce the Name Roosevelt," *Theodore Roosevelt Association Journal*, 84.
   14. Stephen Jeffries, interview with the author by telephone and e-mail (8 March 2014); Douglas Brinkley, *The Wilderness Warrior*, 81–86.
   15. *Ibid.*, 77–80.
   16. *Ibid.*, 84–86.
   17. Edmund Morris, *The Rise of Theodore Roosevelt*, 242; H.W. Brand, *T.R.*, 11–12, 46.
   18. David McCullough, *Mornings on Horseback*, 20–25, 110, 112, 141, 149–150, 231–232, 252–254, 279, 365.
   19. Stephen Jeffries, interview with the author by telephone and e-mail (8 March 2014).
   20. *Ibid.*
   21. *Ibid.*
   22. Timothy Field Beard and Henry B. Hoff, ed., "The Roosevelt Family in America," *Theodore Roosevelt Association Journal*, 161.
   23. *Ibid.*, 92; Ann Keating Luskey, interview with the author by telephone (10 March 2014).
   24. Timothy Field Beard and Henry B. Hoff, ed., "The Roosevelt Family in America," *Theodore Roosevelt Association Journal*, 67, 82; F. Martin Harmon, *The Warm Springs Story: Legacy and Legend*, 270–273.

Chapter 8

   1. Ann Keating Luskey, interview with the author by telephone (10 April 2014).
   2. *Ibid.*
   3. H.W. Brands, *T.R.*, 642–647; Peter Collier with Michael Horowitz, *The Roosevelts*, 156–157.
   4. Douglas Brinkley, *The Wilderness Warrior*, 263–264.
   5. Dorothy Clarke Wilson, *Alice and Edith*, 306, 309, 328, 333, 334, 337–338.
   6. James Chace, *1912*, 8.
   7. Douglas Brinkley, *The Wilderness Warrior*, 177–216; H.W. Brands, *T.R.*, 641–659.
   8. Ann Keating Luskey, interview with the author by telephone (10 March 2014).
   9. "Alfred V. Kidder." Retrieved from www.britannica.com (accessed April 2014).
   10. *Ibid.*; Edmund Morris, *Theodore Rex*, 516–518; H.W. Brands, *T.R.*, 186–187, 738–744.

11. H.W. Brands, *Traitor to His Class*, 606–607; Nina Roosevelt Gibson, interviews with the author (2 November 2013, 27 February 2016); Doris Kearns Goodwin, *No Ordinary Time*, 636.
12. F. Martin Harmon, *The Warm Springs Story*, 272–273; Ellie Roosevelt, *With Love, Aunt Eleanor*, 160–161.
13. H.W. Brands, *Traitor to His Class*, 580–581.
14. F. Martin Harmon, *The Warm Springs Story*, 270–271.
15. *Ibid.*; Nina Roosevelt Gibson, interview with the author by telephone (27 August 2014).
16. F. Martin Harmon, *The Warm Springs Story*, 270–272.
17. *Ibid.*, 272.

Chapter 9

1. Mary Roosevelt, interview with the author by telephone (12 May 2014).
2. *Ibid.*; interview by author with Mary Roosevelt in person (2 November 2013).
3. Interviews by author with Mary Roosevelt in person (2 November 2013, 12 May 2014).
4. *Ibid.*; Winston Skinner, "Descendants Hold Reunion," *Newnan Times-Herald*, November 10, 2013.
5. Mary Roosevelt, interviews with the author (2 November 2013, 12 May 2014).
6. David Nasaw, *The Patriarch: The Remarkable Life and Turbulent Times of Joseph P. Kennedy*, 179–180.
7. *Ibid.*, 193.
8. *Ibid.*, 79–81; Mary Roosevelt, interview with the author by telephone (12 May 2014).
9. David Nasaw, *The Patriarch*, 275; Anna Eleanor Roosevelt, *The Autobiography of Eleanor Roosevelt*, 194.
10. David Nasaw, *The Patriarch*, 437, 443, 459, 464–465, 470–477, 519–520; Mary Roosevelt, interview with the author by telephone (12 May, 2014).
11. *Ibid.*

12. *Ibid.*
13. Peter Collier with Michael Horowitz, *The Roosevelts*, 457; David McCullough, *Truman*, 612; David Nasaw, *The Patriarch*, 65–76, 91–146, 154–170.
14. Mary Roosevelt, interview with the author by telephone (12 May 2014); Bill Billiter, "Polio Foundation Set Up by F.D.R. Is moving to UCI," *Los Angeles Times*, April 28, 1988.
15. "Mrs. James Roosevelt, Community Leader," www.ucifoundation.org (accessed April 2014).
16. Mary Roosevelt, interview with author (2 November 2013).
17. *Ibid.*; *Time*, "Medals: Carlson's Heroes," January 25, 1943; "With Roosevelt in Iraq" June 2, 1941; "The U.S. at War: Roosevelts at War," December 29, 1941.

Chapter 10

1. Chris Roosevelt, interview with the author (1 November 2013).
2. Anna Eleanor Roosevelt, *The Autobiography of Eleanor Roosevelt*, 211; Nathan Miller, *F.D.R.*, 459, 477–480; Peter Collier with Michael Horowitz, *The Roosevelts*, 402.
3. *Ibid.*, 402–404; Wikipedia, "John Roosevelt," "Elliott Roosevelt," and "Franklin Roosevelt, Jr.," www.en.m.wikipedia.org (accessed September 2014); Nathan Miller, *The Roosevelts*, 403–404, 416–417; *Time*, "The U.S. at War: Roosevelts at War (29 December 1941).
4. H.W. Brands, *T.R.*, 786, 790; Ken Burns, *The Roosevelts* (documentary).
5. James MacGregor Burns, *Roosevelt: The Soldier of Freedom, 1940–1945*, 527.
6. Peter Collier with Michael Horowitz, *The Roosevelts*, 414.
7. "Medals: Carlson's Heroes," *Time*, January 25, 1943.
8. "Battle of the Pacific: Forty Hours on Makin," *Time*, September 7, 1942.
9. "Middle Eastern Theater: With Roosevelt in Iraq," *Time*, June 2, 1941.

10. Peter Collier with Michael Horowitz, *The Roosevelts*, 322, 350–351, 366; "James Roosevelt," www.en.m.wikipedia.org (accessed May 2014); H.W. Brands, *Traitor to His Class*, 231–232.
11. "The Press: Jimmy Gets It," *Time*, November 6, 1939.
12. Wikipedia, "James Roosevelt" and "Elliott Roosevelt," www.en.m.wikipedia.org (accessed May 2014); Peter Collier with Michael Horowitz, *The Roosevelts*, 374–375, 478.
13. F. Martin Harmon, *The Warm Springs Story*, 74–75; interviews with FDR/ER grandchildren (1, 2 November 2013).
14. "Franklin Roosevelt Jr.," "Anna Roosevelt," and "John Roosevelt," www.en.m.wikipedia.org (accessed May 2014); interviews with FDR/ER grandchildren and great grandchildren (1, 2 November 2013).
15. Peter Collier with Michael Horowitz, *The Roosevelts*, 453–454.
16. *Ibid.*, 174–179, 381, 383, 395, 397, 410–411, 413; Anna Eleanor Roosevelt, *The Autobiography of Eleanor Roosevelt*, 6, 224–225; *1912*, 239–240.
17. Peter Collier with Michael Horowitz, *The Roosevelts*, 413, 444; "Death of a Lady," *Time*, October 11, 1948.
18. Peter Collier with Michael Horowitz, *The Roosevelts*, 381–382.
19. Stacy A. Cordery, *Alice*, 100, 106, 164, 303–305, 309–312, 314–316, 322–324, 447.

Chapter 11

1. Anna Fierst, interview with the author (1 November 2013).
2. Peter Collier with Michael Horowitz, *The Roosevelts*, 317, 364, 373–374, 456, 477; Curtis Roosevelt, *Too Close to the Sun: Growing Up in the Shadow of My Grandparents*, preface x–xi, 6–7, 30.
3. *Ibid.*, 6, 30, 61–77.
4. *Ibid.*, preface xi, 80, 89–90, 110–112.
5. *Ibid.*
6. *Ibid.*, 288–289.
7. *Ibid.*, 287–288; Anna Fierst, interview with the author (1 November 2013).
8. *Ibid.*
9. "Curtis Roosevelt," www.en.m.wikipedia.org (accessed July 2014).
10. Curtis Roosevelt, *Too Close to the Sun*, 30–31.
11. "Eleanor Roosevelt Seagraves," www.en.m.wikipedia.org (accessed July 2014).
12. *Ibid.*
13. Eleanor R. Seagraves, ed., *Delano's Voyages of Commerce and Discovery*, introduction, xvii–xix; "Mutiny On The Bounty," www.en.m.wikipedia.org (accessed July 2014).
14. Eleanor R. Seagraves, *Delano's Voyages of Commerce and Discovery*, 79–116.
15. *Ibid.*, introduction, xxi–xxii.
16. "Delano Family," www.en.m.wikipedia.org (accessed July 2014).
17. Anna Eleanor Roosevelt, *The Autobiography of Eleanor Roosevelt*, 44–45.
18. Eleanor R. Seagraves, *Delano's Voyages of Commerce and Discovery*, introduction, xxiii.

Chapter 12

1. David Roosevelt, *Grandmère*, preface, xi.
2. "Southern Governors to Celebrate 75th Anniversary at Warm Springs," *The Spirit of Warm Springs* (Fall/Winter 2009); David Roosevelt, *Grandmère*, 106.
3. David Stout, "Clinton Calls for Sculpture of Roosevelt in Wheelchair," *New York Times*, April 24, 1997.
4. *Ibid.*; Virginia Lewick (FDR Library archivist), e-mail answer to author inquiry (7 July 2016); Stella K. Hershan, *The Candles She Lit*; Peter Collier with Michael Horowitz, *The Roosevelts*, 442, 459, 457, 467–468; David Roosevelt, *Grandmère*, 240, 244.

5. Petter Collier with Michael Horowitz, *The Roosevelts*, 459.
6. David Roosevelt, *Grandmère*, 42, 54.
7. *Ibid.*, 29.
8. *Ibid.*, 34.
9. *Ibid.*, 42.
10. *Ibid.*, 51–52, 53, 61.
11. *Ibid.*
12. Peter Collier with Michael Horowitz, *The Roosevelts*, 344–345, 374–375, 438–439, 440, 458, 469; David Roosevelt, *Grandmère*, 214.
13. Peter Collier with Michael Horowitz, *The Roosevelts*, 453.
14. Susan Dunn, "Roosevelts—Betrayed and Betrayers—But Loyal in Some Ways," *Los Angeles Times,* October 8, 2000.

Chapter 13

1. F. Martin Harmon, "Who Was the Man on FDR's Bedroom Wall," *Columbus and the Valley* (online magazine) (April 2014).
2. "Samuel Irving Rosenman," www.en.m.wikipedia.org (accessed December 2015).
3. Samuel I. Rosenman, *Working with Roosevelt*, xiii.
4. Nathan Miller, *F.D.R.*, 95–98, 193–195, 211–212, 223–224, 228, 445–446, 493; F. Martin Harmon, *The Warm Springs Story*, 70; Doris Kearns Goodwin, *No Ordinary Time*, 10.
5. Nathan Miller, *F.D.R.*, 223, 432.
6. *Ibid.*
7. "Grace Tully," www.en.m.wikipedia.org (accessed January 2015).
8. "Archibald Butt," www.en.m.wikipedia.org (accessed January 2015).
9. *Ibid.*
10. *Ibid.*
11. Lawrence F. Abbott, *The Letters of Archie Butt, Personal Aide to President Roosevelt*, 18, 29.
12. *Ibid.*, 19.
13. *Ibid.*, 20–21.
14. *Ibid.*, 33–34.
15. *Ibid.*, 35.
16. *Ibid.*, 55.
17. *Ibid.*, 42.
18. *Ibid.*, 265–266.
19. *Ibid.*, 62.
20. *Ibid.*, 63–64, 70–71.
21. *Ibid.*, 65, 66, 72.
22. *Ibid.*, 74.
23. *Ibid.*, 88.
24. Grace Tully, *F.D.R., My Boss*, 8–9.
25. *Ibid.*, 15–16.
26. Jonathan W. Jordan, *American Warlords*, 67.
27. Grace Tully, *F.D.R., My Boss*, 58.
28. *Ibid.*, 59.
29. *Ibid.*, 101–102.
30. *Ibid.*, 118.
31. *Ibid.*, 130.
32. *Ibid.*, 113.
33. *Ibid.*, 237–238.
34. *Ibid.*, 309.
35. *Ibid.*; *Webster's Seventh New Collegiate Dictionary*, 366.
36. Grace Tully, *F.D.R., My Boss*, 340.
37. Sam I. Rosenman, *Working with Roosevelt*, 68.
38. *Ibid.*, 32.
39. *Ibid.*, 36.
40. *Ibid.*, 36, 104.
41. *Ibid.*, 37.
42. *Ibid.*
43. *Ibid.*, 38.
44. *Ibid.*, 41–42.
45. *Ibid.*, 128–129.
46. *Ibid.*, 47.
47. *Ibid.*, 122.
48. *Ibid.*, 120.
49. *Ibid.*, 357.
50. *Ibid.*, 347.
51. *Ibid.*, 84.
52. *Ibid.*, 422.

Chapter 14

1. Ken Burns, *The Roosevelts* (documentary), Florentine Films, 2014.
2. Peter Collier with Michael Horowitz, *The Roosevelts*, 346.

3. David Herbert Donald, *Lincoln*, 377; David Pietrusza, *1920*, 59.
4. Jonathan Alter, *The Defining Moment*, 92, 165.
5. Nathan Miller, *F.D.R.*, 63; Peter Collier with Michael Horowitz, *The Roosevelts*, 164–165, 335–336.
6. *Ibid.*, 22, 258–260, 330–331, 334, 388–389; Stacy A. Cordery, *Alice*, 366–367.
7. Peter Collier with Michael Horowitz, *The Roosevelts*, 394; Stacy A. Cordery, *Alice*, 368.
8. Ken Burns, *The Roosevelts* (documentary), Florentine Films, 2014.
9. Peter Collier with Michael Horowitz, *The Roosevelts*, 442–443, 450–451, 465, 478–479.
10. *Ibid.*, 362, 478.
11. Joseph Berger, "Roosevelts and the Quirks of Destiny," *New York Times*, March 3, 2005; Mary Roosevelt, interview with the author by telephone (12 May 2014).
12. Michael Hiltzik, *The New Deal: A Modern History*, 37.
13. Stacy A. Cordery, *Alice*, 137, 148–163.
14. James Chace, *1912*, 118.
15. Rob Goodman, "What Happened to the Roosevelts?" *Politico*, October 7, 2014.
16. Nina Roosevelt Gibson, e-mail response to author inquiry (30 November 2015).

Chapter 15

1. Joseph Berger, "Roosevelts and the Quirks of Destiny," *New York Times*, March 16, 2005.
2. *Ibid.*
3. *Ibid.*
4. Timothy Field Beard and Henry B. Hoff, ed., "The Roosevelt Family in America: A Genealogy," *Theodore Roosevelt Association Journal*, 35.
5. *Ibid.*, 37.
6. Douglas Brinkley, *The Wilderness Warrior*, 78–80; "Robert Roosevelt," www.en.m.wikipedia.org (accessed September 2014); "Robert Barnwell Roosevelt," www.geni.com (accessed September 2014).
7. Douglas Brinkley, *The Wilderness Warrior*, 79–86.
8. Peter Collier and Michael Horowitz, *The Roosevelts*, 49; Timothy Field Beard and Henry B. Hoff, ed., "The Roosevelt Family in America: A Genealogy," *Theodore Roosevelt Association Journal*, 55.
9. *Ibid.*; Peter Collier with Michael Horowitz, *The Roosevelts*, 50; "John Jacob Astor," www.encyclopedia-titantica.org (accessed 1 October, 2014).
10. Timothy Field Beard and Henry B. Hoff, ed., "The Roosevelt Family in America: A Genealogy," *Theodore Roosevelt Association Journal*, 63, 76; Peter Collier with Michael Horowitz, *The Roosevelts*, 441.
11. Elizabeth Winthrop, interview with the author (12 April 2016).
12. Timothy Field Beard and Henry B. Hoff, ed., "The Roosevelt Family in America: A Genealogy," *Theodore Roosevelt Association Journal*, p. 58; "Andre Roosevelt," www.en.m.wikipedia.org (accessed October 2014); Stephen Kinzer, *All the Shah's Men: An American Coup and the Roots of Middle East Terror*, 4.
13. Timothy Field Beard and Henry B. Hoff, ed., "The Roosevelt Family in America: a Genealogy," *Theodore Roosevelt Association Journal*, 88.
14. *Ibid.*, 55, 74, 88, 78.

Chapter 16

1. Doris Kearns Goodwin, *The Bully Pulpit*, 468.
2. Greg Herken, *The Georgetown Set: Friends and Rivals in Cold War Washington*, 25.
3. Doris Kearns Goodwin, *The Bully Pulpit*, 170.
4. Doris Kearns Goodwin, *No Ordinary Time*, 57.

5. Robert W. Merry, *Taking On the World: Joseph and Stewart Alsop*, 47, 87, 178, 290, 303, 305; Greg Herken, *The Georgetown Set*, 74.
6. Robert W. Merry, *Taking On the World*, 335–336, 413; Greg Herken, *The Georgetown Set*, 48.
7. *Ibid.*, 111; Robert W. Merry, *Taking On the World*, 170–171, 172–173, 235, 252, 406, 416–418.
8. *Ibid.*, 335–336; Greg Herken, *The Georgetown Set*, 31, 33, 37–38, 56–57.
9. *Ibid.*, 21, 47, 57.
10. Robert W. Merry, *Taking On the World*, 161; Greg Herken, *The Georgetown Set*, 21.
11. *Ibid.*, 110; Robert W. Merry, *Taking On the World*, 160–161, 172.
12. *Ibid.*, 94, 98–99, 105, 110, 113, 114–115, 117–118, 119–121, 123, 127, 129, 131–132, 133, 135–136, 137, 141, 143, 144–145.
13. *Ibid.*, 59, 98–99; Gregg Herken, *The Georgetown Set*, 34.
14. Robert W. Merry, *Taking On the World*, 93, 94.
15. *Ibid.*, 97, 98–99; Edmund Morris, *The Rise of Theodore Roosevelt*, 613, 614.
16. Robert W. Merry, *Taking On the World*, 95–97.
17. *Ibid.*, 99–104.
18. *Ibid.*, 123–132; Gregg Herken, *The Georgetown Set*, 20.
19. Robert W. Merry, *Taking On the World*, 67, 90; Gregg Herken, *The Georgetown Set*, 48.
20. Robert W. Merry, *Taking On The World*, 42, 70; "Theodore Roosevelt Jr.," www.en.m.wikipedia.org (accessed 15 October 2015).
21. Robert W. Merry, *Taking On the World*, 105–107.
22. *Ibid.*, 106, 108–109, 111.
23. *Ibid.*, 112–113.
24. *Ibid.*, 114.
25. *Ibid.*
26. *Ibid.*, 114–115.
27. *Ibid.*, 118–119.
28. *Ibid.*, 120.
29. *Ibid.*, 171–172; Gregg Herken, *The Georgetown Set*, 56.
30. Robert W. Merry, *Taking On the World*, 120–121, 143–145.
31. *Ibid.*, 150–151, 161.

Chapter 17

1. *Ibid.*, 546.
2. Gregg Herken, *The Georgetown Set*, 33.
3. *Ibid.*, 32.
4. Robert W. Merry, *Taking On the World*, 150–153.
5. Gregg Herken, *The Georgetown Set*, 21.
6. *Ibid.*, 24–25, 28.
7. *Ibid.*, 31–32.
8. *Ibid.*, 21, 32.
9. *Ibid.*
10. *Ibid.*, 37.
11. *Ibid.*, 39, 114.
12. *Ibid.*, 47, 111.
13. *Ibid.*, 103, 111, 148.
14. *Ibid.*, 114.
15. Robert W. Merry, *Taking On the World*, 299–305.
16. *Ibid.*, 171–172, 174, 186, 357, 385–395, 403–406, 417–442.
17. *Ibid.*, 225–226.
18. *Ibid.*, 178–181, 243–253, 316–318, 456–466, 511–531.
19. *Ibid.*, 361.
20. Gregg Herken, *The Georgetown Set*, 35, 406, 441, 667; Robert W. Merry, *Taking On the World*, 348, 363, 415–416.
21. *Ibid.*, 374, 385, 397, 402, 464–465, 488.
22. *Ibid.*, 245–246.
23. *Ibid.*, 337–338.
24. *Ibid.*, 187–188, 318–321.
25. *Ibid.*, 320–321.
26. *Ibid.*, 61–62, 79–81, 151, 336–337, 339, 410–411, 466, 522–523, 538.
27. *Ibid.*, 466–470.
28. *Ibid.*, 471–472, 473.
29. *Ibid.*, 494–510, 513–532.
30. *Ibid.*, 539.
31. *Ibid.*, 541–542.

Chapter 18

1. Stephen Kinzer, *All the Shah's Men*, 4, 212–215.
2. *Ibid.*, 10.
3. *Ibid.*, 39–40, 47–52, 57–61, 76–82, 89, 91, 93–96, 97–110, 115–118, 128–131, 134, 149, 150, 152–155, 161.
4. *Ibid.*, 4.
5. Peter Collier with David Horowitz, *The Roosevelts*, 335–337, 345, 387–388; Stephen Kinzer, *All the Shah's Men*, 5–6.
6. *Ibid.*, 148; Peter Collier with David Horowitz, *The Roosevelts*, 406, 446–449.
7. *Ibid.*, 448, 152–161; Stephen Kinzer, *All the Shah's Men*, 5.
8. *Ibid.*, 1–16, 163–166, 167–187.
9. *Ibid.*, 178–182.
10. *Ibid.*, 181, 184, 189, 212.
11. David Halberstam, *The Fifties*, 368.
12. *Ibid.*, 202, 212; Peter Collier with David Horowitz, *The Roosevelts*, 471.
13. Stephen Kinzer, *All the Shah's Men*, 209.
14. *Ibid.*, 202.
15. *Ibid.*, 203.

Chapter 19

1. Joseph Alsop and Robert Kintner, "The Roosevelt Family Album," *Life*, September 9, 1940.
2. Catrina Clay, *King, Kaiser, Czar: Three Royal Cousins Who Led the World to War*, 1–2.
3. *Ibid.*, 202–203; Joseph Alsop and Robert Kintner, "The Roosevelt Family Album, *Life*, September 9, 1940.
4. *Ibid.*
5. Hugh Gallagher Gregory, *FDR's Splendid Deception*, xiii–xiv; Joseph Alsop and Robert Kintner, "The Roosevelt Family Album," *Life*, September 9, 1940.
6. James MacGregor Burns and Susan Dunn, *The Three Roosevelts: Patrician Leaders Who Transformed America*, 85; Kenneth S. Davis, *FDR: The Beckoning of Destiny*, 654; Conrad Black, *Franklin Delano Roosevelt: Champion of Freedom*, 175; F. Martin Harmon, *The Warm Springs Story*, 169.
7. Kenneth S. Davis, *FDR*, 32–33; Joseph Alsop and Robert Kintner, "The Roosevelt Family Album," *Life*, September 9, 1940.
8. Kenneth S. Davis, *FDR*, 62; Joseph Alsop and Robert Kintner, "The Roosevelt Family Album," *Life*, September 9, 1940; Peter Collier with David Horowitz, *The Roosevelts*, 101.
9. *Ibid.*
10. Geoffrey Ward, *Before the Trumpet: Young Franklin Roosevelt, 1882–1905*, p. 390.
11. Joseph Alsop and Robert Kintner, "The Roosevelt Family Album," *Life*, September 9, 1940.
12. *Ibid.*

Chapter 20

1. James MacGregor Burns and Susan Dunn, *The Three Roosevelts*, 8–142.
2. *Ibid.*, 32–61.
3. *Ibid.*, 122–142.
4. *Ibid.*, 13.
5. *Ibid.*, 15, 17.
6. *Ibid.*, 19–21, 25–26.
7. *Ibid.*, 27, 33, 43.
8. *Ibid.*, 68.
9. *Ibid.*, 56, 78, 80, 85, 91, 140.
10. *Ibid.*, 78, 113, 114, 136, 140, 142.
11. *Ibid.*, 87, 89, 129, 150–151, 164, 171.
12. *Ibid.*, 165, 171, 184–185, 188.
13. *Ibid.*, 167, 175.
14. David Emblidge, ed., *My Day: The Best of Eleanor Roosevelt's Acclaimed Newspaper Columns, 1936–1962*, p. 310 (epilogue: quote by Joseph Lash).
15. James MacGregor Burns and Susan Dunn, *The Three Roosevelts*, 131.
16. *Ibid.*, 140–141.
17. *Ibid.*, 135.

Chapter 21

1. Dayton Duncan and Ken Burns, *The National Parks: America's Best Idea*, episodes 4, 5.
2. *Ibid.*
3. Douglas Brinkley, *The Wilderness Warrior*, 788, 811; *Joshua Tree National Park*, video, Scrub Oak Productions, 2009.
4. "André Roosevelt," www.IMDb.com and www.en.m.wikipedia.org (accessed 27 October 2015).
5. "Bali," www.en.m.wikipedia.org (accessed 27 October 2015).
6. *Ibid.*; "André Roosevelt," www.IMDb.com and www.en.m.wikipedia.org (accessed 27 October 2015).
7. "Goona-goona epic," www.en.m.wikipedia.org (accessed 28 October 2015).
8. "André Roosevelt," www.en.m.wikipedia.org (accessed 28 October 2015).
9. *Ibid.*
10. "Roosevelt Campobello International Park: A Legacy of Friendship," www.fdr.net (accessed October 2015).
11. Miguel Covarrubias, *Island of Bali*, 14–20.
12. *Ibid.*, 21.
13. *Ibid.*, 29.
14. *Ibid.*, 20, 25–28.
15. *Ibid.*, 41.

Chapter 22

1. Upton Sinclair, *The Jungle*, chapter 13; "*The Jungle*," www.en.m.wikipedia.org (accessed February 2016); Roosevelt Reunion Address/Information List, Courtesy Roosevelt Warm Springs (accessed August 2013).
2. *Ibid.*
3. *Ibid.*; *Lowell: The Mill City*, Lowell Historical Society, 7–9.
4. Roosevelt Reunion/Address List, Courtesy Roosevelt Warm Springs (accessed August 2013); "Eleanor Swift Reeve" (obituary), www.findagrave.com (accessed February 2016); "Gustavus Franklin Swift," www.en.m.wikipedia.org (accessed February 2016); Shane Hamilton, *Trucking Country: The Road to America's Wal-Mart Economy*, 44–51.
5. Roosevelt Reunion Address/Information List, Courtesy Roosevelt Warm Springs (accessed August 2013); Noah Feldman, *Scorpions: The Battles and Triumphs of FDR's Great Supreme Court Justices*, 43–44.
6. Jonathan W. Jordan, *American Warlords: How Roosevelt's High Command Led America to Victory in World War II*, 42.
7. "Robert H. Jackson," www.en.m.wikipedia.org (accessed February 2016).
8. "Robert H. Jackson and William E. Jackson at Yale University," www.robertjackson.org (accessed February 2016); Noah Feldman, *Scorpions*, 274.
9. Roosevelt Reunion Address/Information List, Courtesy Roosevelt Warm Springs (accessed August 2013).
10. Noah Feldman, *Scorpions*, 275–302.
11. *Ibid.*, 277.
12. *Ibid.*, 293–298.
13. *Ibid.*, 298.
14. *Ibid.*, 299, 300, 301, 302.
15. Ann and John Tusa, *The Nuremberg Trial*, 504; "Nuremberg Trials," www.en.m.wikipedia.org (accessed February 2016).
16. Noah Feldman, *Scorpions*, 302.
17. Roosevelt Reunion Address/Information List, Courtesy Roosevelt Warm Springs (accessed August 2013); "Melissa Jackson," Wikipedia, www.en.m.wikipedia.org (accessed February 2016); Robert H. Jackson Center, www.robertjackson.org (accessed February 2016).
18. James MacGregor Burns and Susan Dunn, *The Three Roosevelts*, 312, 290–293.
19. Peter Collier with David Horowitz, *The Roosevelts*, 362.
20. Joseph P. Lash, *Franklin and Eleanor: The Story of Their Relationship*

Based on Eleanor Roosevelt's Private Papers, 489.
21. "A Du Pont And Roosevelt Marry ... But It's Anything but Happily Ever After," A Short History, www.ashistoryblog.com (accessed February 2016).
22. Leonard Mosley, *Blood Relations: The Rise and Fall of the du Ponts of Delaware*, 117–118, 249.
23. *Ibid.*, 4, 7, 28, 44–46, 62, 144–145, 233–237, 251–252, 377, 378.
24. *Ibid.*, 4, 75–77, 366–367, 371, 377.
25. *Ibid.*, 21, 22–23.
26. Joseph Frazier Wall, *Alfred I. Dupont: The Man and His Family*, 67.
27. Leonard Mosley, *Blood Relations*, 23–24.
28. *Ibid.*, 29, 30, 48; Joseph Wall Frazier, *Alfred I. Dupont*, 67–94.
29. Leonard Mosley, *Blood Relations*, 68–70.
30. *Ibid.*, 210–211.
31. *Ibid.*, 165–177; Joseph Wall Frazier, *Alfred I. Dupont*, 197–216.
32. Joseph Mosley, *Blood Relations*, 213–214, 224, 227, 228, 229, 249, 253–266.
33. Joseph Frazier Wall, *Alfred I. Dupont*, 256–401.
34. *Ibid.*, 254.
35. *Ibid.*, 291–293, 378.

Chapter 23

1. Joshua Boettiger, interview with the author (2 October 2015); John Boettiger, interview with the author (13 October 2015); "William Randolph Hearst," www.en.m.wikipedia.org (accessed October 27, 2015); Joseph Berger, "Roosevelts and the Quirks of Destiny," *New York Times*, May 16, 2005.
2. John Boettiger, interview with the author (13 October 2015).
3. *Ibid.*; "Mercer Island, Washington," www.en.m.wikipedia.org (accessed 31 October 2015).
4. Curtis Roosevelt, *Too Close to the Sun*, 195, 197; John Boettiger, interview with the author (13 October 2015).
5. *Ibid.*, Curtis Roosevelt, *Too Close to the Sun*, 159, 218, 233–234.
6. John Boettiger, interview with the author (13 October 2015).
7. Curtis Roosevelt, *Too Close to the Sun*, 219, 235, 283–286.
8. John Boettiger, interview with the author (13 October 2015); Peter Collier with David Horowitz, *The Roosevelts*, 425–426; Curtis Roosevelt, *Too Close to the Sun*, 221–222.
9. *Ibid.*, 215–218, 281–283; Peter Collier with David Horowitz, *The Roosevelts*, 402, 404, 416, 428.
10. *Ibid.*, 451–452; John Boettiger, interview with the author (13 October 2015); Curtis Roosevelt, *Too Close to the Sun*, 287.
11. *Ibid.*; John Boettiger, interview with the author (13 October 2015).
12. Curtis Roosevelt, *Too Close to the Sun*, 287; Peter Collier with Michael Horowitz, *The Roosevelts*, 477; John Boettiger, interview with the author (13 October 2015).
13. *Ibid.*
14. John Boettiger, *A Love in Shadow: The Story of Anna Roosevelt and John Boettiger*, 13–279.
15. John Boettiger, interview with the author (13 October 2015).

Chapter 24

1. "The Author," www.theodoreroosevelt.org (accessed 20 April 2016); Edmund Morris, *The Rise of Theodore Roosevelt*, 331–335, 378–381, 705–707.
2. Theodore Roosevelt, *The Naval War of 1812*, preface, viii, cover endorsement, *New York Times*, April 1882.
3. *Ibid.*, 251.
4. Andrew Burnstein and Nancy Isenberg, *Madison and Jefferson*, 285, 482, 530.
5. "Keeping the Spirit Alive" and "Executive Committee," www.theodoreroosevelt.org (accessed 22 April, 2016).
6. Elizabeth Winthrop, interview with the author (12 April 2016).

7. *Ibid.*
8. Stacy Cordery, *Alice*, 455.
9. Elizabeth Winthrop, interview with the author (12 April 2016).
10. Theodore Roosevelt, *The Naval War of 1812*, introduction, ix–x.

Chapter 25

1. Linda Creekbaum, interview with the author (27 February 2016).
2. "Franklin A. Thomas Biography: Philanthropist, Administrator, Lawyer," www.biography.jrank.org (accessed March 2016).
3. *Ibid.*
4. "John Hay Whitney," www.en.m.wikipedia.org (accessed March 2016).
5. *Ibid.*; Nora Ephron, "Oh Haddad, Poor Haddad," *New York Magazine*, November 25, 1968.
6. Joseph P. Lash, *Eleanor and Franklin*, 526–527; H.W. Brands, *T.R.: The Last Romantic*, 421–423.
7. Jonathan W. Jordan, *American Warlords*, 56–57.
8. Michael Eric Dyson, *The Black Presidency: Barack Obama and the Politics of Race.*

Epilogue

1. Epilogue sources: Wikipedia; F. Martin Harmon, *The Warm Springs Story: Legacy and Legend;* Carrie Currie, "Information on Oak Terrace, Eleanor Roosevelt's Childhood Home," Demand Media; Anthony P. Musso, "Eleanor Roosevelt's Parents Interred in Tivoli's Hall Vault," *Poughkeepsie Journal*, June 16, 2015; and Anna Eleanor Roosevelt, *The Autobiography of Eleanor Roosevelt.*

Appendix

1. Appendix based on excerpts from *My Day: The Best of Eleanor Roosevelt's Newspaper Columns, 1936–1962*, by Eleanor Roosevelt.

Selected Bibliography

Articles

"Alfred v. Kidder." *Encyclopædia Britannica*. www.britannica.com (accessed April 22, 2014).
"Army and Navy—Medals: Carlson's Heroes." *Time*, January 25, 1943.
"Battle of the Pacific: Forty Hours on Makin." *Time*, September 7, 1942.
Beard, Timothy Field, and Henry B. Hoff, eds. "The Roosevelt Family in America: A Genealogy." *Theodore Roosevelt Association Journal*. Centereach, New York: Jenie, 1990.
Berger, Joseph. "Roosevelts and the Quirks of Destiny." *New York Times*, March 3, 2005.
"Canada–U.S. Relations." Roosevelt Campobello International Park. www.fdr.net (accessed February 19, 2014).
Goodman, Rob. "What Happened to the Roosevelts?" *Politics*, October 7, 2014.
"Medals: Carlson's Heroes." *Time*, January 25, 1943.
"Middle Eastern Theater: With Roosevelt in Iraq." *Time*, June, 2, 1941.
"Mrs. James Roosevelt." www.ucifoundation.org (accessed August 1, 2014).
"The Press: Jimmy Gets It." *Time*, November 6, 1939.
"Rogina Louisa Jeffries." *Beacon Hill Times*. www.beaconhilltimes.com (accessed April 12, 2012).
Skinner, Winston. "Descendants Hold Reunion," *Newnan Times Herald*, November 10, 2013.
"Southern Governors Celebrate 75th Anniversary at Warm Springs." *Spirit of Warm Springs* (Fall/Winter, 2009).
Stout, David. "Clinton Calls for Sculpture of Roosevelt in Wheelchair." *New York Times*, April 24, 1997.
"The U.S. at War: Roosevelts at War." *Time*, December 29, 1941.
"Women: Death of a Lady." *Time*, October 11, 1948.

Books

Abbott, Lawrence F., ed. *The Letters of Archie Butt*. New York: Doubleday, Page & Company, 1924.

Bibliography

Alter, Jonathan. *The Defining Moment: FDR's Hundred Days and the Triumph of Hope.* New York: Simon & Schuster, 2006.

Atkinson, Rick. *The Day of Battle: The War in Sicily and Italy, 1943–1944.* New York: Henry Holt, 2007.

———. *The Guns at Last Light: The War in Western Europe, 1944–1945.* New York: Henry Holt, 2013.

Beatty, Jack. *The Lost History of 1914: Reconsidering the Year the Great War Began.* New York: Walker, 2012.

Black, Conrad. *Franklin Delano Roosevelt: Champion of Freedom.* New York: Public Affairs, Perseus, 2003.

Boettiger, John R. *A Love in Shadow: The Story of Anna Roosevelt and John Boettiger, Told by Their Son.* New York: W.W. Norton, 1978.

Brands, H.W. *T.R.: The Last Romantic.* New York: Basic, 1997.

———. *Traitor to His Class: The Privileged Life and Radical Presidency of Franklin Delano Roosevelt.* New York: Doubleday, 2008.

Brinkley, Douglas. *The Wilderness Warrior: Theodore Roosevelt and the Crusade for America.* New York: HarperCollins, 2009.

Burns, James MacGregor. *Roosevelt: The Soldier of Freedom, 1940–1945.* New York: Harcourt, 1970.

Burns, James MacGregor, and Susan Dunn. *The Three Roosevelts: Patrician Leaders Who Transformed America.* New York: Grove, 2001.

Chace, James. *1912: Wilson, Roosevelt, Taft and Debs—The Election That Changed the Country.* New York: Simon & Shuster, 2004.

Clay, Catrine. *King, Kaiser, Tsar: Three Royal Cousins Who Led the World to War.* New York: Walker, 2006.

Collier, Peter. *The Roosevelts: An American Saga.* With David Horowitz. New York: Simon & Schuster, 1994.

Cooper, John Milton, Jr. *Woodrow Wilson: A Biography.* New York: Alfred A. Knopf, 2009.

Cordery, Stacy A. *Alice: Alice Roosevelt Longworth, from White House Princess to Washington Power Broker.* New York: Viking, 2007.

Covarrubias, Miguel. *Island of Bali.* New York: Alfred A. Knopf, 1937.

Davis, Kenneth. S. *FDR: The Beckoning of Destiny, 1882–1928.* New York: History, 2003.

Donald, David Herbert. *Lincoln.* London: Simon & Schuster, 1995.

Duncan, Dayton with Ken Burns. *The National Parks, America's Best Idea.* Washington, D.C.: Florentine Films, 2009.

Emblidge, David, ed. *My Day: The Best of Eleanor Roosevelt's Acclaimed Newspaper Columns, 1936–1962.* Cambridge, MA: Da Capo, 2001.

Emerson, Jason. *Giant in the Shadows: The Life of Robert T. Lincoln.* Carbondale: Southern Illinois University Press, 2012.

Feldman, Noah. *Scorpions: The Battles and Triumphs of FDR's Great Supreme Court Justices.* New York: Twelve, Hatchett, 2010.

Freidel, Frank. *Franklin D. Roosevelt: A Rendezvous with Destiny.* New York: Little, Brown, 1990.

Gallagher, Hugh. *FDR's Splendid Deception.* Arlington, VA: Vandamere, 1994.

Goodman, Rob. "What Happened to the Roosevelts." *Politico*, October 7, 2014.

Bibliography

Goodwin, Doris Kearns. *The Bully Pulpit: Theodore Roosevelt, William Howard Taft, and the Golden Age of Journalism*. New York: Simon & Schuster, 2013.
_____. *No Ordinary Time: Franklin and Eleanor Roosevelt and the Home Front in World War II*. New York: Touchstone, 1994.
Halberstam, David. *The Fifties*. New York: Villard, 1993.
Harmon, F. Martin. *The Warm Springs Story: Legacy and Legend*. Macon, GA: Mercer University Press, 2014.
Herken, Gregg. *The Georgetown Set: Friends and Rivals in Cold War Washington*. New York: Knopf Doubleday, 2014.
Hershan, Stella. *The Candles She Lit*. Hyde Park, NY: Eleanor Roosevelt Center, 2000.
Hiltzik, Michael. *The New Deal: A Modern History*. New York: Free Press, 2011.
Jordan, Jonathan W. *American Warlords: How Roosevelt's High Command Led America to Victory in World War II*. New York: NAL Caliber, 2015.
Kinzer, Stephen. *All the Shah's Men*. Hoboken, NJ: John Wiley & Sons, Inc., 2003.
Lash, Joseph P. *Franklin and Eleanor: The Story of Their Relationship*. New York: W.W. Norton, 1971.
Lowell Historical Society. *Lowell: The Mill City*. Charleston, SC: Arcadia, 2005.
McCartney, Laton. *The Teapot Dome Scandal*. New York: Random House, 2008.
McCullough, David. *Mornings on Horseback*. New York: Touchstone, 1981.
_____. *Truman*. New York: Simon & Schuster, 1992.
Meecham, Jon. *American Lion: Andrew Jackson in the White House*. New York: Random House, 2008.
Merry, Robert W. *Taking on the World: Joseph and Stewart Alsop, Guardians of the American Century*. New York: Viking, 2012.
Miller, Nathan. *F.D.R.: An Intimate History*. New York: Meridian, 1983.
Morris, Edmund. *The Rise of Theodore Roosevelt*. New York: Ballantine, 1979.
_____. *Theodore Rex*. New York: Random House, 2001.
Mosley, Leonard. *Blood Relations: The Rise and Fall of the du Ponts of Delaware*. New York: Atheneum, 1980.
Nasaw, David. *The Patriarch: The Remarkable Life and Turbulent Times of Joseph P. Kennedy*. New York: Penguin, 2012.
Pietrusza, David. *1920: The Year of the Six Presidents*. New York: Carroll & Graf, 2007.
Roosevelt, Anna Eleanor. *The Autobiography of Eleanor Roosevelt*. Cambridge, MA: Da Capo, 1992.
Roosevelt, Curtis. *Too Close to the Sun: Growing Up in the Shadow of My Grandparents, Franklin and Eleanor*. New York: Public Affairs, 2008.
Roosevelt, David. *Grandmère: A Personal History of Eleanor Roosevelt*. New York: Warner, 2002.
Roosevelt II, Eleanor (Ellie). *With Love, Aunt Eleanor*. Petaluma, CA: Scrapbook, 2004.
Roosevelt, Theodore. *The Naval War of 1812*. New York: Random House, 1996.
Rosenman, Sam. *Working with Roosevelt*. New York: Harper & Brothers, 1952.
Seagraves, Eleanor Roosevelt, ed. *Delano's Voyages of Commerce and Discovery*. Stockbridge, MA: Berkshire House, 1994.
Sinclair, Upton. *The Jungle*. New York: Doubleday, 1906.
Tuchman, Barbara. *The Guns of August*. New York: Macmillan, 1962.

Bibliography

Tully, Grace. *F.D.R.: My Boss.* Chicago: Peoples Book Club, 1949.
Tusa, Ann, and John Tusa. *The Nuremberg Trial.* New York: Skyhorse, 2010.
Wall, Joseph Frazier. *Alfred I. Dupont: The Man and His Family.* New York: Oxford University Press, 1990.
Ward, Geoffrey. *Before the Trumpet: Young Franklin Roosevelt.* New York: Harper & Row, 1985.
Wilson, Dorothy Clark. *Alice and Edith: The Two Wives of Theodore Roosevelt.* New York: Doubleday, 1989.
Winthrop, Elizabeth. *Dear Mr. President: Franklin Delano Roosevelt Letters from a Mill Town Girl.* New York: Winslow, 2001.

Author Interviews

Nina Roosevelt Gibson, March 15, 2012; November 2, 2013; April 18, 2014; August 27, 2014, February 27, 2016.
Anna Fierst, November 1, 2013.
Christopher Roosevelt, November 1, 2013.
Elizabeth Roosevelt, November 1, 2013.
Eleanor Calkin, November 2, 2013.
Haven Roosevelt, November 2, 2013.
Lauren Elliott, November 2, 2013.
Mary Roosevelt, November 2, 2013; May 12, 2014.
Stewart Elliott, November 2, 2013.
Ted Elliott, November 2, 2013.
Theodore Roosevelt IV (TR IV), November 2, 2013.
Tweed Roosevelt, November 2, 2013.
Stephen Jeffries, March 8, 2014.
Ann Luskey, April 10, 2014.
Joshua Boettiger, October 2, 2015.
John Boettiger, October 13, 2015.
Linda Creekbaum, February 27, 2016.
Elizabeth Winthrop, April 12, 2016.

Other Sources

Bill Urbin. National Park Service Tour of Top Cottage. Eleanor Roosevelt National Historic Site, Hyde Park, New York, July 28, 2014.
Roosevelt Reunion Address and Information List (Roosevelt Warm Springs, July–November 2013).
Val-Kill National Park Service Tour. Eleanor Roosevelt National Historic Site, Hyde Park, New York, July 28, 2014.

Index

Abbott, Lawrence F. 95, 200
Actor's Guild 72
African Wildlife Federation 65
Air Medal 75
Albany, New York 92, 105, 183
Albuquerque, New Mexico 155
Algiers, Libya 126
Alsop, Corrine Robinson 12, 124, 126, 173, 174
Alsop, John 122
Alsop, Joseph (Joe) 2, 117, 121–125, 127–130, 132–134, 141–142, 160, 172–174, 203, 209
Alsop, Katie 173
Alsop, Nick 173
Alsop, Patricia Hankey (Tish) 125–127
Alsop, Stewart 117, 119, 121, 124–127, 129–130, 132–134, 172, 174, 202, 209
Alter, Jonathan 2, 109, 193, 195, 201, 207
The Amazon jungle 79
Amazon River 23, 68
American Express 125
American Historical Association 175
American Liberty League 159
American Museum of Natural History 51, 180
American Revolution 5, 161
American Tobacco Company 162
American Volunteer Group (AVG) 122–124
Amherst College 168–169
Anderson, Marian 178
Antioch College 23
Antiquities Act 10, 150
Appeal to Reason (newspaper) 154
Arizona Republic (newspaper) 167

Arizona Times (newspaper, also *Phoenix Shopper*) 167
Armour Meats 154
Associated Press 58
Astor, Caroline (Lady Astor) 142
Astor, John Jacob 116, 201
Atkinson, Rick 53, 196, 207
Atlanta Constitution (newspaper) 96
Avon, Connecticut 126
Ayatollah Khomeini 135

The Badlands 6–8, 10–11, 97, 179, 190
Baker, Ray Stannard 119
Bali (Island of) 151–153
"Bali craze" 151, 153
Bartoletti, Emma 174
Bassanese, Lynn 88
"Battle Hymn of the Republic" 96–97
Battle of New Orleans 171
Beaty, Jack 52
Bedford-Stuyvesant, Brooklyn, New York 177
Bedford-Stuyvesant Restoration Corporation 177
Belafonte, Harry 37
Benton, Thomas Hart 170
Berger, Joseph 114–115, 193, 201, 205, 207
Berkley, California 168
Berkshire Eagle newspaper 173
Berkshire Mountains 174
Berlin, Germany 52
Berlin Airlift 131
Berlin Crisis (or Wall) 121, 131
Berne, Switzerland 24
Bethesda, Maryland 81

211

Index

Bill and Melinda Gates Foundation 164
Black, Hugo 157
Bligh, William 84
Boettiger, Adam 164
Boettiger, John 79, 82, 164
Boettiger, John Roosevelt 2, 79, 164–168, 205, 208, 210
Boettiger, Joshua 115, 164–165, 205, 210
Boettiger, Paul 164–165
Boettiger, Sara de Noyelles 164
Bond, James 137
Borah, William 80
Boston, Massachusetts 60
Boston Symphony Orchestra 38
HMS *Bounty* (ship) 84
Braden, Tom 125, 127
Brando, Marlon 84
Brands, H.W. 2, 19, 53, 62, 76, 193–199, 206, 208
Brandywine River 57, 162–163
Brinkley, Douglas 2, 62, 66, 116, 193, 196–197, 201, 204, 208
Brooklyn, New York 23, 51, 177
Buffalo, New York 180
Burns, James MacGregor 76, 114, 145–148, 198, 203–204, 208
Burns, Ken 2, 11, 22, 109–110, 150, 173, 179, 193, 195, 198, 200–201, 204, 208
Bush, George H.W. 3, 59
Bush, George W. 3, 90–91, 142
Bush, Neil 142
Butt, Archibald 94–99, 108, 116, 200

Cairo, Egypt 75
Calkin, Eleanor Elliott 34, 38, 195–196, 210
Cambridge, England 168
Camelback Mountain 167
Campobello Island (and Roosevelt Home Historic Site) 11, 58–59, 142, 152, 179–181, 204, 207
Capitol Reef National Park 150
Carlson, Evans F. 76, 198
"Carlson's Raiders" 76
Carr, Caleb 170
Carter, Billy 142
Carter, Jimmy 31, 72, 139, 142
Casablanca, Morocco 75, 126, 167
Chace, James 31, 195, 197, 201, 208
Channel Islands National Park 150

Chapman, Bruce Kerry 118
Chappaqua, New York 24
Charlottesville, Virginia 21, 166
Chennault, Claire 122–124
Chia-ling River 122
Chicago, Illinois 23, 154
Chicago Tribune (newspaper) 164
China-U.S. Center for Sustainable Development 51
Chongqing, China 122
Churchill, Winston 76, 138, 167
CIA Near East and Asia Division 136
Citicorp 176
civil rights 33, 131, 178
Civil War 5, 30, 62, 96–97, 144, 161
Cleveland, Grover 143
Cleveland, Ohio 77
Clinton, Bill 21, 37, 58, 149, 197, 199
Clinton, Hillary 24, 149
Cold War 139, 172
College of Physicians and Surgeons of New York 115
Colleville-sur-Mer Cemetery 55
Collier, Peter 13–14, 19, 88, 109, 193–201, 203–205, 208
Columbia University 142, 168, 177
Columbia University Law School 22, 30, 177
Columbus, Georgia 11
Columbus Colonnade 11
Coney Island 98,
Coolidge, Calvin 86, 111
Cooper, John Milton, Jr. 31, 195, 208
Cordery, Stacey 2, 14, 112, 193, 199, 201, 206, 208
Corona del Mar 24, 70
Court of St. James (United Kingdom) 72
Covarrubias, Miguel 152–153, 204, 208
Cowles, Anna Roosevelt (TR's sister, Bamie and/or Bye) 24, 28, 32
Cowles, William Sheffield 24,
Crater Lake National Park 150
Creekbaum, Linda 2, 176, 206, 210
Crimean War 161
Croix de Guerre 127
Cromwell, Oliver 170
Cuban Missile Crisis 121, 131
Cushing, Betsy Maria 77–78, 178
Cushing, Harvey 77, 178

Index

D-Day 53–55, 126–127
Dakota Territory 8, 10
Dall, Curtis 81, 84
Dartmouth College 125
Dear Mr. President book (series) 173
Debs, Eugene 145
De Gaulle, Charles 127
Delano, Amasa 84, 86
Delano, Pablo 86
Delano, Samuel 86
Delano, Warren, Jr. 86
de Lavoisier, Antoine-Laurent 161
Democratic National Committee (DNC) 93
"Democrats for Nixon and Reagan" 72
Dennis, Armand 151–152
Dewey, Thomas E. 100
Distillers Company 71
Distinguished Flying Cross 75
"Dixie" 96
"Doctrinaire Democracy" 171
Doubleday Books 125–126, 154
Douglas, William O. 157
Dry Tortugas National Park 150
Dubuque, Iowa 125
Dulles, Allen 136
Dulles, John Foster 136
Dunn, Susan 90, 145–148, 200, 203–204, 208
du Pont, Alfred I. 162–163
du Pont, Coleman 162–163
du Pont, Eleuthere Irenee 161–162
du Pont, Ethel 57, 75, 79, 158
du Pont, Eugene, Jr. 159
du Pont, Pierre Samuel, II (P.S.) 162–163
du Pont de Nemours, Pierre Samuel 161
DuPont 162–163
Dutchess County, New York 49

Easter Sunday 43
Edward R. Murrow Award 23
Edward VII 141
E.I. du Pont de Nemours and Company 161
Eisenhower, Dwight (Ike) 73, 111, 131–132, 136–139
El Alamein (Battles of) 126
Eleanor Roosevelt Center 88
Eleanor Roosevelt Memorial 181

Eleanor Roosevelt National Historic Site 36, 441, 45, 180
Elliott, Lauren 34, 41, 195, 196, 210
Elliott, Stewart Spencer 34, 38, 196, 210
Elliott, Ted 34, 38, 196, 210
Emblidge, David 187, 203
Emerson, Faye 79
Emmy Awards 23
Equon, Wisconsin 155
Eton, Berkshire, England 125
Evanston, Illinois 23
Exodus (film) 48

Fala (FDR's dog) 99, 103
Fall Kill Creek 36–37
F.D. Roosevelt State Park 180
FDR Library and Museum 2
FDR Memorial Commission 58
Federal Bureau of Investigation (FBI) 132
Federal Housing and Home Finance Agency 177
Federalist Party 171
Feldman, Noah 2, 157, 204, 208
Fiat Spider 45
Field Museum 23
Fierst, Anna 81, 83, 199, 210
Fierst, David 81
La Figaro (newspaper) 84
"Fighting Tigers" 122
"First Lady of the World" 33, 187
Florentine Films 2
For France film 151
Ford, Edsel 177
Ford, Henry 155, 177
Ford Foundation 176–177
"Four Hundred" (New York City's) 146
"Fourth Estate" 119
France-Amerique (magazine) 84
Franklin & Eleanor Roosevelt Institute 59
Franklin D. Roosevelt Four Freedoms Park 180
Franklin D. Roosevelt Lake 180
Franklin D. Roosevelt Mid-Hudson Bridge 181
Franklin D. Roosevelt National Memorial 58, 180
Franklin Delano Roosevelt Home National Historic Site 59, 180
French Resistance 127
French Revolution 161

213

INDEX

Gable, Clark 84
Gable, John Allen 175
Gallagher, Hugh 8, 203, 208
Gannett, Robert T. 23
Garland, Lynn 92
Garland, Merrick 92
Garner, John Nance 111
General Motors 163
Geneva, Switzerland 73, 79
Geneva School of Diplomacy 84
George Washington Carver National Monument 178
Georgetown, Washington, D.C. 130
Georgia Warm Springs Foundation (GWSF) 21, 176
The Gestapo (Nazi secret police) 127
Gibson, Nina Roosevelt (also Anne Sturgis Roosevelt) 34, 38, 41, 43, 45–49, 51, 64, 68, 112, 195–196, 198, 210
Gold Medal 151
Goodman, Rob 112, 201, 207
Goodwill Industries 23
Goodwin, Doris Kearns 2, 7, 114, 119, 193, 195, 198, 200–201, 208
Goona-Goona (film) 151, 152, 204
Grand Canyon National Park 150, 181, 182
Grand Ole Party (Republican GOP) 149
Grand Teton National Park 150
Grant, Ulysses S. 86
Great Depression 19, 36, 100, 173
Great Smoky Mountains National Park 150
"Great White Fleet" 156
Greenville, Delaware 158
Greenwich, Connecticut 24
Groton School 120, 144
Guadalcanal (Island of) 76
Gulf Oil 138
Gung Ho (film) 76

Haddad, Camilla Cushing (Lulie) 115
Haddad, William 178
Hagedorn, Hermann 97
Halberstam, David 138, 203, 208
Halifax, Nova Scotia, Canada 125
Halprin, Lawrence 58
Halsted, James 168
Hampshire College 168
Hanford, Washington 163

Harding, Warren G. 111
Harris, Joel Chandler 96
Harvard University 29, 63
Harvard University History Department 137
Hearst, William Randolph 164–165
Henry Luce Foundation 59
Herken, Gregg 130, 201, 202, 209
The Hermitage 19
Highland, New York 181
Hiltzik, Michael 2, 111, 201, 209
Hitler, Adolf 110, 127
Hong Kong 122–123
Hoover, Herbert 100–101, 111
Hopkins, Harry 93, 124
Hopper, Hedda 77–78
Hornblower, Samuel Roosevelt 23
USS *Hornet* (ship) 75
Horowitz, David 13, 193–194, 203–205, 208
"House of Virginia" 171
Howe, Louis 30, 72, 93
Howland, Rebecca 142
Hudson River 37, 81, 141, 149, 183, 185
Hudson River Valley 2, 5, 36–37, 142, 144
Hughes, Howard 79
Hussein, Saddam 139
Hyde Park, New York 2, 5, 11, 14, 19–20, 34–38, 41, 45, 48–49, 58–59, 64, 68, 81–82, 88, 110, 114, 118, 141, 143, 164, 168, 180, 182, 185, 189–190

Ickes, Harold 110
International Herald Tribune (newspaper) 84
International School 73
Ipswich, Massachusetts 155
Iranian Hostage Crisis 139
Iron Mountain, Tennessee 23
Ivy League (or Ivy Leaguers) 125, 137, 177

Jackson, Andrew 19
Jackson, Melissa Carow 158
Jackson, Nancy Roosevelt 24, 156
Jackson, Robert H. 155–159
Jackson, William E. 155–156
Jamestown, New York 158
Jefferson, Thomas 21, 93, 171

Index

Jeffries, Stephen 60–63, 197, 210
Johnson, Lyndon B. 94, 172
Jordan, Jonathan 178, 200, 204, 206, 209
Joshua Tree National Park 150

Kaiser Wilhelm 52–53
Kai-shek, Chiang 122
Kalman, Laura 2
Keller, Helen 58
Kennedy, Ethel 72
Kennedy, Joe III 72
Kennedy, John F. (JFK) 37, 59, 111, 131
Kennedy, Joseph P. 71–73, 111–112
Kennedy, Robert 72, 177
Kettle Hill 55
The KGB (Soviet secret police) 132
Khartoum, Sudan 66
Khrushchev, Nikita 37, 41
Khrushchev, Nina 37
Kidder, Alfred 67
King County, Washington 166
Kings Canyon National Park 150
King's Royal Rifle Corps 125
Kintiner, Robert 122–123, 130, 141, 203
Kinzer, Stephen 135–137, 139, 201, 203, 209
Kipling, Rudyard 97
"Knickerbockers" 146
Korean War 121, 131

Lacey, John 10
LaGuardia, Fiorello 110
Lake Forest, Illinois 155
Landon, Alf 100–101
Lash, Joe 160
Lawrence, Massachusetts 174
Lee, Robert E. 97
Lehand, Marguerite (Missy) 93
Lend-Lease (Act) 101, 106, 124, 156
Liberation Trilogy book (series) 53
Liebling, A.J. 53
Life (magazine) 141–142, 203
Lincoln, Abraham 30, 58, 93, 97, 109
Lincoln, Robert 74
Lincoln Memorial 178
Lindsley, Ruth Chandler 87
Little Rock, Arkansas 173
The Little White House (also State Historic Site) 58, 68, 92, 95, 180–181
Lochridge, James (code name) 137
Loire Valley 43
London, England 116, 125–127, 143, 181
Long Beach, California 73
Long Island 5, 18, 63, 75
Longworth, Alice Roosevelt (TR's daughter, Mrs. L) 14–16, 28, 80, 98, 110, 112, 137, 173–174
Longworth, Nicholas 80, 112
Los Angeles, California 73, 167–168
Los Angeles Times (newspaper) 23, 77–78, 90, 121, 194, 198, 200
Lou Gehrig's Disease (also ALS) 168
Louisville Courier-Journal (newspaper) 121
Lowell, Francis Cabot 155
Lowell, Massachusetts 155
"Lowell Experiment" 155
Lubec, Maine 59, 180
Lucent Technologies 176
Luskey, Anne Keating 63, 65, 67, 197, 210

Madison, James 171
Madison Square Garden 142
Makin Island 76
Manchester by the Sea, Massachusetts 154
Manhattan, New York 37, 62, 110
Manhattan Project 163
March of Dimes 176
Marianne (magazine) 84
Marshall, George 124, 127
Marshall Plan 127, 131
Martha's Vineyard, Massachusetts 24
Massachusetts (ship) 84
Mayflower (ship) 86
Mayflower Compact 86
Mayflower Hotel 102
Mayo Clinic 77
McCarthy, Eugene 131
McCarthy, Leighton 181
McCarthy Cottage 181
McClure's (magazine) 119
McGovern, George 72
McKinley, William 145
Meadow Croft 63
Meat Inspection Act 154

215

Index

Mercer, Lucy 32
Mercer Island, Washington 165
Merrimack River 155
Merry, Robert W. 124, 129, 131, 133, 202, 209
Mesa Verde National Park 150
Metro Goldwin Meier 73
Miami, Florida 111
Miller, Nathan 2, 193–195, 198, 200–201, 209
Mission Impossible (film) 137
Mombasa, Kenya 66
Monroe, James 171
Morris, Edmund 2, 15–16, 62, 93, 194, 197, 202, 205, 209
Morris, Gouverneur 170
Morris Meats 154
Mosaddegh, Mohammad 135–139
Mosely, Leonard 160, 205, 209
Mount Rushmore 181
El Mundo (newspaper) 84
Mutiny on the Bounty (films) 84

Napoleon III 186
Nasaw, David 71, 72, 198, 209
National Collegiate Athletic Association (NCAA) 175
National Register of Historic Places 186
National Security Medal 138
Navy Cross 76
"The New Deal" 8, 10, 31, 106, 109–110, 130, 159, 173
"New Freedom" 31
"New Nationalism" 31
New York City, New York 5, 7, 11, 18, 24, 29–30, 63, 73, 75, 77, 111, 158, 168, 172, 180–181, 183, 189
New York Herald Tribune (newspaper) 117, 119, 121, 178
New York Outlook (magazine) 147
New York Post (newspaper) 178
New York Sound 62
New York State Fish Commission 62
New York State Supreme Court 92
New York State Teachers Association 60
New York Times (newspaper) 58, 114, 164, 170, 182, 193–194, 197, 199, 201, 205, 207
Newnan Times-Herald (newspaper) 193–194, 198, 207

Newport Beach, California 24, 73
Newsweek (magazine) 117, 132–133
Nimitz, Chester W. 76
Nixon, Richard 52, 72, 111, 131–133
Nobel Peace Prize 52, 66, 175
Norris, George 10
North Adams, Massachusetts 174
Nuremberg, Germany 157–158
Nuremberg Trials 156

Oak Ridge, Tennessee 163
Oak Terrace (also Oak Hall) 27, 183, 185–186
Obama, Barack 31, 142, 178
Obama, Malik 142
O'Connor, Basil 93
Olympic National Park 150
Onassis, Jackie Kennedy 24
Operation Jedburgh 126
Orange County, California 74
The Oval Office 99
Oyster Bay, New York 5, 11–12, 16, 20, 63, 90, 97–98, 120, 137, 147, 171, 190

Panama Canal 10, 175, 181
Pandora (ship) 85
Paris, France 30, 43, 151, 155, 161, 186
Paris Olympics (1900) 151
Park City, Utah 24
Pastor Hall (film) 77
Peabody Awards 23
Pearl Harbor 75–76, 122, 166
Pecos National Historical Park 67
Pembridge Gardens 24
Pepsico 176
Persian Gulf 139
Peters, Carla 80
Pew Center for Global Climate Change 51
Philadelphia, Pennsylvania 52, 162
Phoenix, Arizona 167
Pierson, Elizabeth 182
Pierson Cottage 181
Pietrusza, David 2, 196, 201, 209
Pine Cay Resort 24
Pine Mountain 180
Pittsburgh Post-Gazette (newspaper) 121
Plymouth Colony 86

Index

The Politburo (Communist executive committee) 55
Porcellian Club 144
Port-au-Prince, Haiti 151
Portland, Maine 23
Pot of Gold (film) 73
Potomac River 58, 180
Poughkeepsie, New York 181
Powder Trust 162
Pravda (newspaper) 131
Presidio Boulevard 24
Prides Crossing, Massachusetts 155
Princeton University 145
Progressive Era 122
Progressive Movement 119
Progressive Party (also Bull Moose Party) 109, 145
Puget Sound 166
Pulitzer Prize 7
Pure Food and Drug Act 154
Purple Heart 75

Queen Frederica (of Greece) 37
Queen Juliana (of the Netherlands) 37
Queen Mother Elizabeth Bowes-Lyon (of United Kingdom) 37
Queen Victoria (of United Kingdom) 141
Quincy, Massachusetts 84

Rainmaker (code name) 137
Reagan, Ronald 72, 111
Reeve, Abbott 155
Reeve, Abbott Lawrence 154
Reeve, Alfred 155
Reeve, Arlana 155
Reeve, Cintra Lowell 155
Reeve, Daphne M. 155
Reeve, Eleanor Swift 155
Reeve, J. Stanley 155
Reeve, Josiah Stanley 155
Reeve, Katherine Roosevelt 155
Reeve, Lawrence Lowell 155
Reeve, Lawrence Roosevelt 155
Revolutionary War 1, 5, 161
Riley, Elizabeth 143
Riverside Park 181
Roach, George William 118
Robert H. Jackson Center 158
Robinson, Corinne Roosevelt (TR's sister) 63, 65, 124

Robinson, Theodore Douglas 141
Rommel, Erwin (The Desert Fox) 126
Roosevelt, André 117, 151, 153
Roosevelt, Anna C. 23
Roosevelt, Anna E. 23
Roosevelt, Anna Eleanor (FDR's daughter, also Dall, Boettiger & Halsted) 30, 79, 81–82, 85, 115, 164, 166–168
Roosevelt Arch 181
Roosevelt, Archibald (TR's son, Archie) 137, 156
Roosevelt, Archibald, Jr. 137
Roosevelt, Christopher duPont (Chris, CDR) 18–19, 56–57, 210
Roosevelt, Cornelius V.S. 137
Roosevelt, Curtis (Buzzie) 2, 58, 81–83, 85, 165–167, 199, 205, 209
Roosevelt, D. Franklin, III (FDR III) 12
Roosevelt, David (Little Texas) 2, 58, 87–88, 193–197, 199–200, 209
Roosevelt, Edith Carow (TR's 2nd wife) 32, 67, 80
Roosevelt, Eleanor (ER, 1st Anna Eleanor): as author 194–195, 198–199, 209; childhood 27–29; family ties 12, 14–16, 18–20, 23, 27, 29, 32, 61, 63–64, 70, 81–83, 85, 87–90, 113, 124, 29, 141–142, 158, 160, 164–165, 168–169, 173, 178–179; in her honor 180–184; individual traits and progressive leanings 36–37, 102, 107, 114, 120, 145, 148–149, 178, 187–189, 191–192; later life 33–36, 38, 41, 43, 45, 47–50, 68, 190; as mother 30
Roosevelt, Eleanor, II (ER's niece, Ellie) 34–35, 37–38, 45, 195–196, 209
Roosevelt, Elizabeth 12, 16, 172, 193, 210
Roosevelt, Elizabeth Riley 143
Roosevelt, Elliott (FDR's son) 90–91, 111–112, 117, 167
Roosevelt, Elliott Bulloch (TR's brother, ER's father) 27, 79, 90
Roosevelt, Elliott, IV (Thatcher) 12, 16, 87, 179
Roosevelt, Elliott, Jr. (Tony) 87–88, 90–91
Roosevelt, Ethel (TR's daughter) 98

217

Index

Roosevelt, Franklin D. (FDR): background and early career 5–10, 19, 21, 24–25, 27, 29, 122, 176; family ties 12, 14, 16, 18–20, 30, 56, 61, 63–64, 68–70, 77–79, 81–88, 93, 112–113, 115–119, 122, 129–130, 137, 141–142, 150–151, 156, 158–160, 164–167, 173–174, 178, 192; in his honor 180–183; individual traits 11, 33, 36–37, 45, 57–59, 94, 99, 100, 102–107, 128, 189–190; as president 72, 75–77, 82–83, 91–92, 96, 187; as progressive 7, 31, 100, 104, 109–111, 114, 120, 143–145, 147–149, 159, 178–179;

Roosevelt, Franklin D., Jr. (the 1st) 30

Roosevelt, Franklin D., Jr. (the 2nd) 73, 75, 79, 111–112, 119, 158, 160, 167

Roosevelt, Hall (ER's brother) 15, 27, 32, 35, 38, 79, 89

Roosevelt, Hall Delano 73, 114

Roosevelt, Haven 34, 38, 43, 45, 68, 195–196, 210

Roosevelt, Helen Astor 141, 142–143

Roosevelt, Isaac 115

Roosevelt, James (FDR's son, Jimmy) 18, 59, 70, 73–74, 76–79, 178

Roosevelt, James Alfred 154

Roosevelt, James I 5, 142–143

Roosevelt, James, Jr. 71–72

Roosevelt, James Roosevelt (FDR's brother, Rosy) 116, 141–144

Roosevelt, Jean S. 63

Roosevelt, John (FDR's son) 35, 38, 71, 73, 75, 77, 111, 112

Roosevelt, John Ellis 63

Roosevelt, John Kean 18

Roosevelt, Katherine Lowell 155

Roosevelt, Kermit (TR's son) 65, 79–80, 98, 110

Roosevelt, Kermit III 23

Roosevelt, Kermit, Jr. (Kim, KR) 118, 135–140

Roosevelt, Lloyd Cartwright 118

Roosevelt, Mark 23

Roosevelt, Mary Winskill 70–74, 78, 198, 201, 210

Roosevelt, Michael 71

Roosevelt, Phillip James 63

Roosevelt, Quentin (TR's son) 24, 52, 55, 98

Roosevelt, Quentin II 137

Roosevelt, Rebecca Howland 142

Roosevelt, Robert Barnwell (TR's uncle, RBR) 61–63, 115–116

Roosevelt, Rosalind (Roddy) 59

Roosevelt, Sara Delano 36, 45, 81, 142

Roosevelt, Theodore (TR, Teddy): background and early career 5–10, 31, 122; family ties 14–16, 18–19, 23–25, 27, 32, 52, 55, 61–62, 65, 67, 78–79, 89, 98, 100, 110, 113, 115–116, 118–119, 122, 125, 129–130, 135–137, 139, 154, 156, 171–172, 174, 179, 192; in his honor 180–182; individual traits 11, 51, 89, 95–98, 106, 170, 175, 190; post presidency 52–53, 65–67, 76, 79, 97; as president 29, 94–96, 119, 133–134, 150–151, 156, 162, 187; as progressive 7, 31, 109, 111, 112, 120, 144–148, 178, 188

Roosevelt, Theodore IV (TR IV) 12, 51, 53, 55, 56, 61

Roosevelt, Theodore, Jr. (TR's son, Ted) 16, 18, 53–56, 61

Roosevelt, Tweed 18, 172, 193, 210

Roosevelt, William Albert 118

Roosevelt Auditorium 21

Roosevelt Campobello International Park Commission 59

Roosevelt Island 180

Roosevelt Lodge 181

Roosevelt Point 181–182

Roosevelt Study Center 19

Roosevelt Warm Springs 21, 176, 182

Roosevelt Warm Springs Archives 2

Roosevelt Warm Springs Foundation 73

The Roosevelts: An Intimate History (film) 2, 11, 22, 109

Rosenman, Sam 92–95, 99, 103–108, 200

Rough Riders 122, 175

Rowe, New Mexico 24

Royal Navy 84

Rural Electrification Administration 10

Russo-Japanese War 52

Sagamore Hill 63, 89, 98, 99

Sagamore Hill National Historic Site 180

Index

St-Bonnet-du-Gard, France 24
St. John's College 73
St. Louis Post-Dispatch (newspaper) 121
St. Patrick's Day 20
St. Paul's Episcopal Church Cemetery 185
Salt River 180
Samuel Goldwyn, Inc. 77
San Francisco, California 24, 58
San Juan Hill 55
San Juan Islands 166
Santa Fe, New Mexico 23
Saturday Evening Post (magazine) 117, 119, 121, 132–133
Savannah, Georgia 96
Sayville, New York 63
Scheider, Romelle 77
Schenck, Joseph 77
Schwartz, Abba 48
Seagraves, Anna Eleanor Roosevelt (Sistie) 81, 82, 84–86, 166, 199
Seagraves, Van 82
Seattle, Washington 82, 165–167
Seattle Post-Intelligencer (newspaper) 164
Second Empire Style 186
Selassie, Haile 37
Shadix, Mike 2
Shah of Iran 24
Silver Star 75
Sinclair, Upton 154–155, 209
Sixtieth Rifles 125
Smith, Al 16, 102
Smithsonian Institution 23, 67
Social Security (Act) 90–91, 149, 181, 191
"Solid South" 10
South Vietnam 131
Southern Governor's Association Conference (75th) 87
Spanish American War 55, 62, 94, 118, 122, 161
Spaulding, Victoria Reeve 155
Springwood 36–37, 180, 183, 185
"Square Deal" 175
Stalin, Joseph 76, 167
Standard Oil 18, 162
"Star-Spangled Banner" 96
Steffens, Lincoln 119
Stevenson, Adlai 37

Stillwell, Joseph (Vinegar Joe) 124
Stimson, Henry 178
Stone, Cassandra Reeve 155
Stone, Harlan 157
Stone Cottage 35–36, 41, 45
Strauss-Kahn, Dominique 158
Sturm, Alexander 80
Sturm, Paulina Longworth 80
Suckley, Margaret (Daisy) 93, 110
Suffolk County, New York 63
Sugarbush Ski Resort 24
Summer Olympics 25, 117
"Sunday Night Suppers" 130
Swift, George Hastings 155
Swift, Gustavus Franklin 154–155
Swift & Company (also Swift Meats) 154–155

Taft, William Howard 31, 67, 97, 109, 145
Taylor, Gustavus F. 155
Teapot Dome 16, 18
Tehran, Iran 75, 136, 138–139, 167
Tennessee Valley Authority (TVA) 10
Theodore Roosevelt Association 19, 63, 171, 175
Theodore Roosevelt Association Journal (quarterly) 61
Theodore Roosevelt Birthplace National Historic Site 180
Theodore Roosevelt Bridge 180
Theodore Roosevelt Dam 180
Theodore Roosevelt Inaugural National Historic Site 180
Theodore Roosevelt Island 180
Theodore Roosevelt Memorial Hall 180
Thomas, Franklin A. 176–178
Thompson, Malvina (Tommy) 37
Time (magazine) 2, 74, 76–77, 133, 158, 198–199, 207
Titanic (ship) 95, 116
Tivoli, New York 27, 183, 185
Toombs, Henry 21
Top Cottage 34, 36, 58–59, 88
La Tribune (newspaper) 84
Truman, Harry 31, 33, 157
Truman Doctrine 127, 131
Tucson, Arizona 69
Tully, Grace 93, 101–103, 108, 200, 210

219

INDEX

United Nations (UN) 33–35, 47, 118
United Nations Charter 33
U.S. Army 76, 124–126
U.S. Army Air Corps 32, 75
U.S. Army Reserve 75
U.S. Bureau of Internal Revenue 156
U.S. Census Bureau 118
U.S. Central Intelligence Agency (CIA) 131, 135–138
U.S. Department of Agriculture 49
U.S. Department of State 49
U.S. District Court, Southern District of New York 177
U.S. Embassy, Tehran 139
U.S. Federal Housing and Home Finance Agency 177
U.S. Forest Service 175
U.S. House Judiciary Committee 157
U.S. Joint Chiefs 124
U.S. Marine Corps (or Marines) 74, 78
U.S. Maritime Commission 72
U.S. National Park Service (or System) 150, 181, 183, 185
U.S. National Register of Historic Places 186
U.S. Naval Intelligence 122
U.S. Navy 16, 52, 75, 123, 171
U.S. Office of Strategic Services (OSS) 127, 137
U.S. Secret Service 95, 103
U.S. Securities and Exchange Commission 72
U.S. Senate Judiciary Committee 157
U.S. Supreme Court 24, 92, 155–157, 159
U.S. Veterans Administration 168
University of Arizona Medical Center 68
University of California–Berkley 164
University of California–Irvine (UCI) 73
University of Pennsylvania 24
University of Virginia 21
Urbin, Bill 210
Uris, Leon 48

Val-Kill 36–38, 41, 43, 45, 47–48, 88, 180, 185, 190
Val-Kill Cottage 35–37, 43
Val-Kill Industries 35
Valparaiso, Chile 86

van Rosenvelt, Jacobus 5, 20
van Rosenvelt, Johannes 5, 20
Vero Beach, Florida 155
Vidal, Gore 37
Vienna, Austria 116, 143
Vietnam War (also Vietnam conflict) 52, 121, 131, 133
Vinson, Fred 157

Wall, Joseph Frazier 162–163, 205, 209
Wall Street 63, 73
War of 1812 161
Ward, Geoffrey 145, 203, 209
Warm Springs, Georgia 1–3, 7–13, 16, 18–19, 21–22, 33, 35, 38, 51, 56–58, 61–62, 65, 69, 71, 173, 176, 178–182, 190
Warm Springs Quadrangle 11, 13, 21, 176
Warm Springs National Historic Landmark District 182
Washington, Booker T. 178
Washington, D.C. 14–15, 23–24, 58, 81–82, 156, 163, 180
Washington Post (newspaper) 58, 121, 197
Watergate 131, 133
Waud, Cornelius B. 155
Waud, Reeve B. 155
Weld, Susan 24
The White House 24, 31, 33, 35, 58, 65–66, 68, 72, 81–83, 85, 94, 98–100, 112, 122, 124, 133, 138, 150, 159, 166, 172–173, 178, 180
Whitney, John Hay (Jock) 115, 178
Whitney, Kate Roosevelt 71, 115, 176, 178
Wilderness Society 51
Wilkie, Wendell 100–102
Williams, Edith Danby 8
Willis, John 97
Wilmington, Delaware 57, 162–163
Wilson, Dorothy Clarke 67, 197, 209
Wilson, Woodrow 30–32, 52, 109–111, 145, 148, 150
Winchell, Walter 77
Winchester, Hampshire, England 125
Wind Cave National Park 150
Winthrop, Elizabeth 2, 117, 172, 201, 205–206, 210

220

Index

Woman's National Democratic Club 82, 84
World War I 32, 52–54, 76, 110, 121, 139, 141, 143, 151, 161
World War II 1, 8, 4, 53–54, 72, 74–77, 93, 106, 115, 119, 121–122, 125–127, 129, 135, 137, 156, 161
Wuthering Heights (film) 73

Yale University 120, 125, 156
Yalta, Crimea, Russia 167
Yangtze River 122
Yellowstone National Park 150, 181
Yosemite National Park 150

Zimmerman, Corinne 23
Zimmerman, Warren 23

www.ingramcontent.com/pod-product-compliance
Ingram Content Group UK Ltd.
Pitfield, Milton Keynes, MK11 3LW, UK
UKHW041952140426
5217IPUK00015B/757